FLESH & STONE

CARLOS PACHECO
Penciler & Co-scripter

JEPH LOEB
Wordsmith

RAFAEL MARIN
Co-scripter

JESUS MERINO
Inks

LIQUID GRAPHICS
Colors

RICHARD STARKINGS'
COMICRAFT & ALBERT
Letters

BOBBIE CHASE
Original Series Editor

MIKHAIL BORTNIK
Book Design

MATTY RYAN
Assistant Editor

BEN ABERNATHY
Collections Editor

BERNADETTE THOMAS
Manufacturing Manager

BOB GREENBERGER
Director: Editorial Operations

JOE QUESADA
Editor In Chief

BILL JEMAS
President

FANTASTIC FOUR®: FLESH AND STONE. Contains material originally published in magazine form as FANTASTIC FOUR Vol. 3 #'s 35-39. Published by MARVEL COMICS, a division of MARVEL ENTERPRISES, INC. Lou Gioia, Executive Vice-President, Publishing; Bob Greenberger, Director, Editorial Operations; Stan Lee, Chairman Emeritus. OFFICE OF PUBLICATION: 387 PARK AVENUE SOUTH, NEW YORK, N.Y. 10016. Copyright © 2000 and 2001 Marvel Characters, Inc. All rights reserved. No similarity between any of the names, characters, persons, and/or institutions in this magazine with those of any living or dead person or institution is intended, and any such similarity which may exist is purely coincidental. This periodical may not be sold except by authorized dealers and is sold subject to the condition that it shall not be sold or distributed with any part of its cover or markings removed, nor in a mutilated condition. FANTASTIC FOUR (including all prominent characters featured in this issue and the distinctive likenesses thereof) is a registered trademark of MARVEL CHARACTERS, INC. No part of this book may be printed or reproduced in any manner without the written permission of the publisher. Printed in Hong Kong. First Printing, August, 2001. ISBN # 0-7851-0793-2. GST. #R127032852. MARVEL COMICS is a division of MARVEL ENTERPRISES, INC. Peter Cuneo, Chief Executive Officer; Avi Arad, Chief Creative Officer.   10 9 8 7 6 5 4 3 2 1

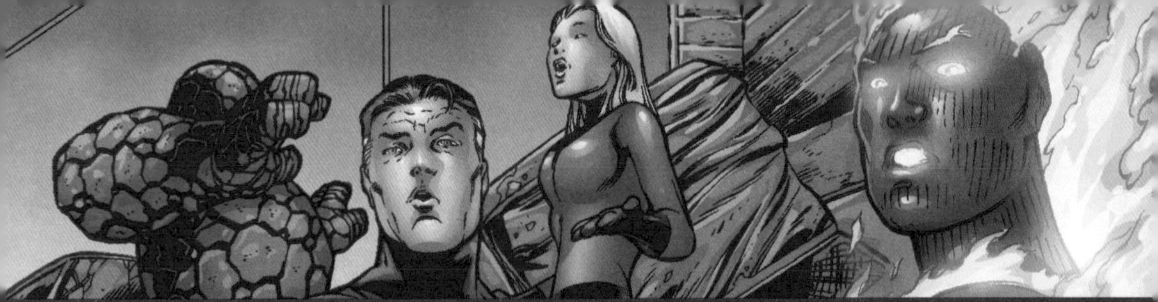

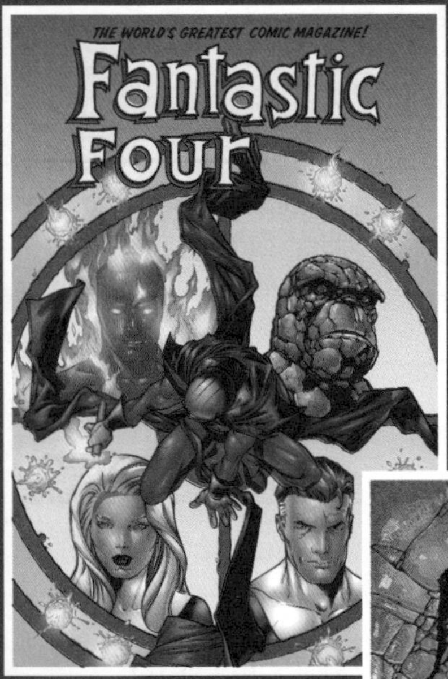
THE WORLD'S GREATEST COMIC MAGAZINE!
Fantastic Four

Chapter 1:
"Shadows in the Mirror!"

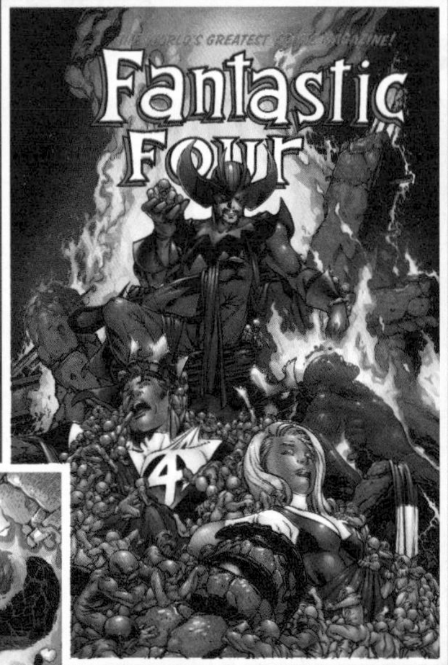
Fantastic Four

Chapter 2:
"Day of the Dark Sun"

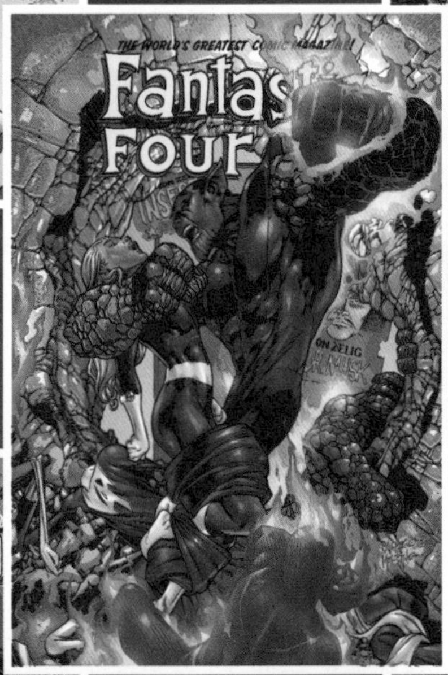
THE WORLD'S GREATEST COMIC MAGAZINE!

Chapter 3:
"There's No Business..."

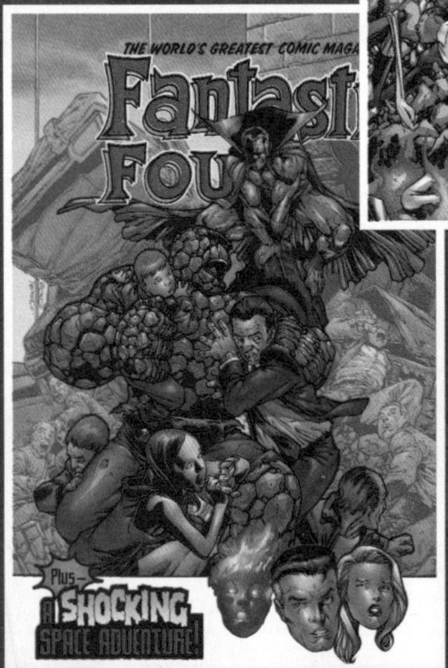
Plus
A SHOCKING
SPACE ADVENTURE!

Chapter 4
"Flesh & Stone"

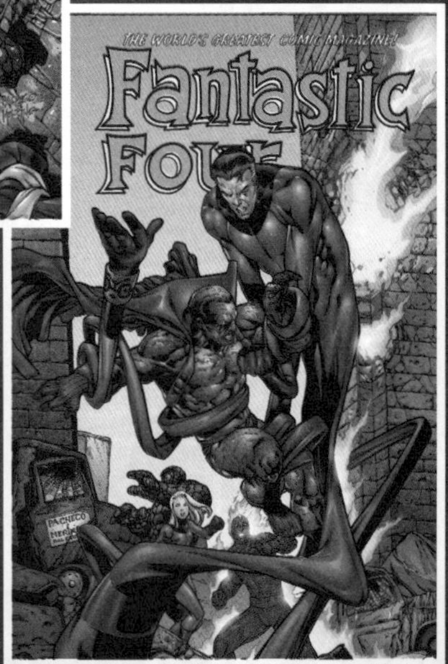
THE WORLD'S GREATEST COMIC MAGAZINE!
Fantastic

Chapter 5:
"Things Change"

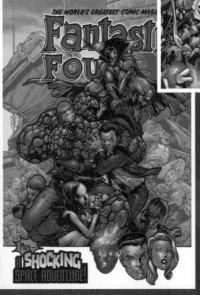

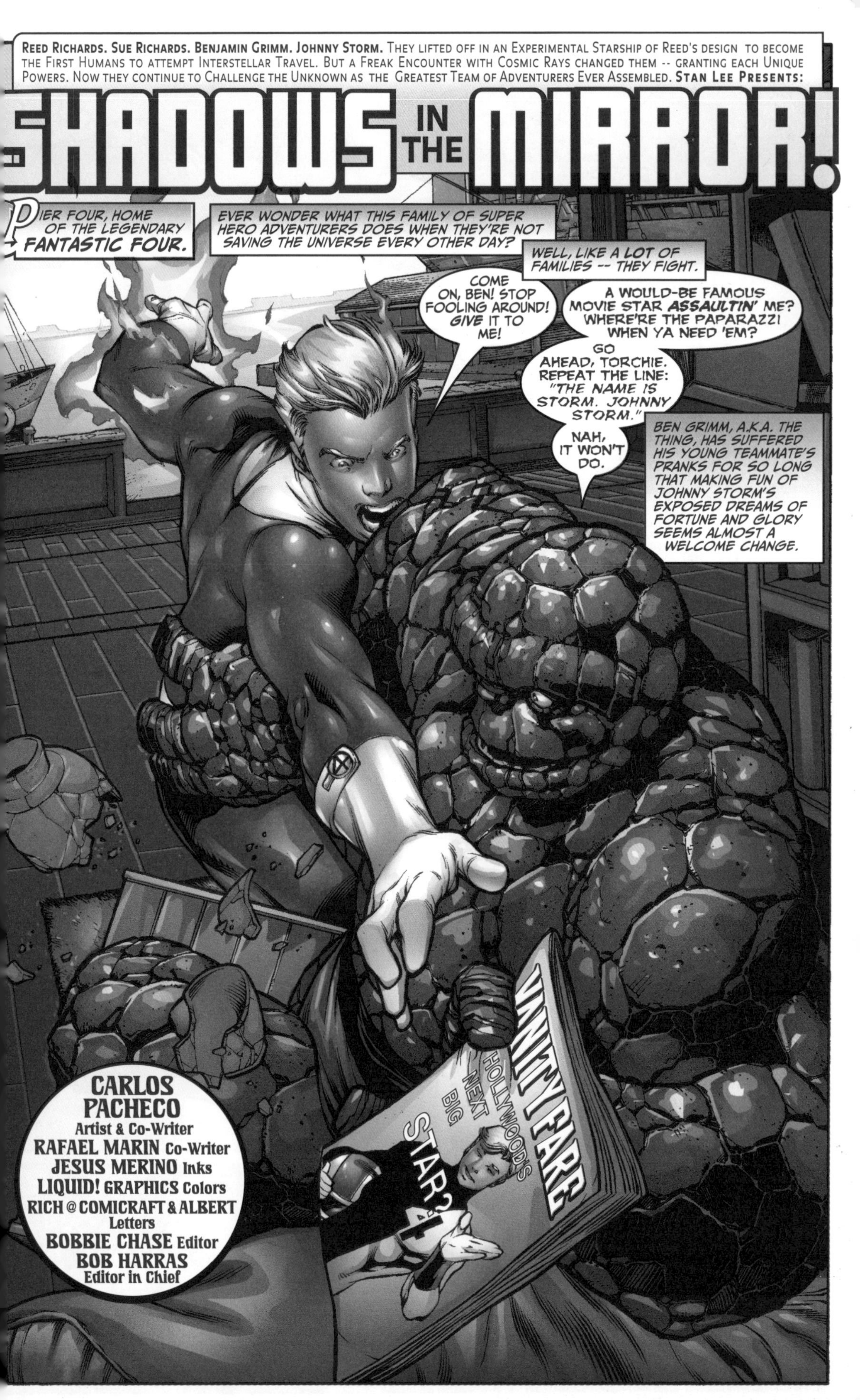

REED RICHARDS. SUE RICHARDS. BENJAMIN GRIMM. JOHNNY STORM. THEY LIFTED OFF IN AN EXPERIMENTAL STARSHIP OF REED'S DESIGN TO BECOME THE FIRST HUMANS TO ATTEMPT INTERSTELLAR TRAVEL. BUT A FREAK ENCOUNTER WITH COSMIC RAYS CHANGED THEM -- GRANTING EACH UNIQUE POWERS. NOW THEY CONTINUE TO CHALLENGE THE UNKNOWN AS THE GREATEST TEAM OF ADVENTURERS EVER ASSEMBLED. STAN LEE PRESENTS:
SHADOWS IN THE MIRROR!
PIER FOUR, HOME OF THE LEGENDARY FANTASTIC FOUR.
EVER WONDER WHAT THIS FAMILY OF SUPER HERO ADVENTURERS DOES WHEN THEY'RE NOT SAVING THE UNIVERSE EVERY OTHER DAY?
WELL, LIKE A LOT OF FAMILIES -- THEY FIGHT.
COME ON, BEN! STOP FOOLING AROUND! GIVE IT TO ME!
A WOULD-BE FAMOUS MOVIE STAR ASSAULTIN' ME? WHERE'RE THE PAPARAZZI WHEN YA NEED 'EM?
GO AHEAD, TORCHIE. REPEAT THE LINE: "THE NAME IS STORM. JOHNNY STORM."
NAH, IT WON'T DO.
BEN GRIMM, A.K.A. THE THING, HAS SUFFERED HIS YOUNG TEAMMATE'S PRANKS FOR SO LONG THAT MAKING FUN OF JOHNNY STORM'S EXPOSED DREAMS OF FORTUNE AND GLORY SEEMS ALMOST A WELCOME CHANGE.
VANITY FARE
HOLLYWOOD'S NEXT BIG STAR?
CARLOS PACHECO Artist & Co-Writer
RAFAEL MARIN Co-Writer
JESUS MERINO Inks
LIQUID! GRAPHICS Colors
RICH @ COMICRAFT & ALBERT Letters
BOBBIE CHASE Editor
BOB HARRAS Editor in Chief

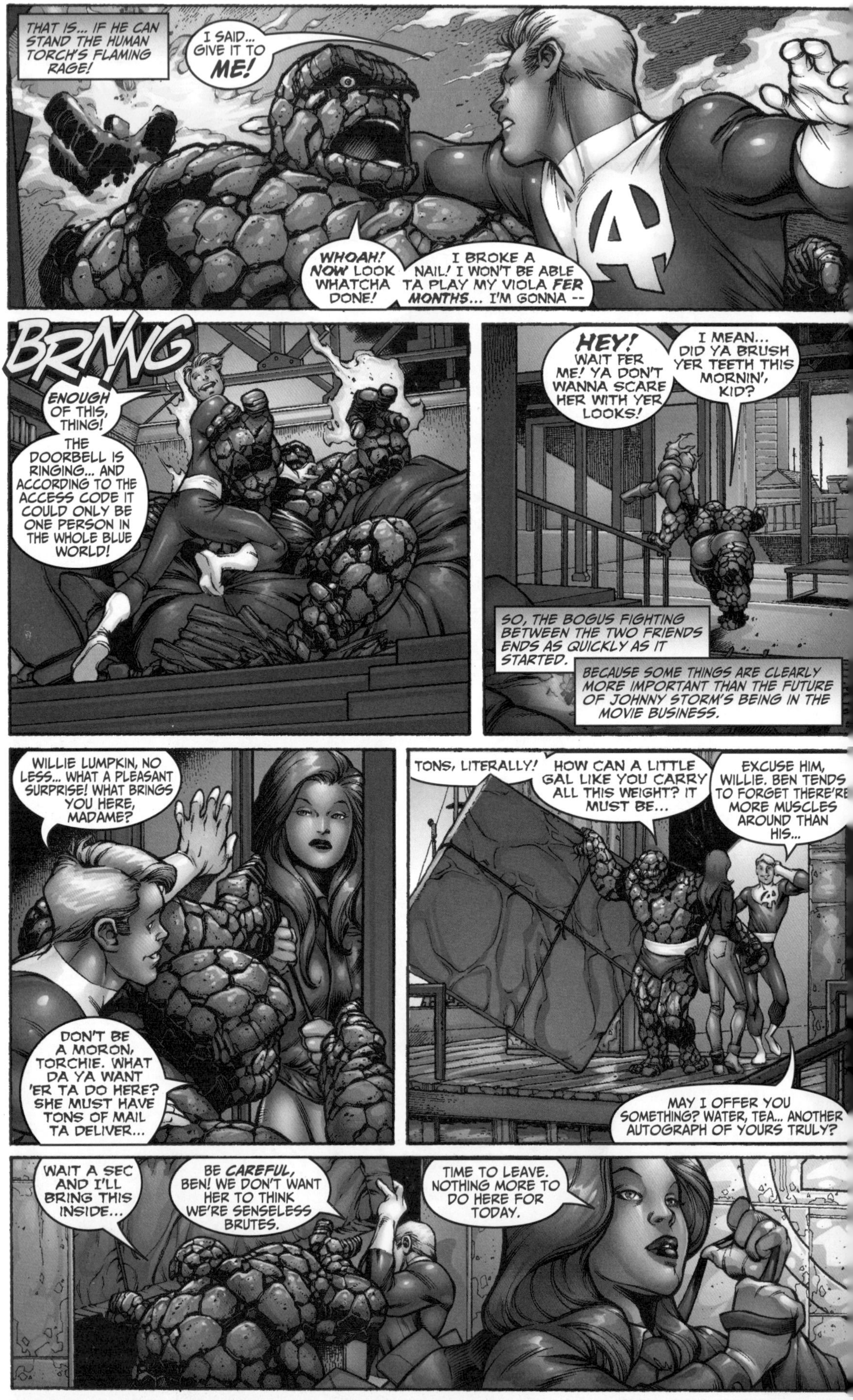
THAT IS... IF HE CAN STAND THE HUMAN TORCH'S FLAMING RAGE!
I SAID... GIVE IT TO ME!
WHOAH! NOW LOOK WHATCHA DONE!
I BROKE A NAIL! I WON'T BE ABLE TA PLAY MY VIOLA FER MONTHS... I'M GONNA --
BRNNG
ENOUGH OF THIS, THING!
THE DOORBELL IS RINGING... AND ACCORDING TO THE ACCESS CODE IT COULD ONLY BE ONE PERSON IN THE WHOLE BLUE WORLD!
HEY! WAIT FER ME! YA DON'T WANNA SCARE HER WITH YER LOOKS!
I MEAN... DID YA BRUSH YER TEETH THIS MORNIN', KID?
SO, THE BOGUS FIGHTING BETWEEN THE TWO FRIENDS ENDS AS QUICKLY AS IT STARTED.
BECAUSE SOME THINGS ARE CLEARLY MORE IMPORTANT THAN THE FUTURE OF JOHNNY STORM'S BEING IN THE MOVIE BUSINESS.
WILLIE LUMPKIN, NO LESS... WHAT A PLEASANT SURPRISE! WHAT BRINGS YOU HERE, MADAME?
DON'T BE A MORON, TORCHIE. WHAT DA YA WANT 'ER TA DO HERE? SHE MUST HAVE TONS OF MAIL TA DELIVER...
TONS, LITERALLY!
HOW CAN A LITTLE GAL LIKE YOU CARRY ALL THIS WEIGHT? IT MUST BE...
EXCUSE HIM, WILLIE. BEN TENDS TO FORGET THERE'RE MORE MUSCLES AROUND THAN HIS...
MAY I OFFER YOU SOMETHING? WATER, TEA... ANOTHER AUTOGRAPH OF YOURS TRULY?
WAIT A SEC AND I'LL BRING THIS INSIDE...
BE CAREFUL, BEN! WE DON'T WANT HER TO THINK WE'RE SENSELESS BRUTES.
TIME TO LEAVE. NOTHING MORE TO DO HERE FOR TODAY.

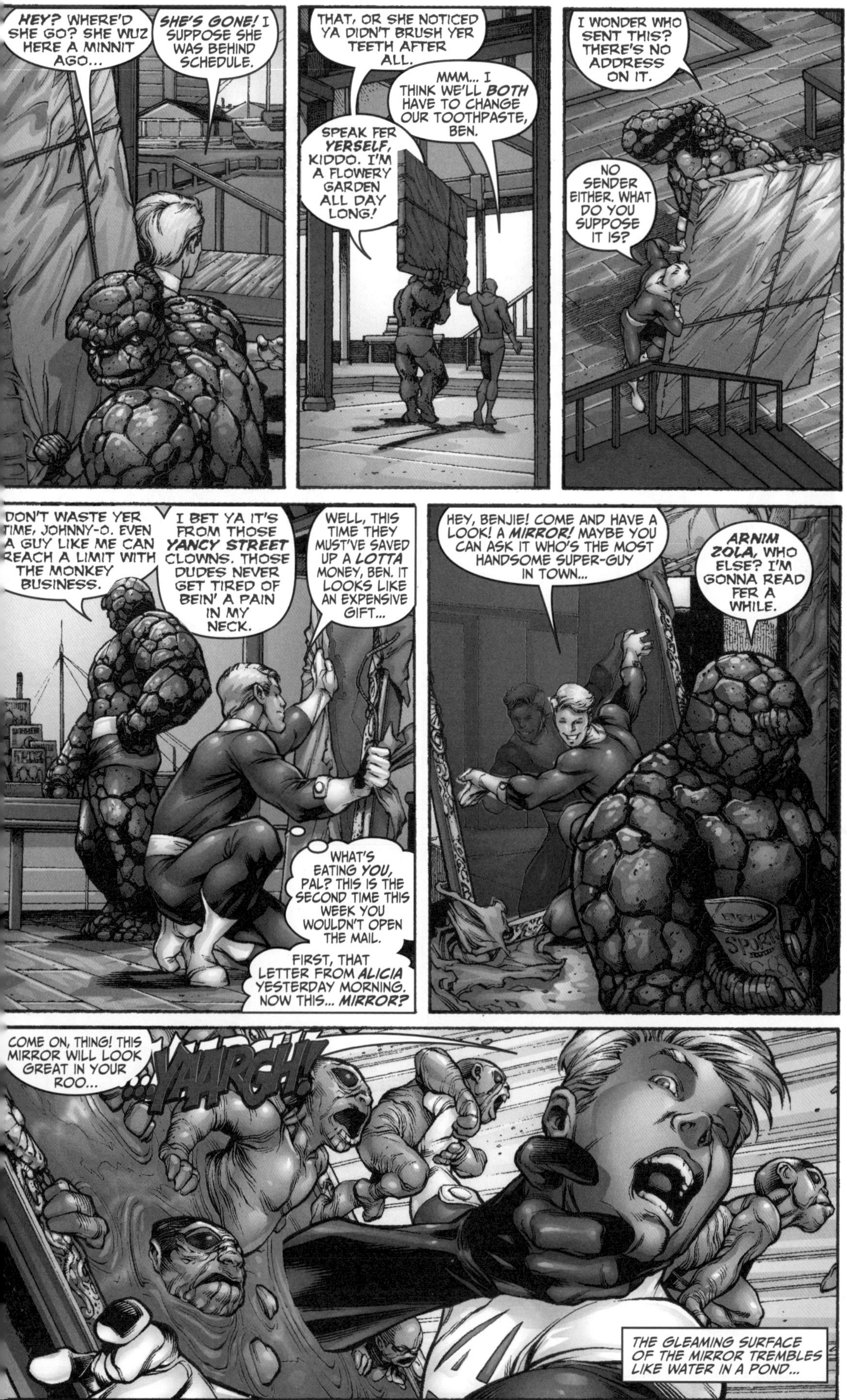

HEY? WHERE'D SHE GO? SHE WUZ HERE A MINNIT AGO...
SHE'S GONE! I SUPPOSE SHE WAS BEHIND SCHEDULE.
THAT, OR SHE NOTICED YA DIDN'T BRUSH YER TEETH AFTER ALL.
MMM... I THINK WE'LL BOTH HAVE TO CHANGE OUR TOOTHPASTE, BEN.
SPEAK FER YERSELF, KIDDO. I'M A FLOWERY GARDEN ALL DAY LONG!
I WONDER WHO SENT THIS? THERE'S NO ADDRESS ON IT.
NO SENDER EITHER. WHAT DO YOU SUPPOSE IT IS?
DON'T WASTE YER TIME, JOHNNY-O. EVEN A GUY LIKE ME CAN REACH A LIMIT WITH THE MONKEY BUSINESS.
I BET YA IT'S FROM THOSE YANCY STREET CLOWNS. THOSE DUDES NEVER GET TIRED OF BEIN' A PAIN IN MY NECK.
WELL, THIS TIME THEY MUST'VE SAVED UP A LOTTA MONEY, BEN. IT LOOKS LIKE AN EXPENSIVE GIFT...
WHAT'S EATING YOU, PAL? THIS IS THE SECOND TIME THIS WEEK YOU WOULDN'T OPEN THE MAIL.
FIRST, THAT LETTER FROM ALICIA YESTERDAY MORNING. NOW THIS... MIRROR?
HEY, BENJIE! COME AND HAVE A LOOK! A MIRROR! MAYBE YOU CAN ASK IT WHO'S THE MOST HANDSOME SUPER-GUY IN TOWN...
ARNIM ZOLA, WHO ELSE? I'M GONNA READ FER A WHILE.
COME ON, THING! THIS MIRROR WILL LOOK GREAT IN YOUR ROO...
...YAARGH!!
THE GLEAMING SURFACE OF THE MIRROR TREMBLES LIKE WATER IN A POND...

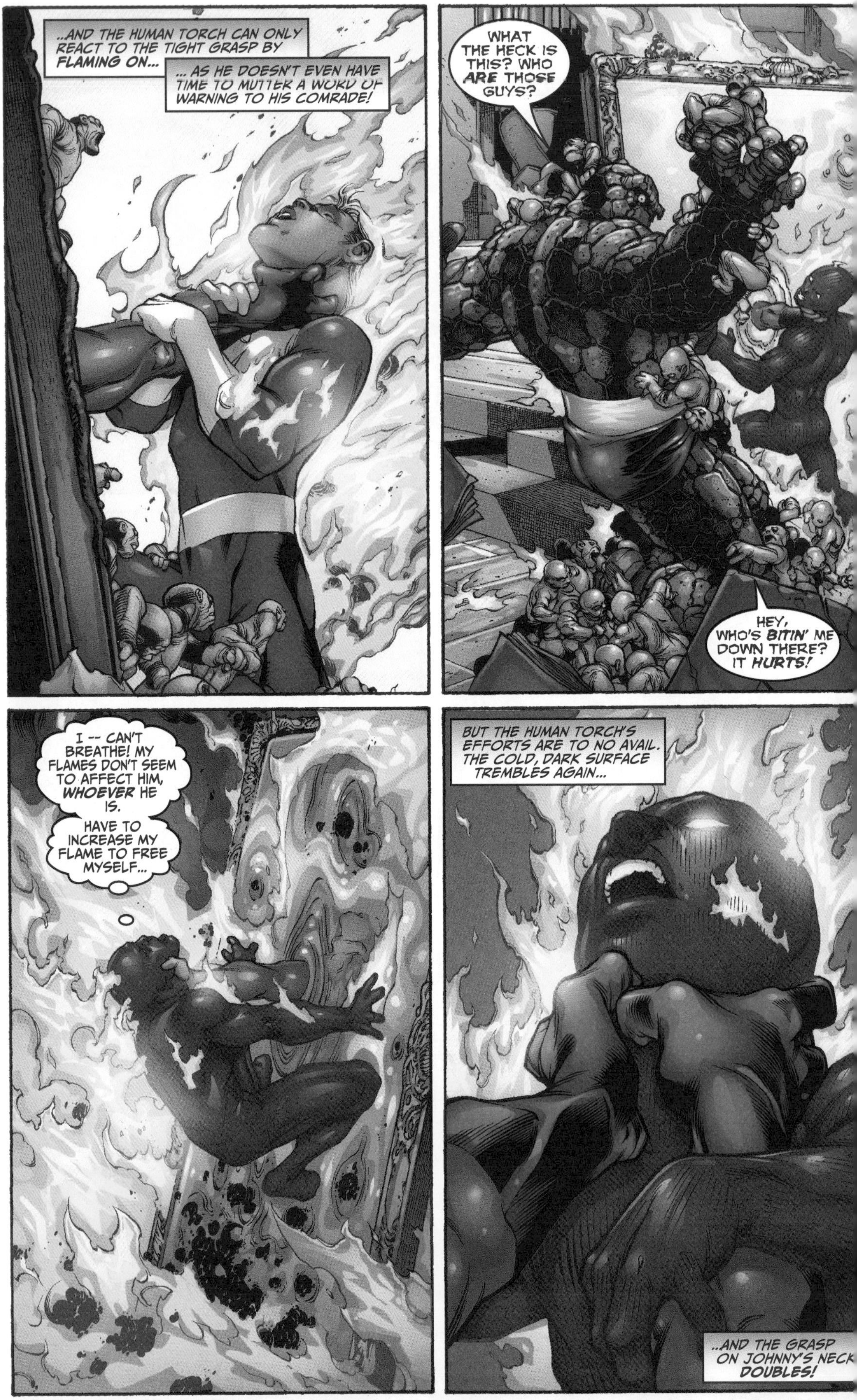
...AND THE HUMAN TORCH CAN ONLY REACT TO THE TIGHT GRASP BY FLAMING ON...
...AS HE DOESN'T EVEN HAVE TIME TO MUTTER A WORD OF WARNING TO HIS COMRADE!
WHAT THE HECK IS THIS? WHO ARE THOSE GUYS?
HEY, WHO'S BITIN' ME DOWN THERE? IT HURTS!
I -- CAN'T BREATHE! MY FLAMES DON'T SEEM TO AFFECT HIM, WHOEVER HE IS.
HAVE TO INCREASE MY FLAME TO FREE MYSELF...
BUT THE HUMAN TORCH'S EFFORTS ARE TO NO AVAIL. THE COLD, DARK SURFACE TREMBLES AGAIN...
...AND THE GRASP ON JOHNNY'S NECK DOUBLES!

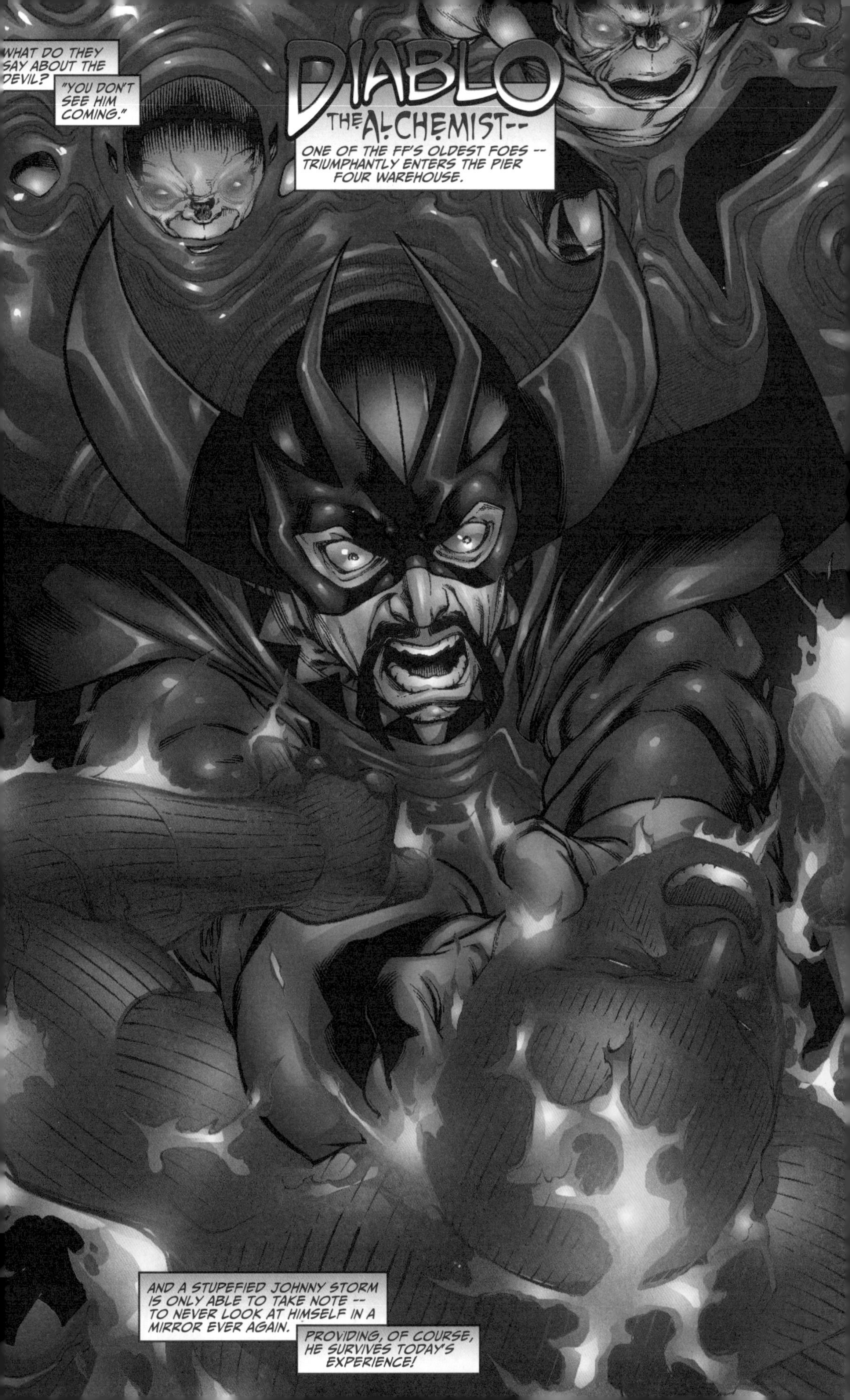
WHAT DO THEY SAY ABOUT THE DEVIL?
"YOU DON'T SEE HIM COMING."
DIABLO
THE ALCHEMIST--
ONE OF THE FF'S OLDEST FOES -- TRIUMPHANTLY ENTERS THE PIER FOUR WAREHOUSE.
AND A STUPEFIED JOHNNY STORM IS ONLY ABLE TO TAKE NOTE -- TO NEVER LOOK AT HIMSELF IN A MIRROR EVER AGAIN.
PROVIDING, OF COURSE, HE SURVIVES TODAY'S EXPERIENCE!

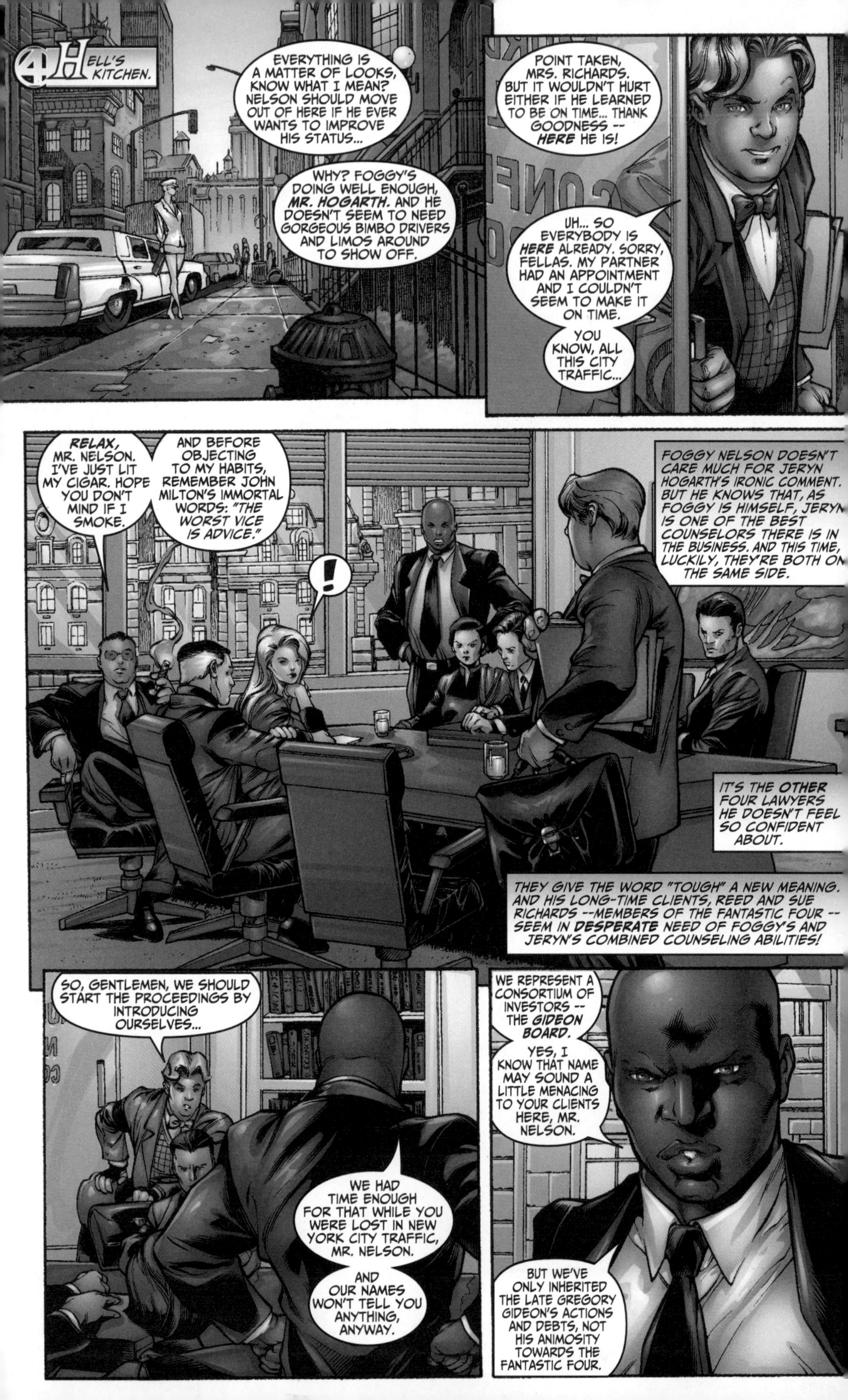

HELL'S KITCHEN.
EVERYTHING IS A MATTER OF LOOKS, KNOW WHAT I MEAN? NELSON SHOULD MOVE OUT OF HERE IF HE EVER WANTS TO IMPROVE HIS STATUS...
WHY? FOGGY'S DOING WELL ENOUGH, MR. HOGARTH. AND HE DOESN'T SEEM TO NEED GORGEOUS BIMBO DRIVERS AND LIMOS AROUND TO SHOW OFF.
POINT TAKEN, MRS. RICHARDS. BUT IT WOULDN'T HURT EITHER IF HE LEARNED TO BE ON TIME... THANK GOODNESS -- HERE HE IS!
UH... SO EVERYBODY IS HERE ALREADY. SORRY, FELLAS. MY PARTNER HAD AN APPOINTMENT AND I COULDN'T SEEM TO MAKE IT ON TIME.
YOU KNOW, ALL THIS CITY TRAFFIC...
RELAX, MR. NELSON. I'VE JUST LIT MY CIGAR. HOPE YOU DON'T MIND IF I SMOKE.
AND BEFORE OBJECTING TO MY HABITS, REMEMBER JOHN MILTON'S IMMORTAL WORDS: "THE WORST VICE IS ADVICE."
!
FOGGY NELSON DOESN'T CARE MUCH FOR JERYN HOGARTH'S IRONIC COMMENT. BUT HE KNOWS THAT, AS FOGGY IS HIMSELF, JERYN IS ONE OF THE BEST COUNSELORS THERE IS IN THE BUSINESS. AND THIS TIME, LUCKILY, THEY'RE BOTH ON THE SAME SIDE.
IT'S THE OTHER FOUR LAWYERS HE DOESN'T FEEL SO CONFIDENT ABOUT.
THEY GIVE THE WORD "TOUGH" A NEW MEANING. AND HIS LONG-TIME CLIENTS, REED AND SUE RICHARDS --MEMBERS OF THE FANTASTIC FOUR -- SEEM IN DESPERATE NEED OF FOGGY'S AND JERYN'S COMBINED COUNSELING ABILITIES!
SO, GENTLEMEN, WE SHOULD START THE PROCEEDINGS BY INTRODUCING OURSELVES...
WE HAD TIME ENOUGH FOR THAT WHILE YOU WERE LOST IN NEW YORK CITY TRAFFIC, MR. NELSON.
AND OUR NAMES WON'T TELL YOU ANYTHING, ANYWAY.
WE REPRESENT A CONSORTIUM OF INVESTORS -- THE GIDEON BOARD.
YES, I KNOW THAT NAME MAY SOUND A LITTLE MENACING TO YOUR CLIENTS HERE, MR. NELSON.
BUT WE'VE ONLY INHERITED THE LATE GREGORY GIDEON'S ACTIONS AND DEBTS, NOT HIS ANIMOSITY TOWARDS THE FANTASTIC FOUR.

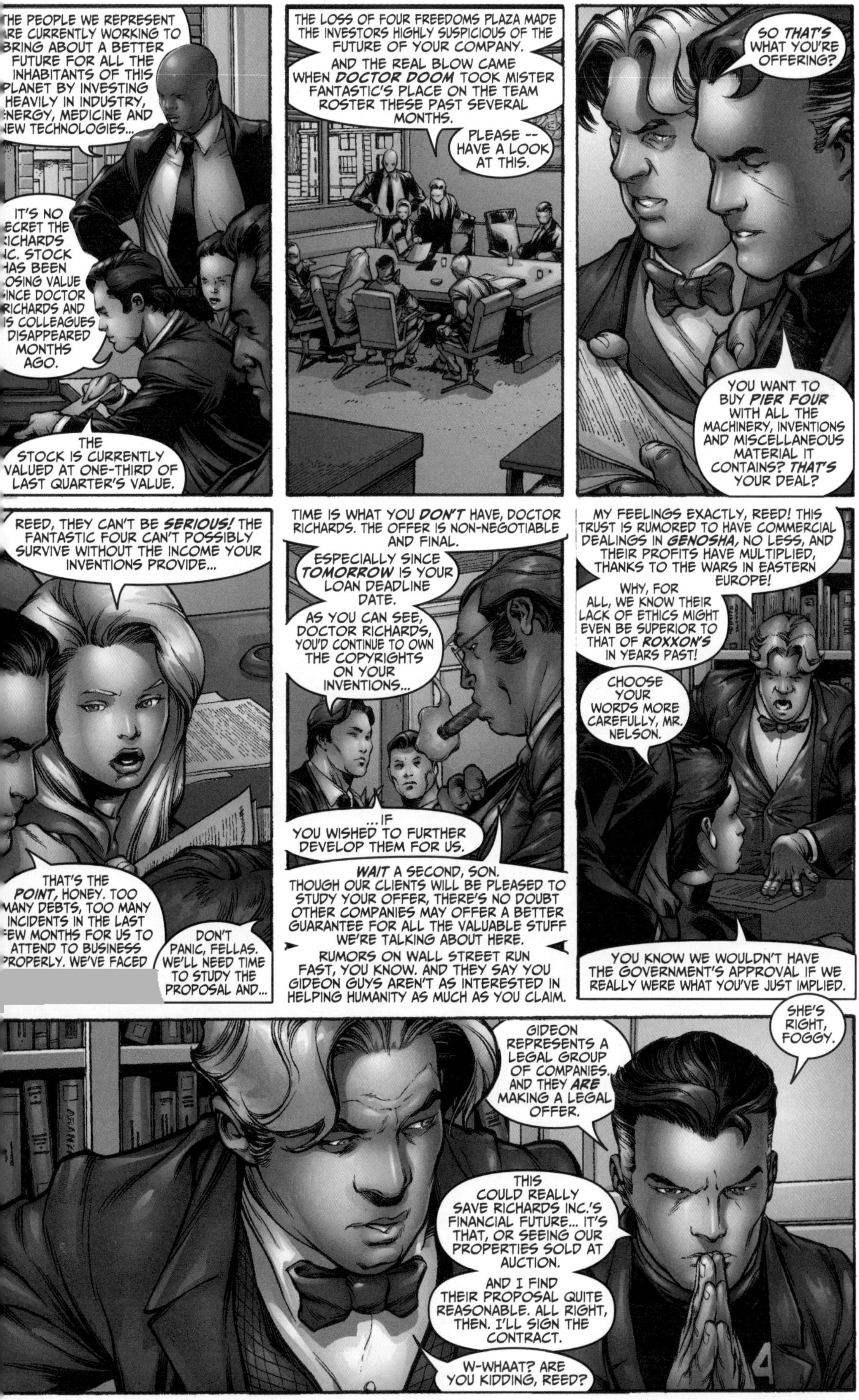

THE PEOPLE WE REPRESENT RE CURRENTLY WORKING TO BRING ABOUT A BETTER FUTURE FOR ALL THE INHABITANTS OF THIS PLANET BY INVESTING HEAVILY IN INDUSTRY, NERGY, MEDICINE AND NEW TECHNOLOGIES...
IT'S NO ECRET THE RICHARDS IC. STOCK HAS BEEN OSING VALUE INCE DOCTOR RICHARDS AND IS COLLEAGUES DISAPPEARED MONTHS AGO.
THE STOCK IS CURRENTLY VALUED AT ONE-THIRD OF LAST QUARTER'S VALUE.
THE LOSS OF FOUR FREEDOMS PLAZA MADE THE INVESTORS HIGHLY SUSPICIOUS OF THE FUTURE OF YOUR COMPANY.
AND THE REAL BLOW CAME WHEN DOCTOR DOOM TOOK MISTER FANTASTIC'S PLACE ON THE TEAM ROSTER THESE PAST SEVERAL MONTHS.
PLEASE -- HAVE A LOOK AT THIS.
SO THAT'S WHAT YOU'RE OFFERING?
YOU WANT TO BUY PIER FOUR WITH ALL THE MACHINERY, INVENTIONS AND MISCELLANEOUS MATERIAL IT CONTAINS? THAT'S YOUR DEAL?
REED, THEY CAN'T BE SERIOUS! THE FANTASTIC FOUR CAN'T POSSIBLY SURVIVE WITHOUT THE INCOME YOUR INVENTIONS PROVIDE...
THAT'S THE POINT, HONEY. TOO MANY DEBTS, TOO MANY INCIDENTS IN THE LAST EW MONTHS FOR US TO ATTEND TO BUSINESS PROPERLY. WE'VE FACED
DON'T PANIC, FELLAS. WE'LL NEED TIME TO STUDY THE PROPOSAL AND...
TIME IS WHAT YOU DON'T HAVE, DOCTOR RICHARDS. THE OFFER IS NON-NEGOTIABLE AND FINAL.
ESPECIALLY SINCE TOMORROW IS YOUR LOAN DEADLINE DATE.
AS YOU CAN SEE, DOCTOR RICHARDS, YOU'D CONTINUE TO OWN THE COPYRIGHTS ON YOUR INVENTIONS...
...IF YOU WISHED TO FURTHER DEVELOP THEM FOR US.
WAIT A SECOND, SON. THOUGH OUR CLIENTS WILL BE PLEASED TO STUDY YOUR OFFER, THERE'S NO DOUBT OTHER COMPANIES MAY OFFER A BETTER GUARANTEE FOR ALL THE VALUABLE STUFF WE'RE TALKING ABOUT HERE.
RUMORS ON WALL STREET RUN FAST, YOU KNOW. AND THEY SAY YOU GIDEON GUYS AREN'T AS INTERESTED IN HELPING HUMANITY AS MUCH AS YOU CLAIM.
MY FEELINGS EXACTLY, REED! THIS TRUST IS RUMORED TO HAVE COMMERCIAL DEALINGS IN GENOSHA, NO LESS, AND THEIR PROFITS HAVE MULTIPLIED, THANKS TO THE WARS IN EASTERN EUROPE!
WHY, FOR ALL, WE KNOW THEIR LACK OF ETHICS MIGHT EVEN BE SUPERIOR TO THAT OF ROXXON'S IN YEARS PAST!
CHOOSE YOUR WORDS MORE CAREFULLY, MR. NELSON.
YOU KNOW WE WOULDN'T HAVE THE GOVERNMENT'S APPROVAL IF WE REALLY WERE WHAT YOU'VE JUST IMPLIED.
GIDEON REPRESENTS A LEGAL GROUP OF COMPANIES. AND THEY ARE MAKING A LEGAL OFFER.
SHE'S RIGHT, FOGGY.
THIS COULD REALLY SAVE RICHARDS INC.'S FINANCIAL FUTURE... IT'S THAT, OR SEEING OUR PROPERTIES SOLD AT AUCTION.
AND I FIND THEIR PROPOSAL QUITE REASONABLE. ALL RIGHT, THEN. I'LL SIGN THE CONTRACT.
W-WHAAT? ARE YOU KIDDING, REED?

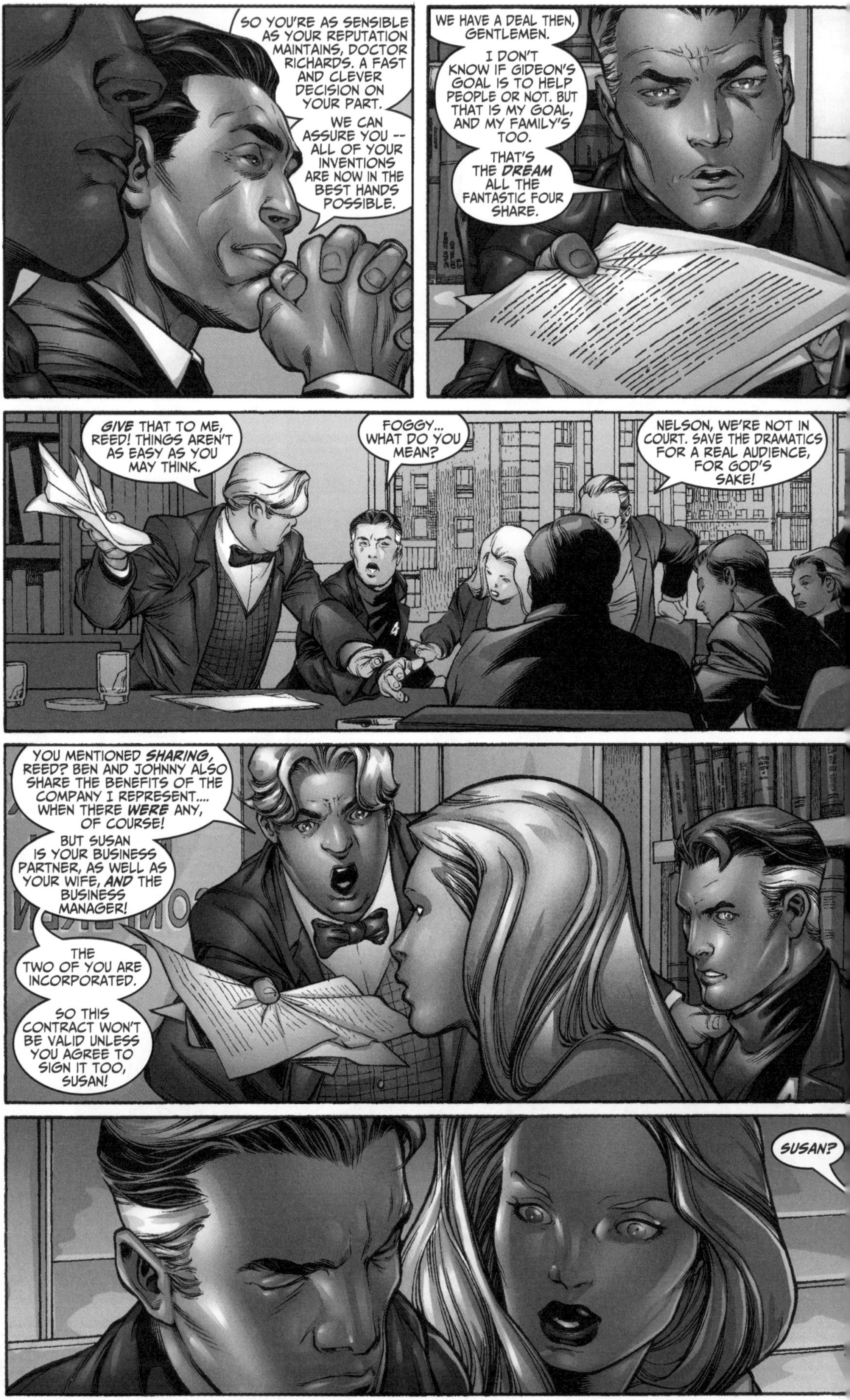
SO YOU'RE AS SENSIBLE AS YOUR REPUTATION MAINTAINS, DOCTOR RICHARDS. A FAST AND CLEVER DECISION ON YOUR PART.
WE CAN ASSURE YOU -- ALL OF YOUR INVENTIONS ARE NOW IN THE BEST HANDS POSSIBLE.
WE HAVE A DEAL THEN, GENTLEMEN.
I DON'T KNOW IF GIDEON'S GOAL IS TO HELP PEOPLE OR NOT. BUT THAT IS MY GOAL, AND MY FAMILY'S TOO.
THAT'S THE DREAM ALL THE FANTASTIC FOUR SHARE.
GIVE THAT TO ME, REED! THINGS AREN'T AS EASY AS YOU MAY THINK.
FOGGY... WHAT DO YOU MEAN?
NELSON, WE'RE NOT IN COURT. SAVE THE DRAMATICS FOR A REAL AUDIENCE, FOR GOD'S SAKE!
YOU MENTIONED SHARING, REED? BEN AND JOHNNY ALSO SHARE THE BENEFITS OF THE COMPANY I REPRESENT.... WHEN THERE WERE ANY, OF COURSE!
BUT SUSAN IS YOUR BUSINESS PARTNER, AS WELL AS YOUR WIFE, AND THE BUSINESS MANAGER!
THE TWO OF YOU ARE INCORPORATED.
SO THIS CONTRACT WON'T BE VALID UNLESS YOU AGREE TO SIGN IT TOO, SUSAN!
SUSAN?

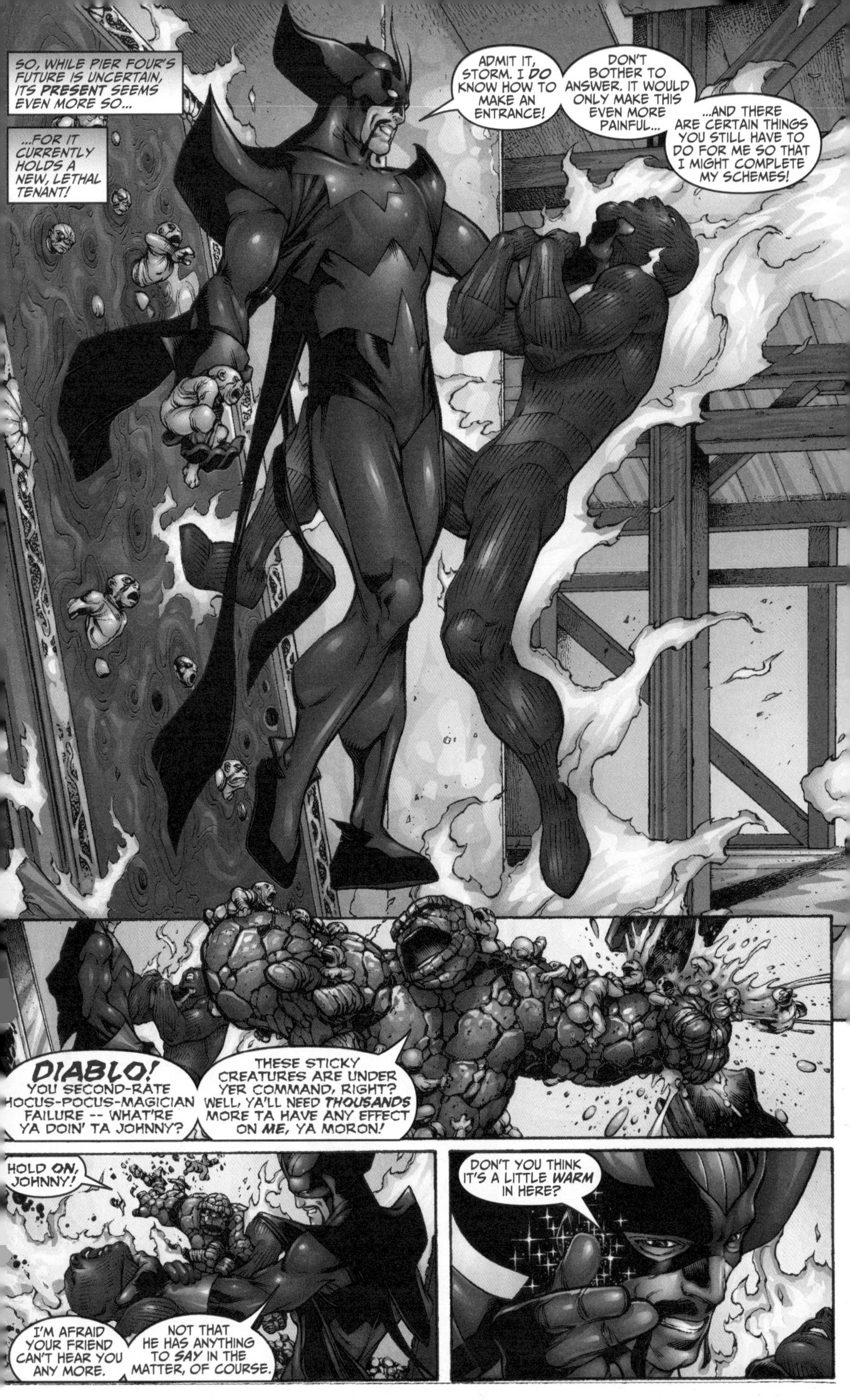
SO, WHILE PIER FOUR'S FUTURE IS UNCERTAIN, ITS PRESENT SEEMS EVEN MORE SO...
...FOR IT CURRENTLY HOLDS A NEW, LETHAL TENANT!
ADMIT IT, STORM. I DO KNOW HOW TO MAKE AN ENTRANCE!
DON'T BOTHER TO ANSWER. IT WOULD ONLY MAKE THIS EVEN MORE PAINFUL...
...AND THERE ARE CERTAIN THINGS YOU STILL HAVE TO DO FOR ME SO THAT I MIGHT COMPLETE MY SCHEMES!
DIABLO! YOU SECOND-RATE HOCUS-POCUS-MAGICIAN FAILURE -- WHAT'RE YA DOIN' TA JOHNNY?
THESE STICKY CREATURES ARE UNDER YER COMMAND, RIGHT? WELL, YA'LL NEED THOUSANDS MORE TA HAVE ANY EFFECT ON ME, YA MORON!
HOLD ON, JOHNNY!
I'M AFRAID YOUR FRIEND CAN'T HEAR YOU ANY MORE.
NOT THAT HE HAS ANYTHING TO SAY IN THE MATTER, OF COURSE.
DON'T YOU THINK IT'S A LITTLE WARM IN HERE?

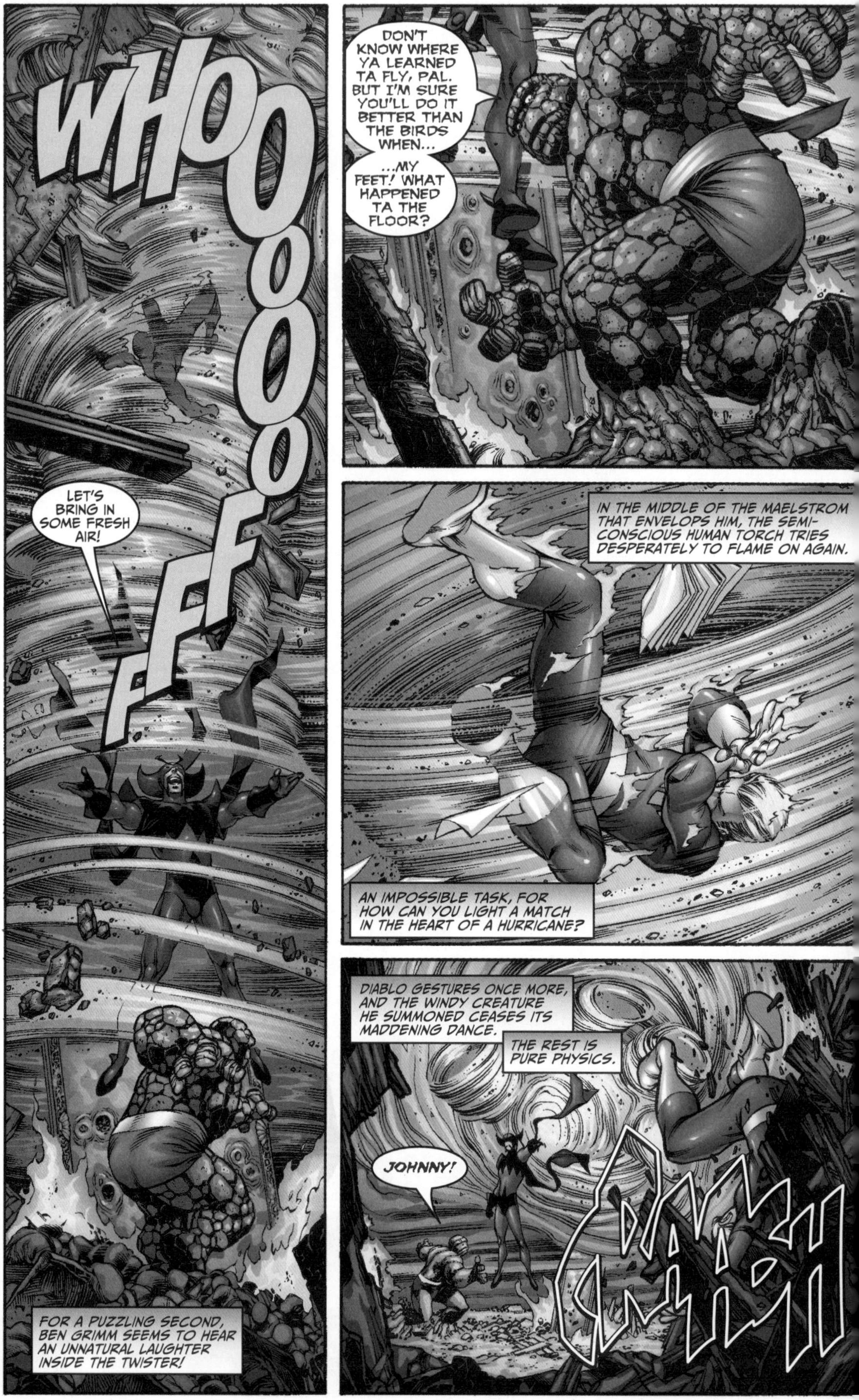
WHOOOOOOOFFFF
LET'S BRING IN SOME FRESH AIR!
FOR A PUZZLING SECOND, BEN GRIMM SEEMS TO HEAR AN UNNATURAL LAUGHTER INSIDE THE TWISTER!
DON'T KNOW WHERE YA LEARNED TA FLY, PAL. BUT I'M SURE YOU'LL DO IT BETTER THAN THE BIRDS WHEN...
...MY FEET! WHAT HAPPENED TA THE FLOOR?
IN THE MIDDLE OF THE MAELSTROM THAT ENVELOPS HIM, THE SEMI-CONSCIOUS HUMAN TORCH TRIES DESPERATELY TO FLAME ON AGAIN.
AN IMPOSSIBLE TASK, FOR HOW CAN YOU LIGHT A MATCH IN THE HEART OF A HURRICANE?
DIABLO GESTURES ONCE MORE, AND THE WINDY CREATURE HE SUMMONED CEASES ITS MADDENING DANCE.
THE REST IS PURE PHYSICS.
JOHNNY!

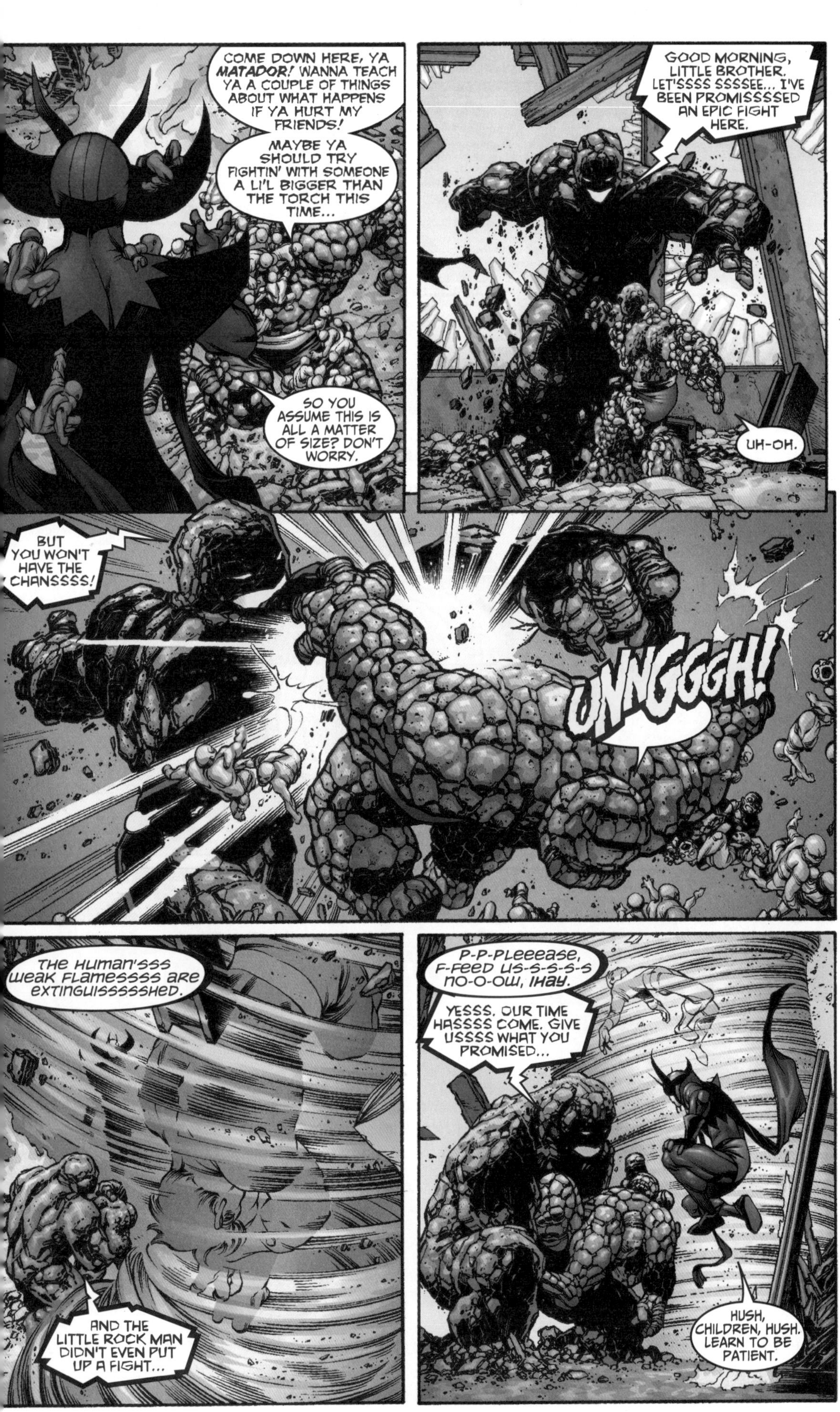
COME DOWN HERE, YA MATADOR! WANNA TEACH YA A COUPLE OF THINGS ABOUT WHAT HAPPENS IF YA HURT MY FRIENDS!
MAYBE YA SHOULD TRY FIGHTIN' WITH SOMEONE A LI'L BIGGER THAN THE TORCH THIS TIME...
SO YOU ASSUME THIS IS ALL A MATTER OF SIZE? DON'T WORRY.
GOOD MORNING, LITTLE BROTHER. LET'SSSS SSSSEE... I'VE BEEN PROMISSSSED AN EPIC FIGHT HERE.
UH-OH.
BUT YOU WON'T HAVE THE CHANSSSS!
UNNGGGH!
THE HUMAN'SSS WEAK FLAMESSSS ARE EXTINGUISSSSSHED.
AND THE LITTLE ROCK MAN DIDN'T EVEN PUT UP A FIGHT...
P-P-PLEEEASE, F-FEED US-S-S-S-S NO-O-OW, IHAY.
YESSS. OUR TIME HASSSS COME. GIVE USSSS WHAT YOU PROMISED...
HUSH, CHILDREN, HUSH. LEARN TO BE PATIENT.

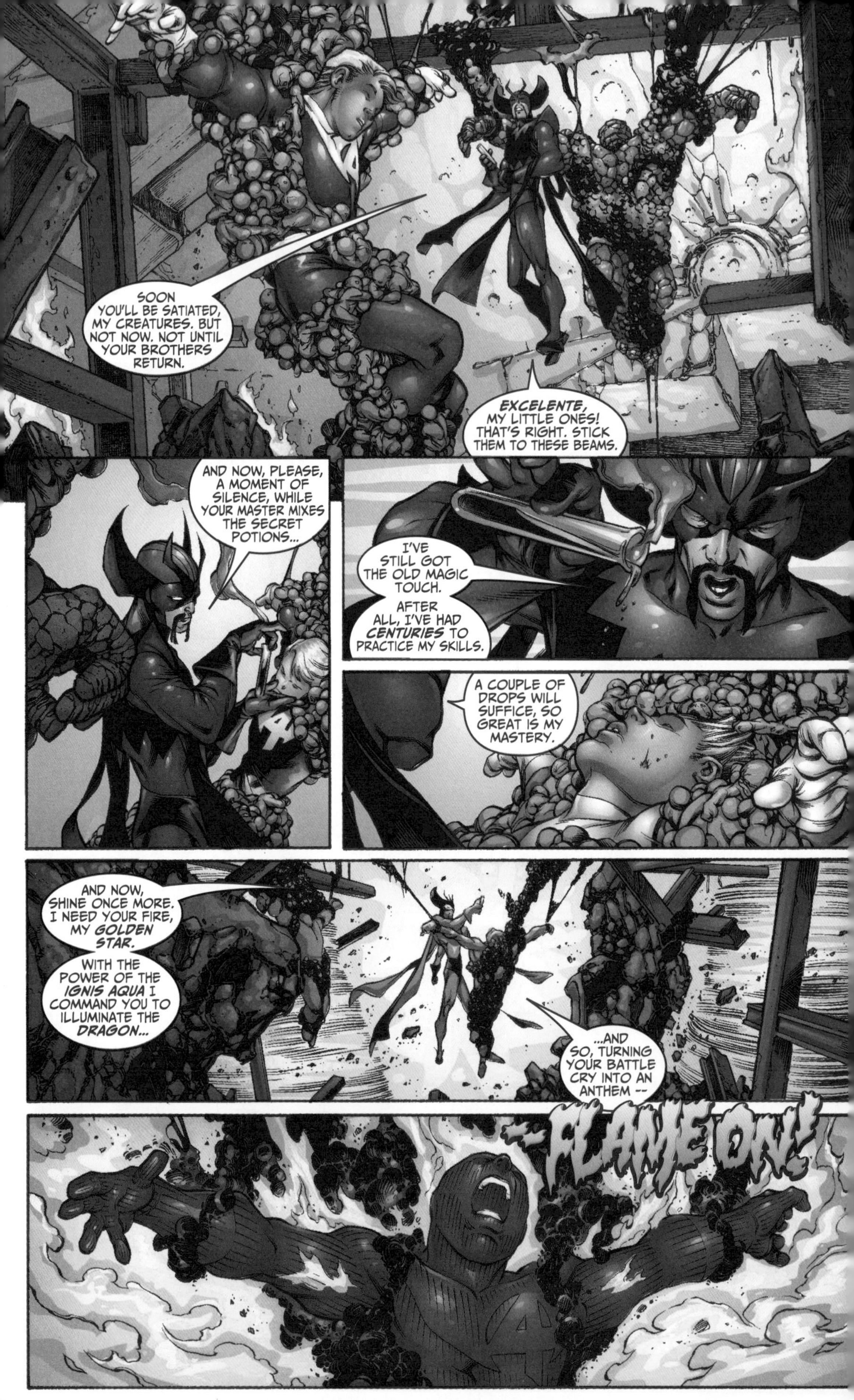
SOON YOU'LL BE SATIATED, MY CREATURES. BUT NOT NOW. NOT UNTIL YOUR BROTHERS RETURN.
EXCELENTE, MY LITTLE ONES! THAT'S RIGHT. STICK THEM TO THESE BEAMS.
AND NOW, PLEASE, A MOMENT OF SILENCE, WHILE YOUR MASTER MIXES THE SECRET POTIONS...
I'VE STILL GOT THE OLD MAGIC TOUCH.
AFTER ALL, I'VE HAD CENTURIES TO PRACTICE MY SKILLS.
A COUPLE OF DROPS WILL SUFFICE, SO GREAT IS MY MASTERY.
AND NOW, SHINE ONCE MORE. I NEED YOUR FIRE, MY GOLDEN STAR.
WITH THE POWER OF THE IGNIS AQUA I COMMAND YOU TO ILLUMINATE THE DRAGON...
...AND SO, TURNING YOUR BATTLE CRY INTO AN ANTHEM --
--FLAME ON!

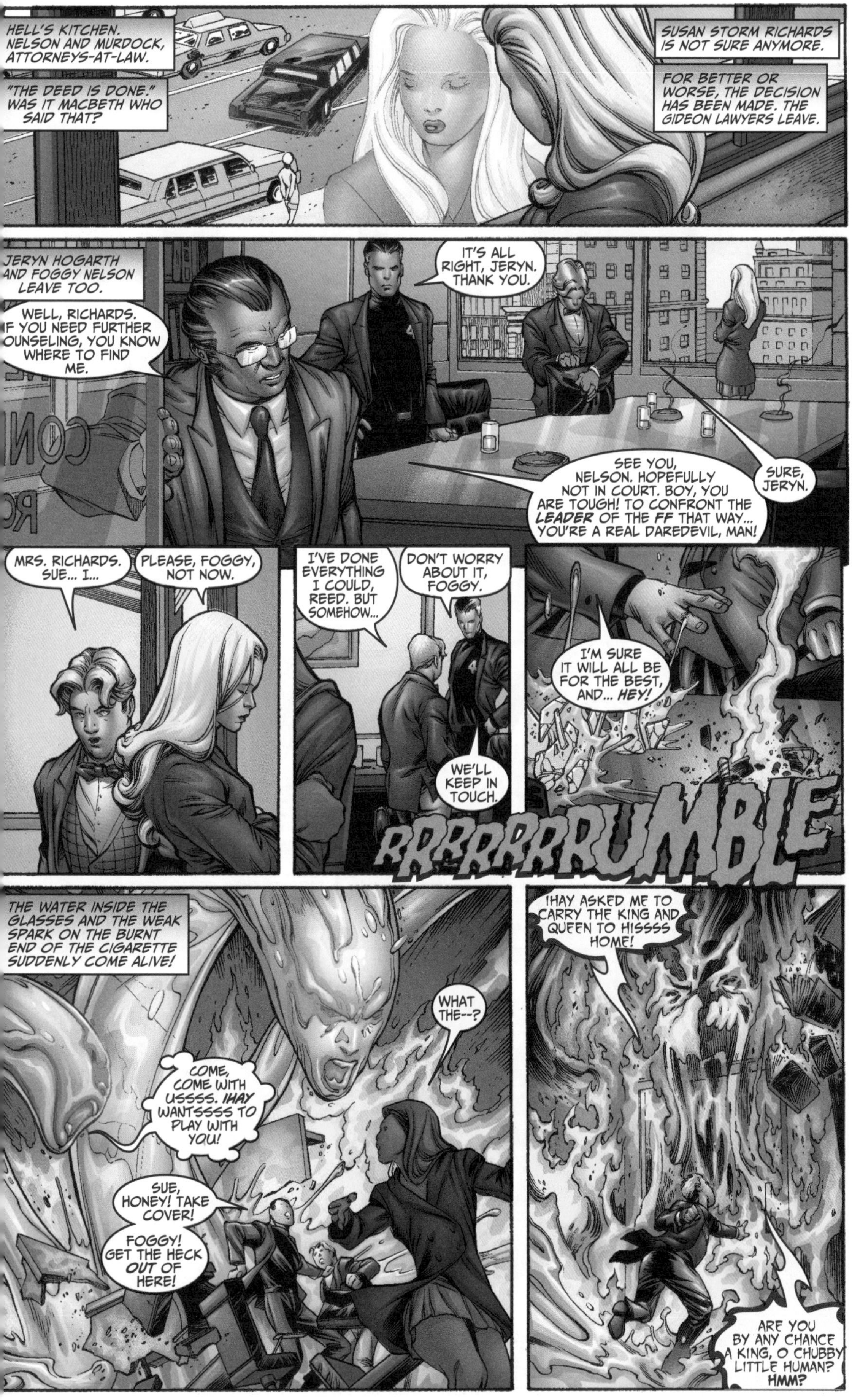
HELL'S KITCHEN. NELSON AND MURDOCK, ATTORNEYS-AT-LAW.
"THE DEED IS DONE." WAS IT MACBETH WHO SAID THAT?
SUSAN STORM RICHARDS IS NOT SURE ANYMORE.
FOR BETTER OR WORSE, THE DECISION HAS BEEN MADE. THE GIDEON LAWYERS LEAVE.
JERYN HOGARTH AND FOGGY NELSON LEAVE TOO.
WELL, RICHARDS. IF YOU NEED FURTHER COUNSELING, YOU KNOW WHERE TO FIND ME.
IT'S ALL RIGHT, JERYN. THANK YOU.
SEE YOU, NELSON. HOPEFULLY NOT IN COURT. BOY, YOU ARE TOUGH! TO CONFRONT THE LEADER OF THE FF THAT WAY... YOU'RE A REAL DAREDEVIL, MAN!
SURE, JERYN.
MRS. RICHARDS. SUE... I...
PLEASE, FOGGY, NOT NOW.
I'VE DONE EVERYTHING I COULD, REED. BUT SOMEHOW...
DON'T WORRY ABOUT IT, FOGGY.
WE'LL KEEP IN TOUCH.
I'M SURE IT WILL ALL BE FOR THE BEST, AND... HEY!
RRRRRRRUMBLE
THE WATER INSIDE THE GLASSES AND THE WEAK SPARK ON THE BURNT END OF THE CIGARETTE SUDDENLY COME ALIVE!
WHAT THE--?
COME, COME WITH USSSS. IHAY WANTSSSS TO PLAY WITH YOU!
SUE, HONEY! TAKE COVER!
FOGGY! GET THE HECK OUT OF HERE!
IHAY ASKED ME TO CARRY THE KING AND QUEEN TO HISSSS HOME!
ARE YOU BY ANY CHANCE A KING, O CHUBBY LITTLE HUMAN? HMM?

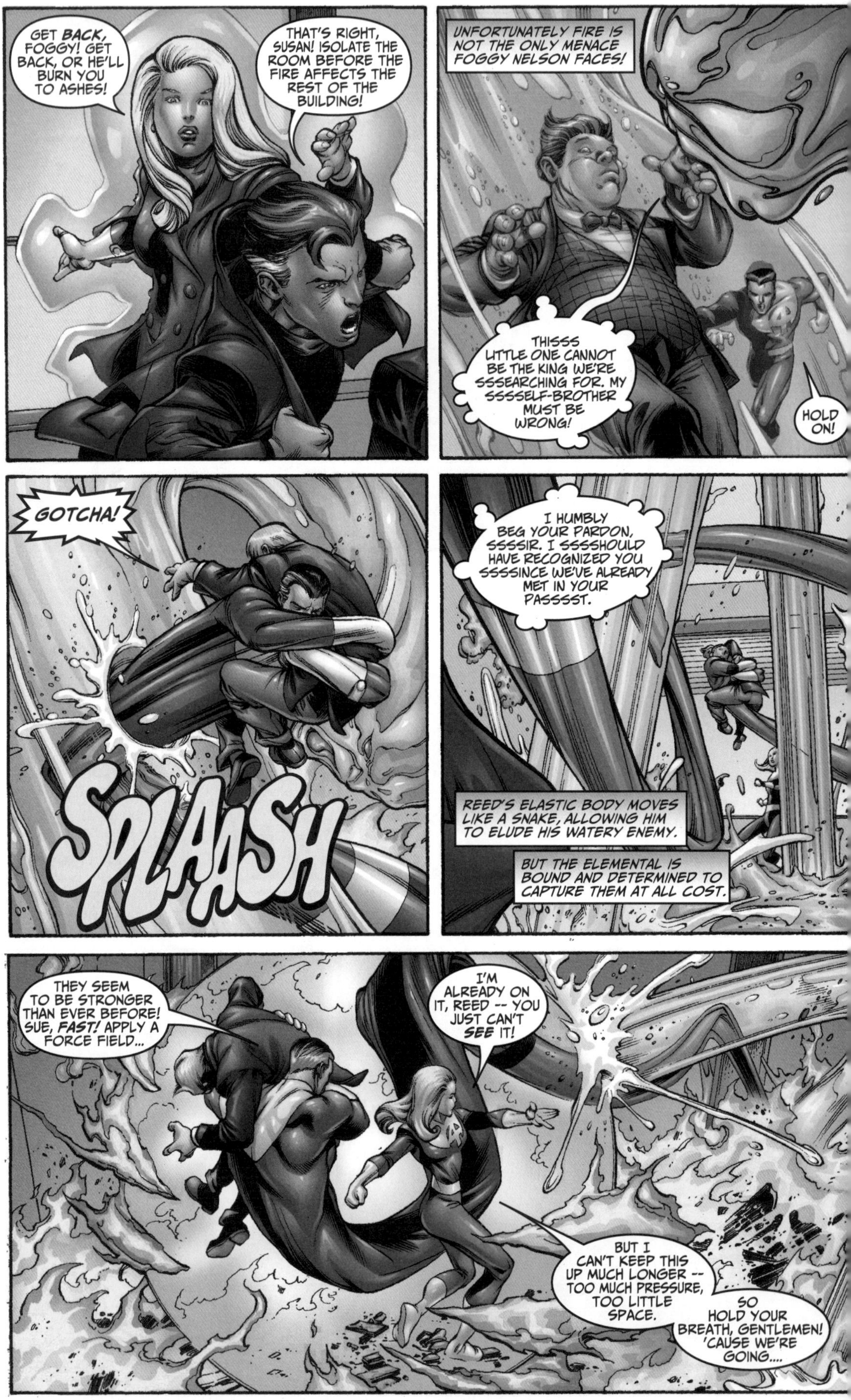
GET BACK, FOGGY! GET BACK, OR HE'LL BURN YOU TO ASHES!
THAT'S RIGHT, SUSAN! ISOLATE THE ROOM BEFORE THE FIRE AFFECTS THE REST OF THE BUILDING!
UNFORTUNATELY FIRE IS NOT THE ONLY MENACE FOGGY NELSON FACES!
THISSS LITTLE ONE CANNOT BE THE KING WE'RE SSSEARCHING FOR. MY SSSSELF-BROTHER MUST BE WRONG!
HOLD ON!
GOTCHA!
SPLAASH
I HUMBLY BEG YOUR PARDON, SSSSIR. I SSSSHOULD HAVE RECOGNIZED YOU SSSSINCE WE'VE ALREADY MET IN YOUR PASSSST.
REED'S ELASTIC BODY MOVES LIKE A SNAKE, ALLOWING HIM TO ELUDE HIS WATERY ENEMY.
BUT THE ELEMENTAL IS BOUND AND DETERMINED TO CAPTURE THEM AT ALL COST.
THEY SEEM TO BE STRONGER THAN EVER BEFORE! SUE, FAST! APPLY A FORCE FIELD...
I'M ALREADY ON IT, REED -- YOU JUST CAN'T SEE IT!
BUT I CAN'T KEEP THIS UP MUCH LONGER -- TOO MUCH PRESSURE, TOO LITTLE SPACE.
SO HOLD YOUR BREATH, GENTLEMEN! 'CAUSE WE'RE GOING....

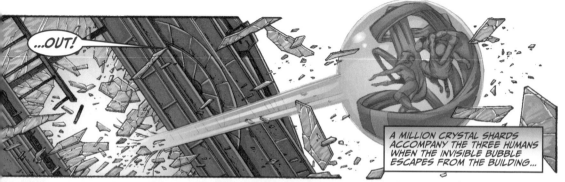

...OUT!

A MILLION CRYSTAL SHARDS ACCOMPANY THE THREE HUMANS WHEN THE INVISIBLE BUBBLE ESCAPES FROM THE BUILDING...

...BUT REED STRETCHES FAST ENOUGH TO PROTECT THE BYSTANDERS ON THE STREETS BELOW.

HEY, WHAT'S THAT...?

COME, COME BACK! YOU CANNOT ESSSSSCAPE! YOU ARE THE QUEEN IN OUR GAME. UUUNNNGGHH!

AIEEEE! WHAT NEW HIDEOUSSS MAGIC ISSS THISSS?

HIDEOUS? CALL IT WHAT YOU WANT!

WITH HER POWERS TURNED TO THE MAX, SUE USES THE INVISIBLE FORCE FIELD THAT SECONDS BEFORE HAD ISOLATED THE ROOM, KEEPING THE ELEMENTALS AT BAY.

AAAAARRGH!

THE TENSION... IT'S ALMOST UNBEARABLE.

THERE THEY ARE, SURROUNDED BY MY CONTAINMENT BUBBLE. ALL I HAVE TO DO IS HOLD... HOLD...

THEY VANISHED!

POP

HEY, BUDDY, WAKE UP. ARE YOU OKAY?

WA... WA... OH, MY. REED? SUE?

IF YOU WANNA TELL THEM ANYTHIN', I HOPE YOU GOT THEIR E-MAIL, SON...

...'CAUSE THERE THEY GO!

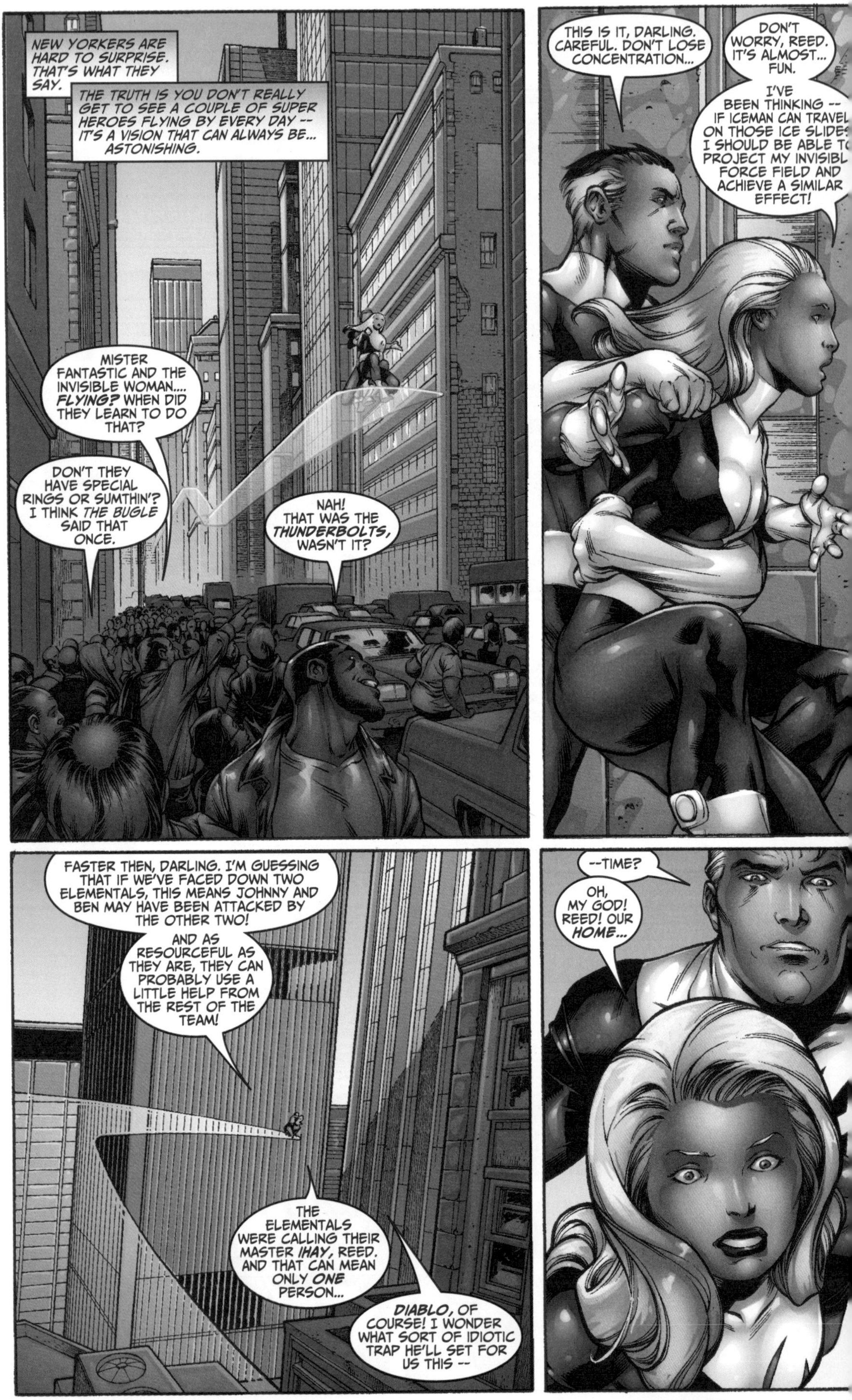
NEW YORKERS ARE HARD TO SURPRISE. THAT'S WHAT THEY SAY.
THE TRUTH IS YOU DON'T REALLY GET TO SEE A COUPLE OF SUPER HEROES FLYING BY EVERY DAY -- IT'S A VISION THAT CAN ALWAYS BE... ASTONISHING.
MISTER FANTASTIC AND THE INVISIBLE WOMAN.... FLYING? WHEN DID THEY LEARN TO DO THAT?
DON'T THEY HAVE SPECIAL RINGS OR SUMTHIN'? I THINK THE BUGLE SAID THAT ONCE.
NAH! THAT WAS THE THUNDERBOLTS, WASN'T IT?
THIS IS IT, DARLING. CAREFUL. DON'T LOSE CONCENTRATION...
DON'T WORRY, REED. IT'S ALMOST... FUN.
I'VE BEEN THINKING -- IF ICEMAN CAN TRAVEL ON THOSE ICE SLIDES I SHOULD BE ABLE TO PROJECT MY INVISIBLE FORCE FIELD AND ACHIEVE A SIMILAR EFFECT!
FASTER THEN, DARLING. I'M GUESSING THAT IF WE'VE FACED DOWN TWO ELEMENTALS, THIS MEANS JOHNNY AND BEN MAY HAVE BEEN ATTACKED BY THE OTHER TWO!
AND AS RESOURCEFUL AS THEY ARE, THEY CAN PROBABLY USE A LITTLE HELP FROM THE REST OF THE TEAM!
THE ELEMENTALS WERE CALLING THEIR MASTER IHAY, REED. AND THAT CAN MEAN ONLY ONE PERSON...
DIABLO, OF COURSE! I WONDER WHAT SORT OF IDIOTIC TRAP HE'LL SET FOR US THIS --
--TIME?
OH, MY GOD! REED! OUR HOME...

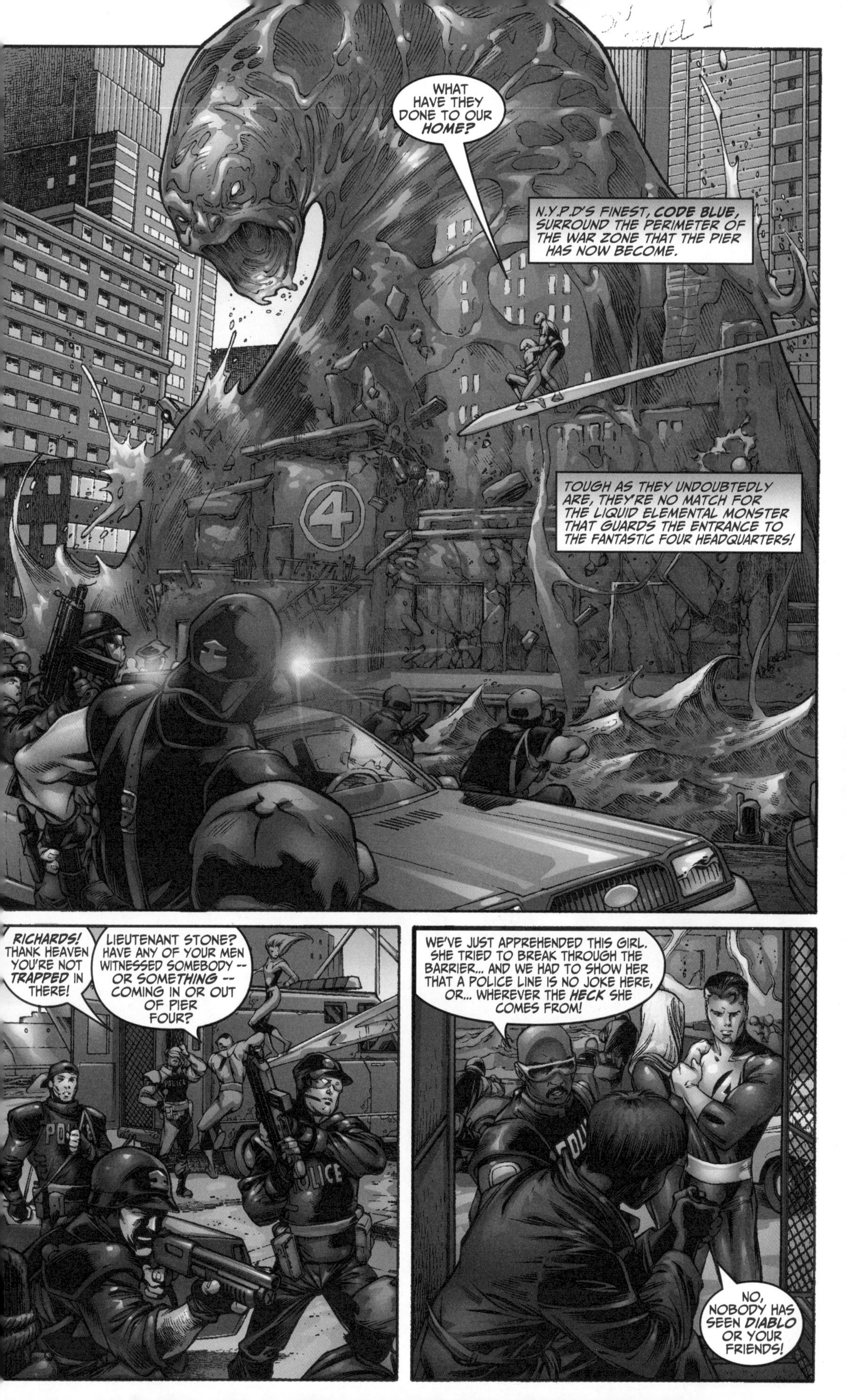
WHAT HAVE THEY DONE TO OUR HOME?
N.Y.P.D'S FINEST, CODE BLUE, SURROUND THE PERIMETER OF THE WAR ZONE THAT THE PIER HAS NOW BECOME.
TOUGH AS THEY UNDOUBTEDLY ARE, THEY'RE NO MATCH FOR THE LIQUID ELEMENTAL MONSTER THAT GUARDS THE ENTRANCE TO THE FANTASTIC FOUR HEADQUARTERS!
RICHARDS! THANK HEAVEN YOU'RE NOT TRAPPED IN THERE!
LIEUTENANT STONE? HAVE ANY OF YOUR MEN WITNESSED SOMEBODY -- OR SOMETHING -- COMING IN OR OUT OF PIER FOUR?
WE'VE JUST APPREHENDED THIS GIRL. SHE TRIED TO BREAK THROUGH THE BARRIER... AND WE HAD TO SHOW HER THAT A POLICE LINE IS NO JOKE HERE, OR... WHEREVER THE HECK SHE COMES FROM!
NO, NOBODY HAS SEEN DIABLO OR YOUR FRIENDS!

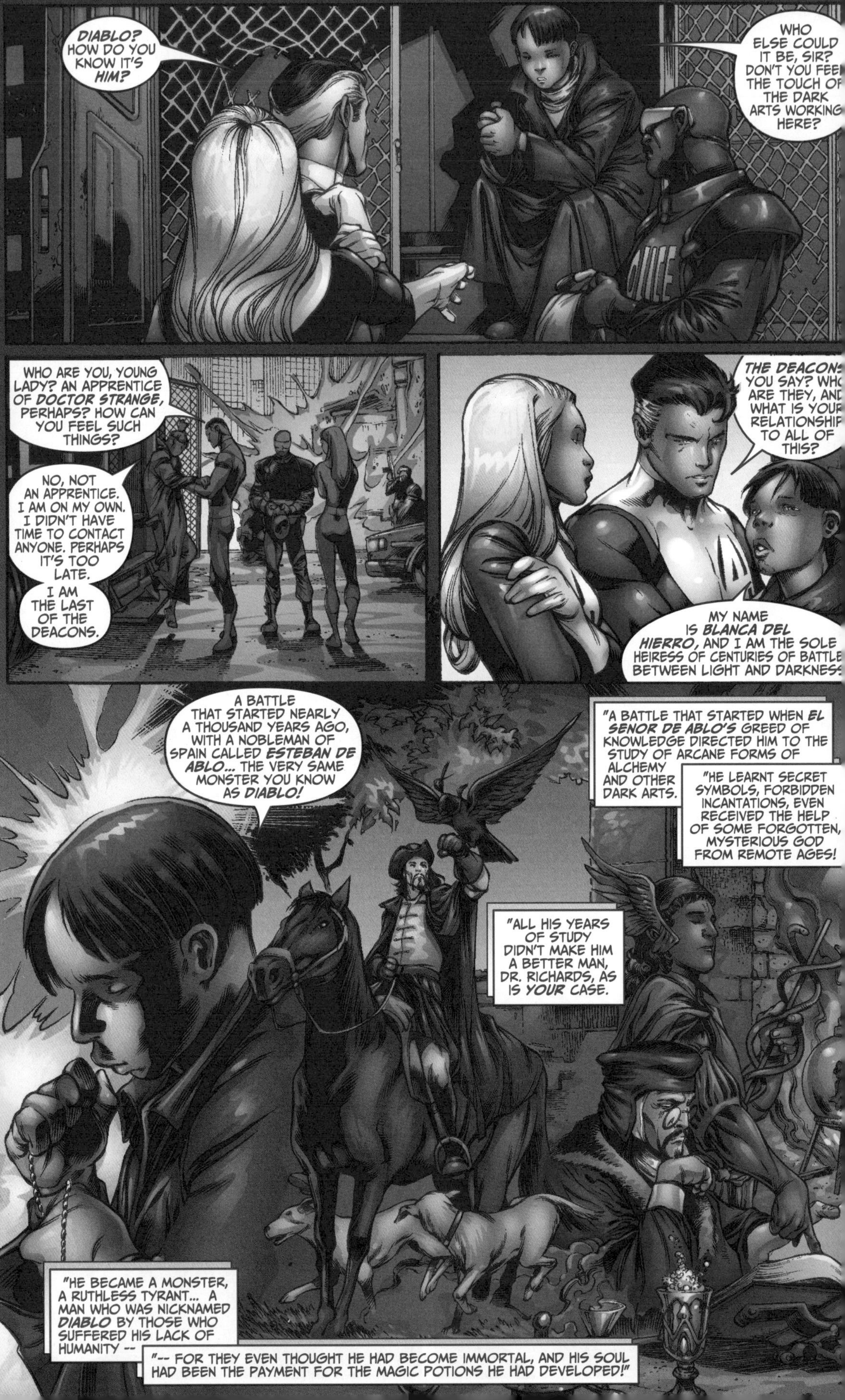
DIABLO? HOW DO YOU KNOW IT'S HIM?
WHO ELSE COULD IT BE, SIR? DON'T YOU FEEL THE TOUCH OF THE DARK ARTS WORKING HERE?
WHO ARE YOU, YOUNG LADY? AN APPRENTICE OF DOCTOR STRANGE, PERHAPS? HOW CAN YOU FEEL SUCH THINGS?
NO, NOT AN APPRENTICE. I AM ON MY OWN. I DIDN'T HAVE TIME TO CONTACT ANYONE. PERHAPS IT'S TOO LATE.
I AM THE LAST OF THE DEACONS.
THE DEACONS YOU SAY? WHO ARE THEY, AND WHAT IS YOUR RELATIONSHIP TO ALL OF THIS?
MY NAME IS BLANCA DEL HIERRO, AND I AM THE SOLE HEIRESS OF CENTURIES OF BATTLE BETWEEN LIGHT AND DARKNESS.
A BATTLE THAT STARTED NEARLY A THOUSAND YEARS AGO, WITH A NOBLEMAN OF SPAIN CALLED ESTEBAN DE ABLO... THE VERY SAME MONSTER YOU KNOW AS DIABLO!
"A BATTLE THAT STARTED WHEN EL SENOR DE ABLO'S GREED OF KNOWLEDGE DIRECTED HIM TO THE STUDY OF ARCANE FORMS OF ALCHEMY AND OTHER DARK ARTS.
"HE LEARNT SECRET SYMBOLS, FORBIDDEN INCANTATIONS, EVEN RECEIVED THE HELP OF SOME FORGOTTEN, MYSTERIOUS GOD FROM REMOTE AGES!
"ALL HIS YEARS OF STUDY DIDN'T MAKE HIM A BETTER MAN, DR. RICHARDS, AS IS YOUR CASE.
"HE BECAME A MONSTER, A RUTHLESS TYRANT... A MAN WHO WAS NICKNAMED DIABLO BY THOSE WHO SUFFERED HIS LACK OF HUMANITY --
"-- FOR THEY EVEN THOUGHT HE HAD BECOME IMMORTAL, AND HIS SOUL HAD BEEN THE PAYMENT FOR THE MAGIC POTIONS HE HAD DEVELOPED!"

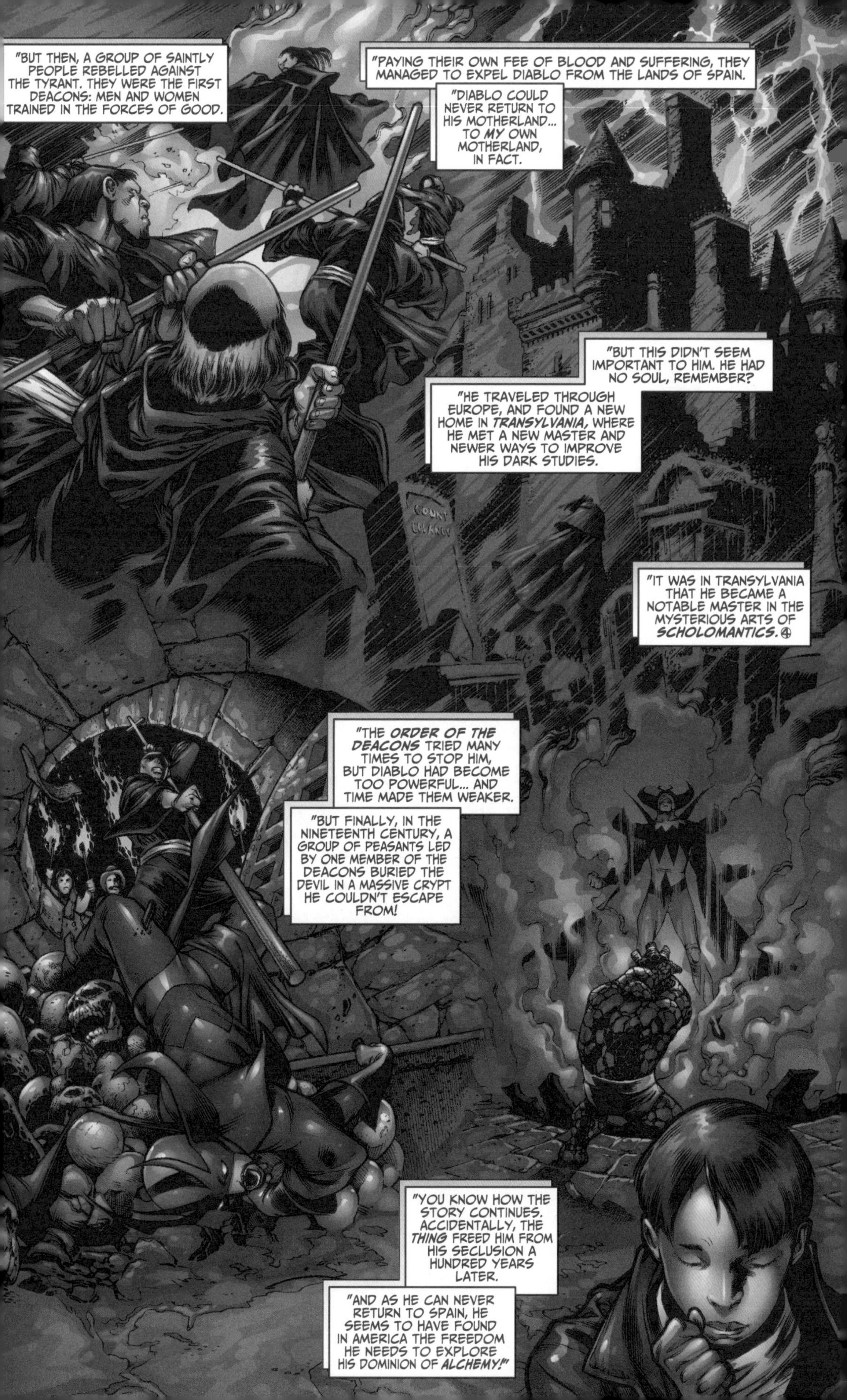
"BUT THEN, A GROUP OF SAINTLY PEOPLE REBELLED AGAINST THE TYRANT. THEY WERE THE FIRST DEACONS: MEN AND WOMEN TRAINED IN THE FORCES OF GOOD.
"PAYING THEIR OWN FEE OF BLOOD AND SUFFERING, THEY MANAGED TO EXPEL DIABLO FROM THE LANDS OF SPAIN.
"DIABLO COULD NEVER RETURN TO HIS MOTHERLAND... TO MY OWN MOTHERLAND, IN FACT.
"BUT THIS DIDN'T SEEM IMPORTANT TO HIM. HE HAD NO SOUL, REMEMBER?
"HE TRAVELED THROUGH EUROPE, AND FOUND A NEW HOME IN TRANSYLVANIA, WHERE HE MET A NEW MASTER AND NEWER WAYS TO IMPROVE HIS DARK STUDIES.
"IT WAS IN TRANSYLVANIA THAT HE BECAME A NOTABLE MASTER IN THE MYSTERIOUS ARTS OF SCHOLOMANTICS.
"THE ORDER OF THE DEACONS TRIED MANY TIMES TO STOP HIM, BUT DIABLO HAD BECOME TOO POWERFUL... AND TIME MADE THEM WEAKER.
"BUT FINALLY, IN THE NINETEENTH CENTURY, A GROUP OF PEASANTS LED BY ONE MEMBER OF THE DEACONS BURIED THE DEVIL IN A MASSIVE CRYPT HE COULDN'T ESCAPE FROM!
"YOU KNOW HOW THE STORY CONTINUES. ACCIDENTALLY, THE THING FREED HIM FROM HIS SECLUSION A HUNDRED YEARS LATER.
"AND AS HE CAN NEVER RETURN TO SPAIN, HE SEEMS TO HAVE FOUND IN AMERICA THE FREEDOM HE NEEDS TO EXPLORE HIS DOMINION OF ALCHEMY!"

I ADMIT I *HAVE* BEEN STUDYING DIABLO'S ORIGIN AND POWERS. THE DEACONS WERE MENTIONED BRIEFLY IN ONE OR TWO BOOKS STEPHEN STRANGE LENT ME...

BUT WHAT WERE YOU TRYING TO DO, HONEY? ENTERING A COMBAT ZONE!

MY WIFE IS RIGHT, BLANCA. THIS IS *OUR* HOME, *OUR* FIGHT.

DO YOU THINK I DON'T KNOW WHAT'S AT *STAKE*, DOCTOR RICHARDS? I AM YOUNG, AND NAIVE, *SI*. BUT I'M ALSO A DEACONESS.

THE LAST OF THE LINEAGE.

IF ANYONE CAN HELP YOU DEFEAT DIABLO AND WHATEVER PLANS HE HAS DEVELOPED NOW, *SOY YO*. IT'S ME.

AND AS A LAMB TO THE SLAUGHTERHOUSE I SHALL GO, WITH OR WITHOUT YOUR APPROVAL. THIS IS MY *FATE*.

YOU REMIND ME OF A CERTAI[N] YOUNG GIRL, BLANCA. SHE STUBBORNLY PREFERRED TO GO ABOARD A STARSHIP THAT WOULD CHANGE HER LIFE FOREVER.

"WHERE YOU GO, I GO." REMEMBER, REED?

HOW COULD I FORGET THE GIRL I MARRIED, DARLING? LIEUTENANT STONE?

"AS YOU SAID, IT'S *YOUR* HOME, RICHARDS."

"BUT TRY TO END THIS *CLEAN* AND *FAST*. THE MAYOR WILL HAVE MY *BADGE* FOR DINNER IF YOU CAN'T SOLVE THE SITUATION BEFORE MY PEOPLE HERE CAN ACT."

THE INVISIBLE WOMAN CONCENTRATES HARD...

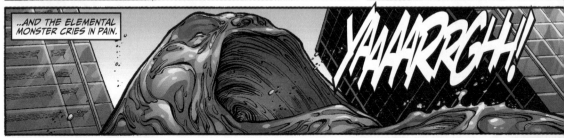

...AND THE ELEMENTAL MONSTER CRIES IN PAIN.

YAAAARRGH!

THE WATERS PART. REED AND SUE, ALONG WITH THE ONLY SURVIVING HEIRESS OF A LINEAGE OF DEVOTION...

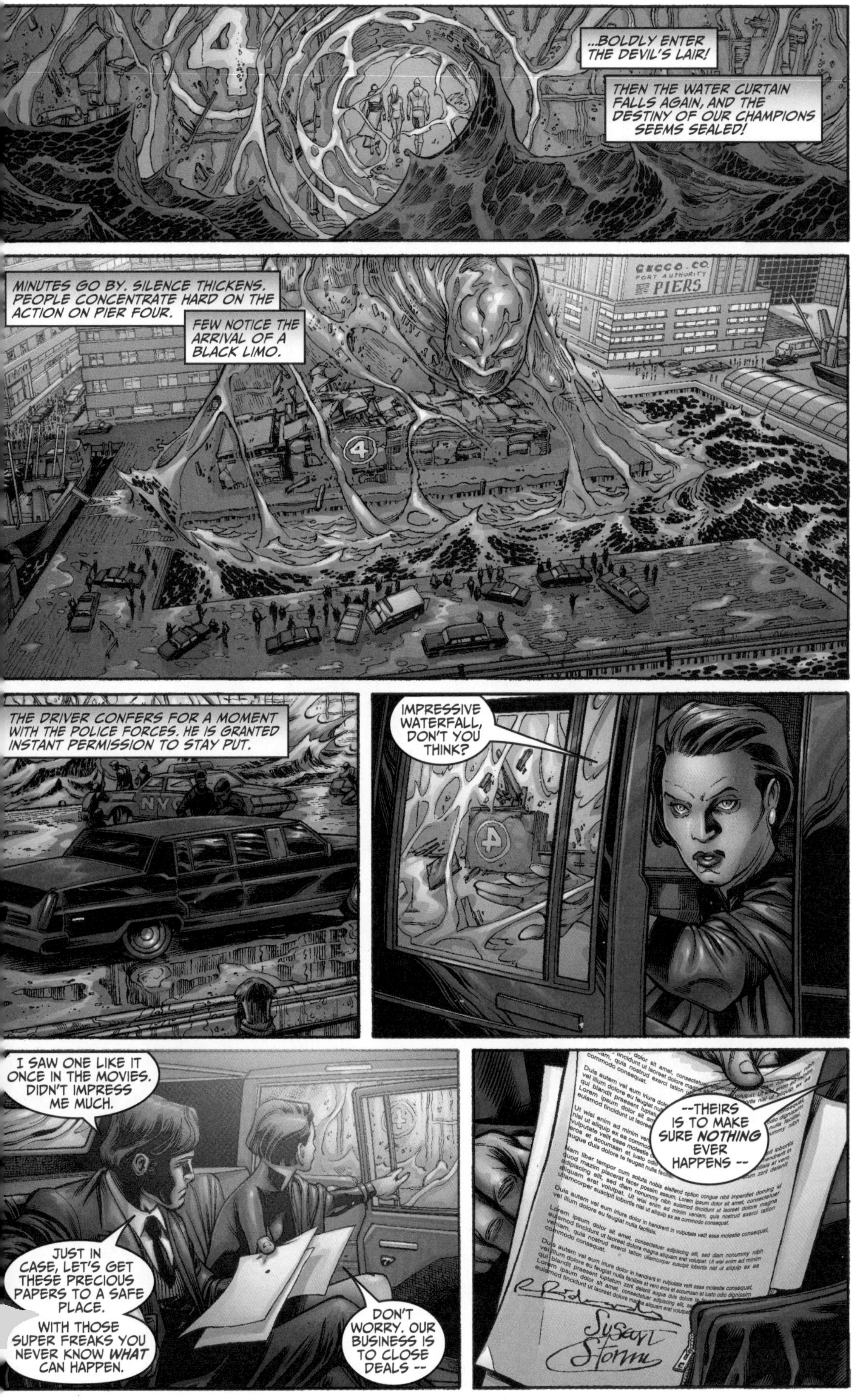
...BOLDLY ENTER THE DEVIL'S LAIR!
THEN THE WATER CURTAIN FALLS AGAIN, AND THE DESTINY OF OUR CHAMPIONS SEEMS SEALED!
MINUTES GO BY. SILENCE THICKENS. PEOPLE CONCENTRATE HARD ON THE ACTION ON PIER FOUR.
FEW NOTICE THE ARRIVAL OF A BLACK LIMO.
PORT AUTHORITY
PIERS
THE DRIVER CONFERS FOR A MOMENT WITH THE POLICE FORCES. HE IS GRANTED INSTANT PERMISSION TO STAY PUT.
IMPRESSIVE WATERFALL, DON'T YOU THINK?
I SAW ONE LIKE IT ONCE IN THE MOVIES. DIDN'T IMPRESS ME MUCH.
JUST IN CASE, LET'S GET THESE PRECIOUS PAPERS TO A SAFE PLACE.
WITH THOSE SUPER FREAKS YOU NEVER KNOW WHAT CAN HAPPEN.
DON'T WORRY. OUR BUSINESS IS TO CLOSE DEALS --
--THEIRS IS TO MAKE SURE NOTHING EVER HAPPENS --
Susan Storm

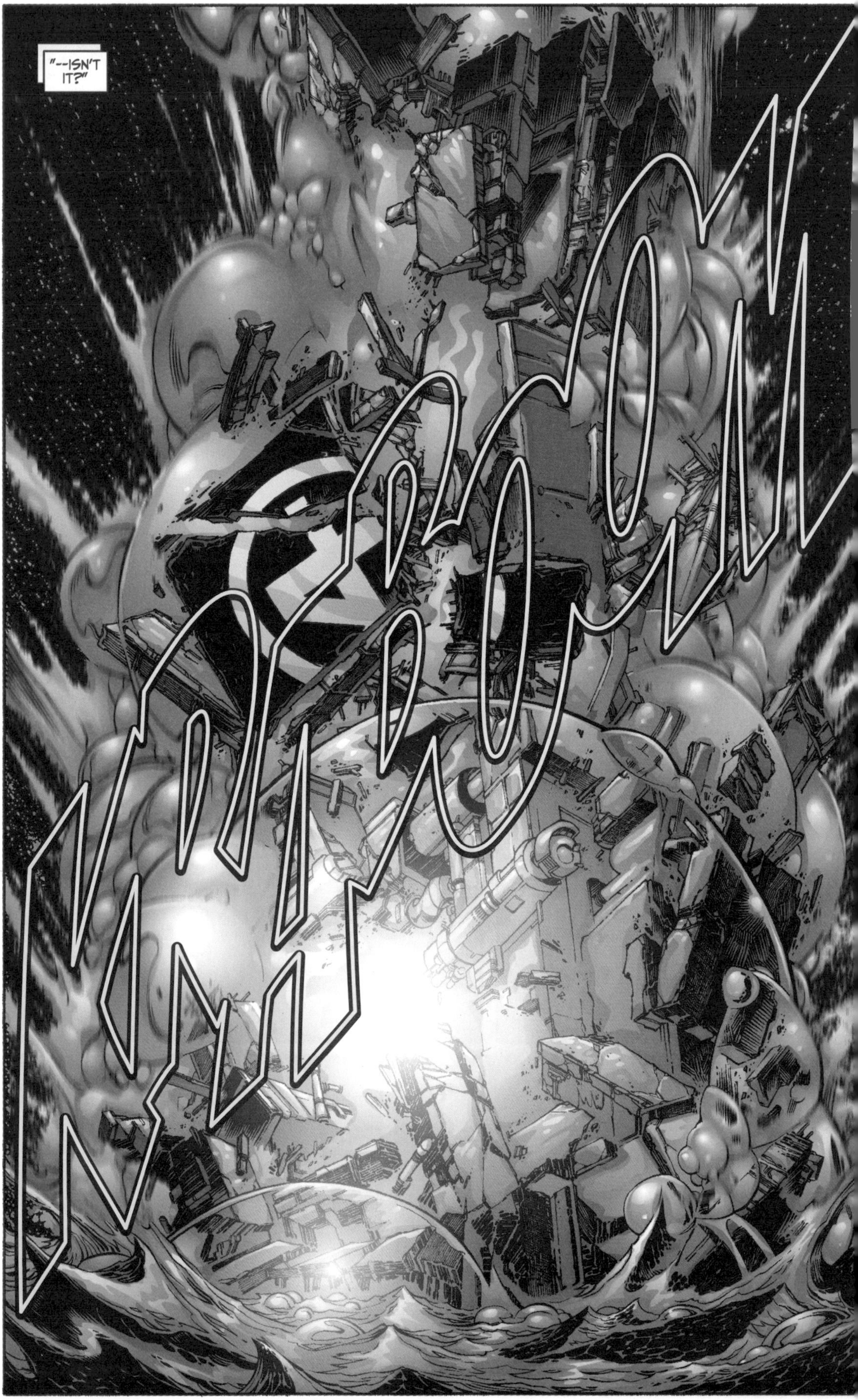
"--ISN'T IT?"

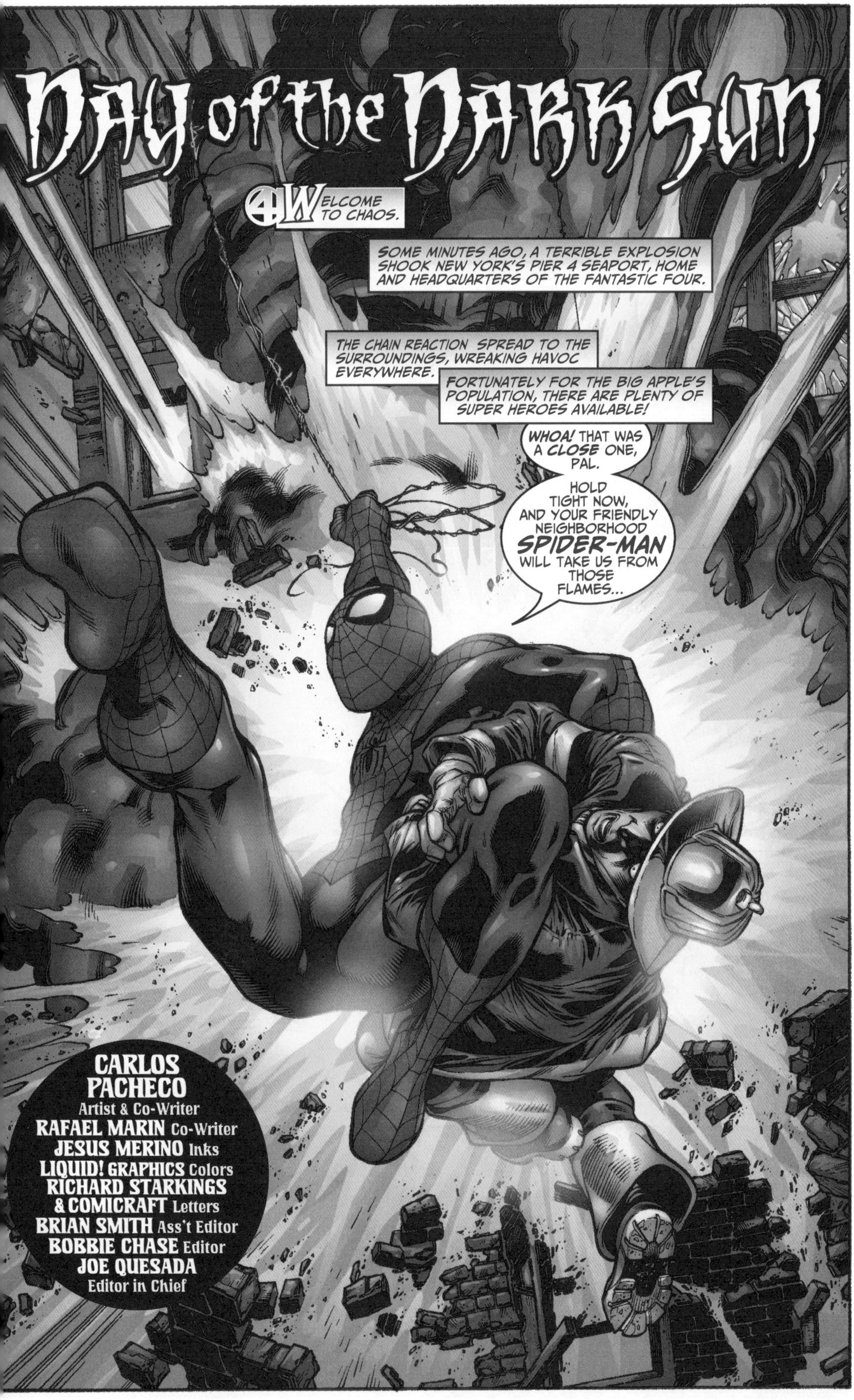

DAY of the DARK SUN
WELCOME TO CHAOS.
SOME MINUTES AGO, A TERRIBLE EXPLOSION SHOOK NEW YORK'S PIER 4 SEAPORT, HOME AND HEADQUARTERS OF THE FANTASTIC FOUR.
THE CHAIN REACTION SPREAD TO THE SURROUNDINGS, WREAKING HAVOC EVERYWHERE.
FORTUNATELY FOR THE BIG APPLE'S POPULATION, THERE ARE PLENTY OF SUPER HEROES AVAILABLE!
WHOA! THAT WAS A CLOSE ONE, PAL.
HOLD TIGHT NOW, AND YOUR FRIENDLY NEIGHBORHOOD SPIDER-MAN WILL TAKE US FROM THOSE FLAMES...
CARLOS PACHECO Artist & Co-Writer
RAFAEL MARIN Co-Writer
JESUS MERINO Inks
LIQUID! GRAPHICS Colors
RICHARD STARKINGS & COMICRAFT Letters
BRIAN SMITH Ass't Editor
BOBBIE CHASE Editor
JOE QUESADA Editor in Chief

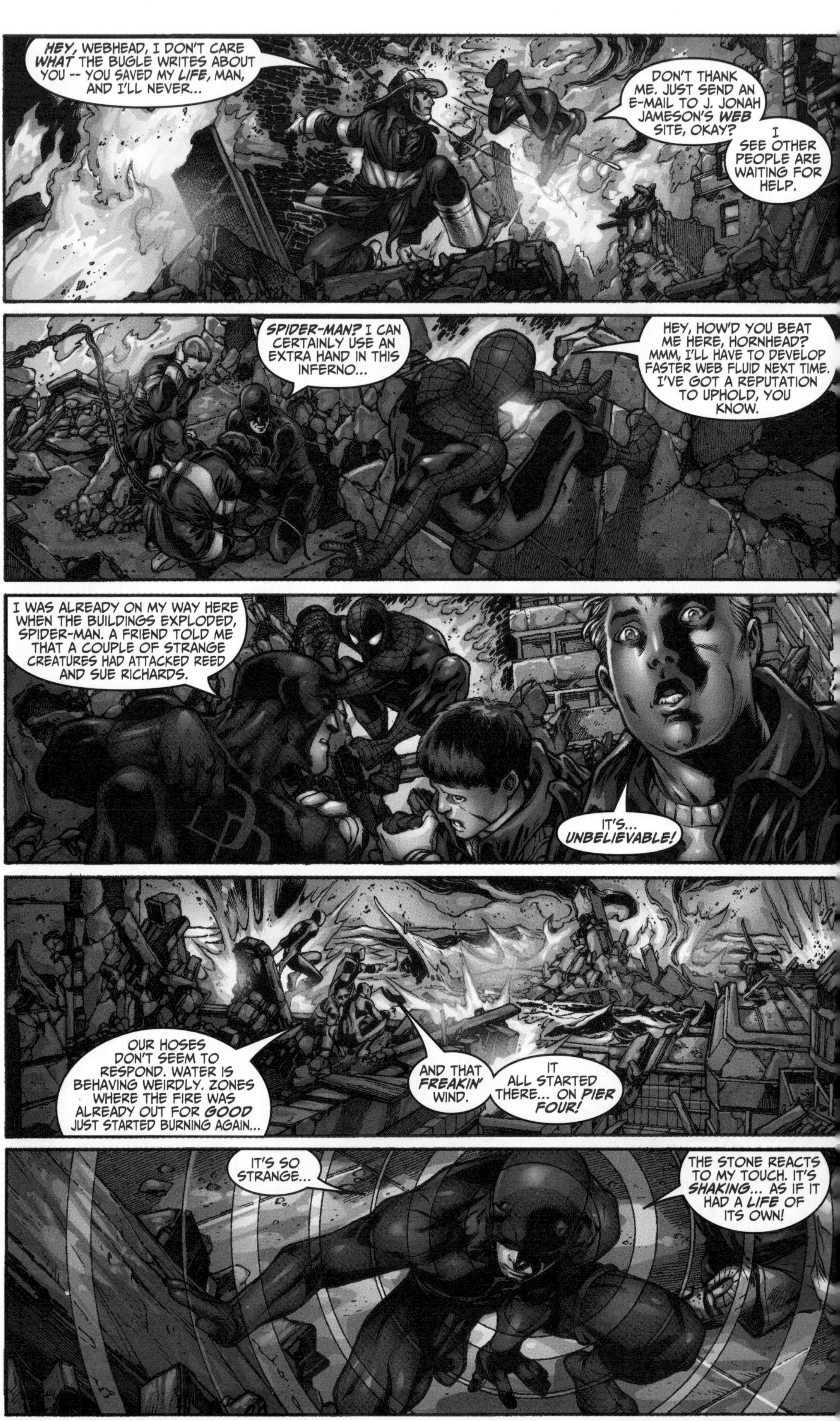
HEY, WEBHEAD, I DON'T CARE WHAT THE BUGLE WRITES ABOUT YOU -- YOU SAVED MY LIFE, MAN, AND I'LL NEVER...
DON'T THANK ME. JUST SEND AN E-MAIL TO J. JONAH JAMESON'S WEB SITE, OKAY?
I SEE OTHER PEOPLE ARE WAITING FOR HELP.
SPIDER-MAN? I CAN CERTAINLY USE AN EXTRA HAND IN THIS INFERNO...
HEY, HOW'D YOU BEAT ME HERE, HORNHEAD? MMM, I'LL HAVE TO DEVELOP FASTER WEB FLUID NEXT TIME. I'VE GOT A REPUTATION TO UPHOLD, YOU KNOW.
I WAS ALREADY ON MY WAY HERE WHEN THE BUILDINGS EXPLODED, SPIDER-MAN. A FRIEND TOLD ME THAT A COUPLE OF STRANGE CREATURES HAD ATTACKED REED AND SUE RICHARDS.
IT'S... UNBELIEVABLE!
OUR HOSES DON'T SEEM TO RESPOND. WATER IS BEHAVING WEIRDLY. ZONES WHERE THE FIRE WAS ALREADY OUT FOR GOOD JUST STARTED BURNING AGAIN...
AND THAT FREAKIN' WIND.
IT ALL STARTED THERE... ON PIER FOUR!
IT'S SO STRANGE...
THE STONE REACTS TO MY TOUCH. IT'S SHAKING... AS IF IT HAD A LIFE OF ITS OWN!

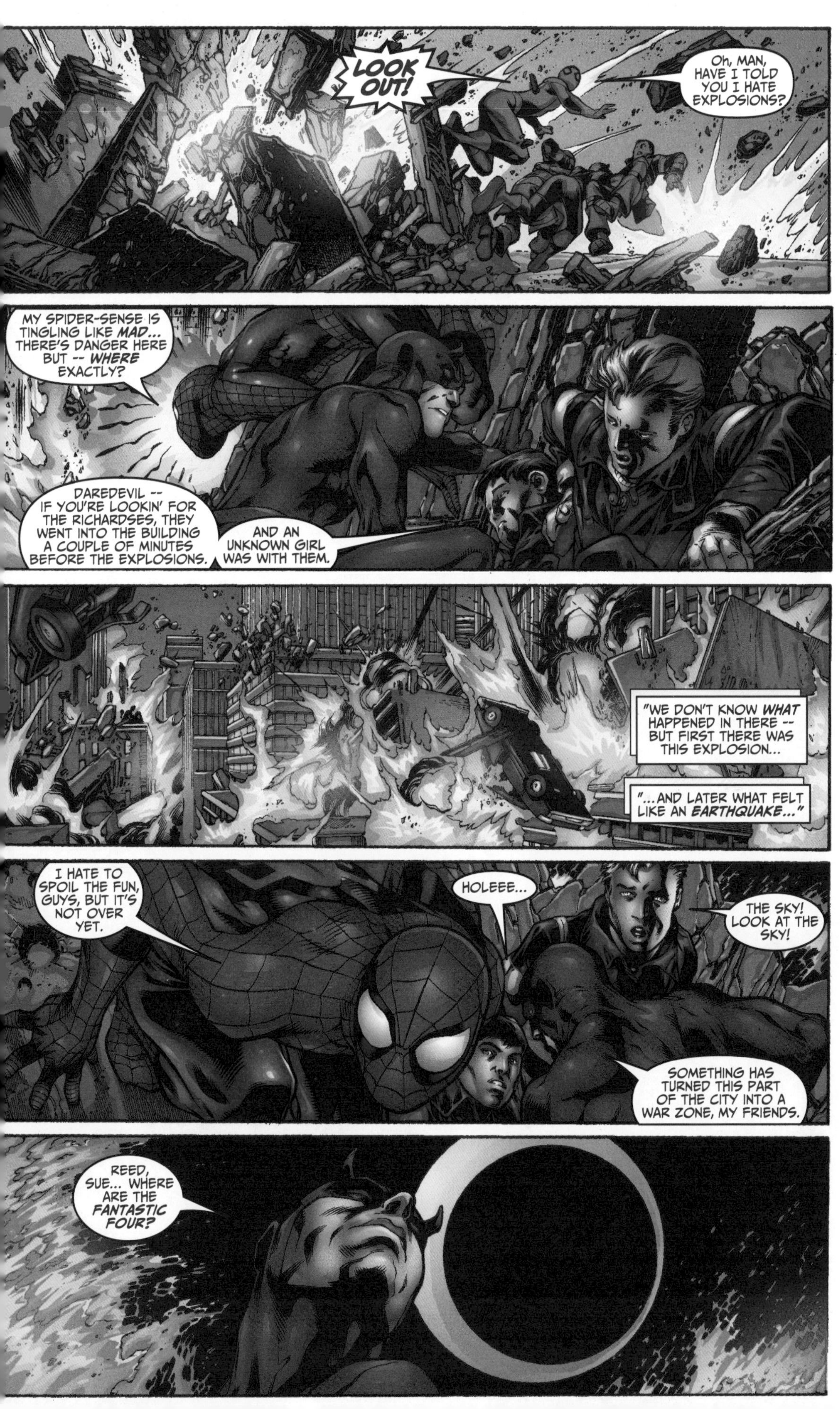
LOOK OUT!
Oh, MAN, HAVE I TOLD YOU I HATE EXPLOSIONS?
MY SPIDER-SENSE IS TINGLING LIKE MAD... THERE'S DANGER HERE BUT -- WHERE EXACTLY?
DAREDEVIL -- IF YOU'RE LOOKIN' FOR THE RICHARDSES, THEY WENT INTO THE BUILDING A COUPLE OF MINUTES BEFORE THE EXPLOSIONS.
AND AN UNKNOWN GIRL WAS WITH THEM.
"WE DON'T KNOW WHAT HAPPENED IN THERE -- BUT FIRST THERE WAS THIS EXPLOSION...
"...AND LATER WHAT FELT LIKE AN EARTHQUAKE..."
I HATE TO SPOIL THE FUN, GUYS, BUT IT'S NOT OVER YET.
HOLEEE...
THE SKY! LOOK AT THE SKY!
SOMETHING HAS TURNED THIS PART OF THE CITY INTO A WAR ZONE, MY FRIENDS.
REED, SUE... WHERE ARE THE FANTASTIC FOUR?

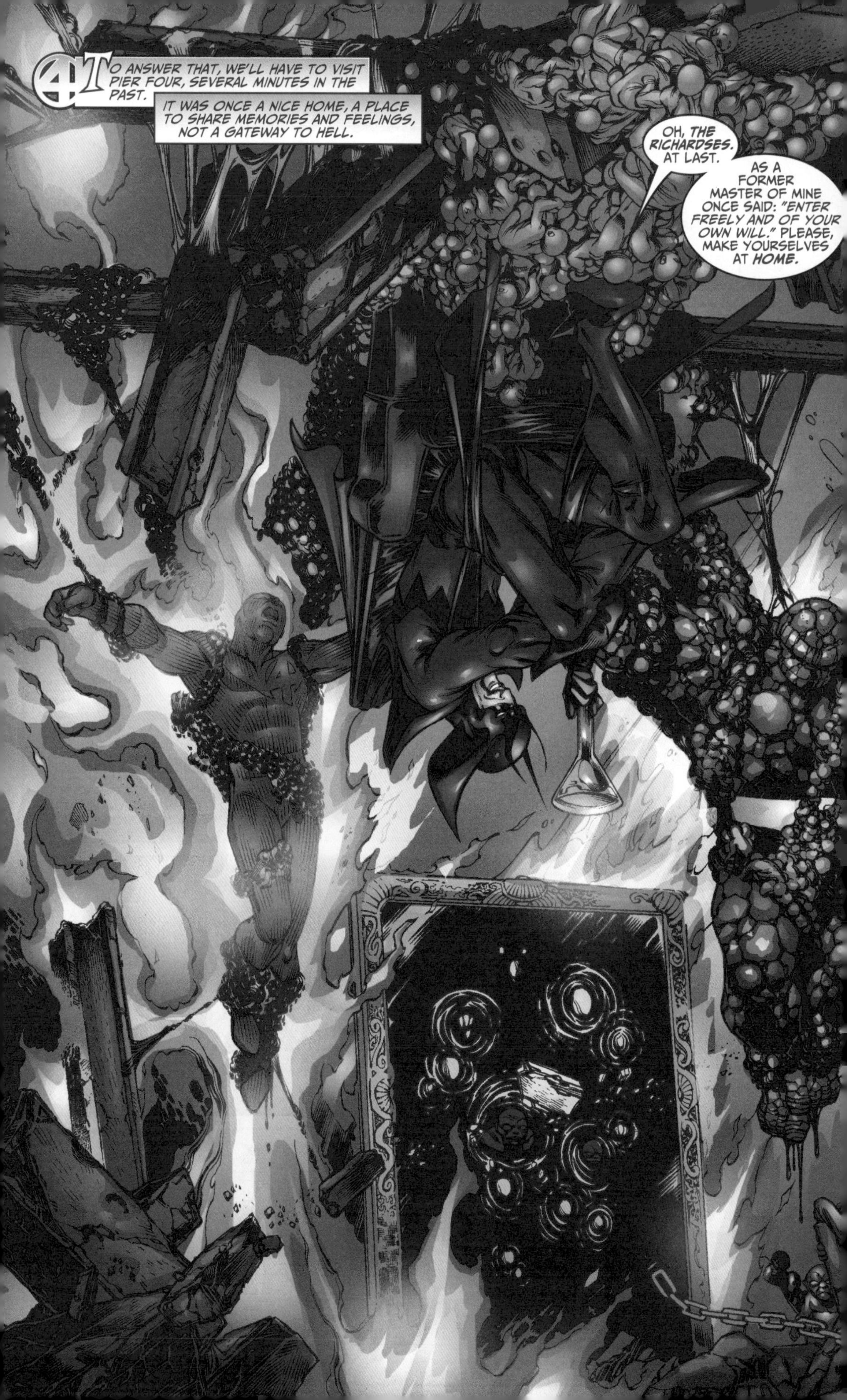

TO ANSWER THAT, WE'LL HAVE TO VISIT PIER FOUR, SEVERAL MINUTES IN THE PAST.
IT WAS ONCE A NICE HOME, A PLACE TO SHARE MEMORIES AND FEELINGS, NOT A GATEWAY TO HELL.
OH, THE RICHARDSES. AT LAST.
AS A FORMER MASTER OF MINE ONCE SAID: "ENTER FREELY AND OF YOUR OWN WILL." PLEASE, MAKE YOURSELVES AT HOME.

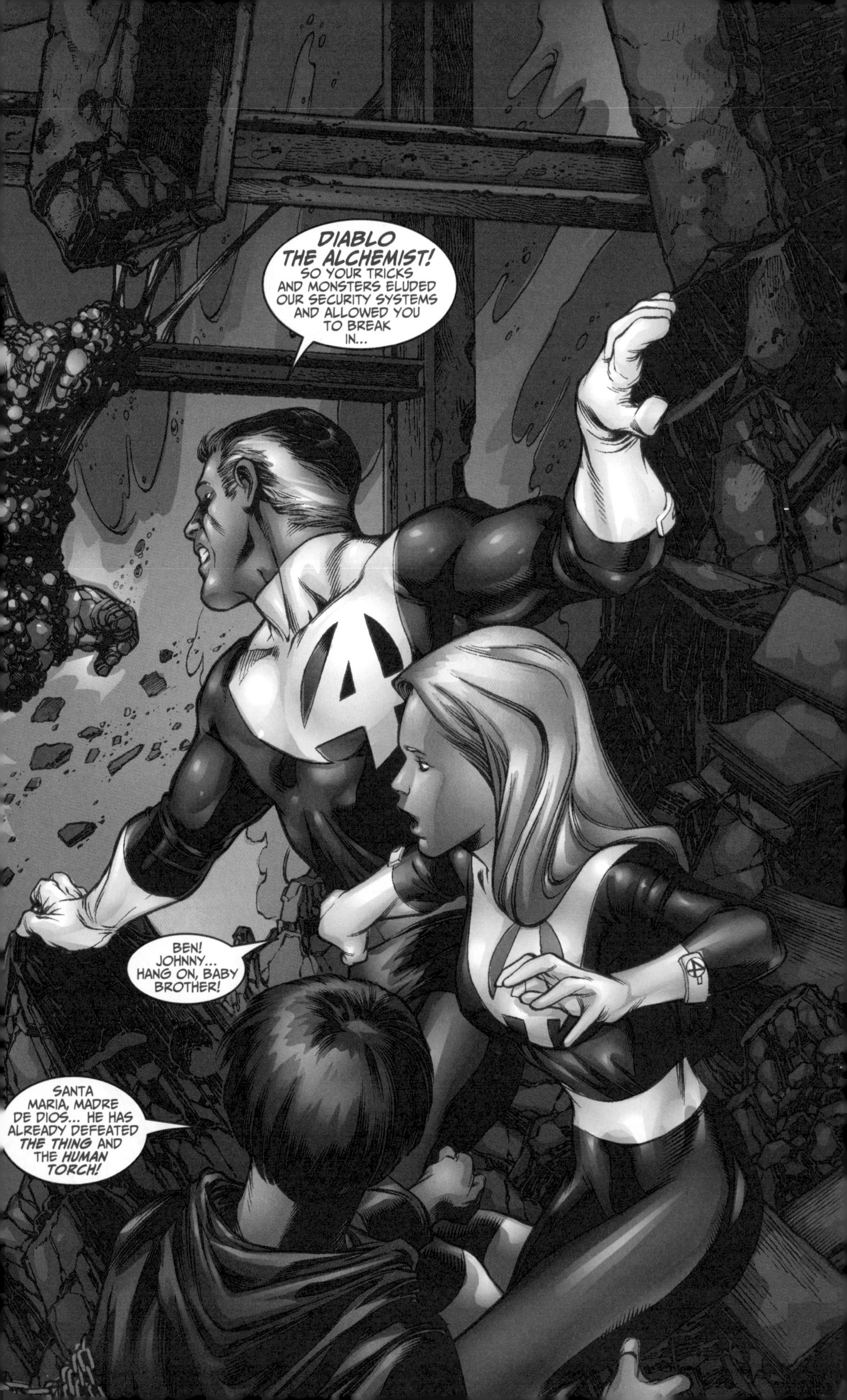
DIABLO THE ALCHEMIST! SO YOUR TRICKS AND MONSTERS ELUDED OUR SECURITY SYSTEMS AND ALLOWED YOU TO BREAK IN...
BEN! JOHNNY... HANG ON, BABY BROTHER!
SANTA MARIA, MADRE DE DIOS... HE HAS ALREADY DEFEATED THE THING AND THE HUMAN TORCH!

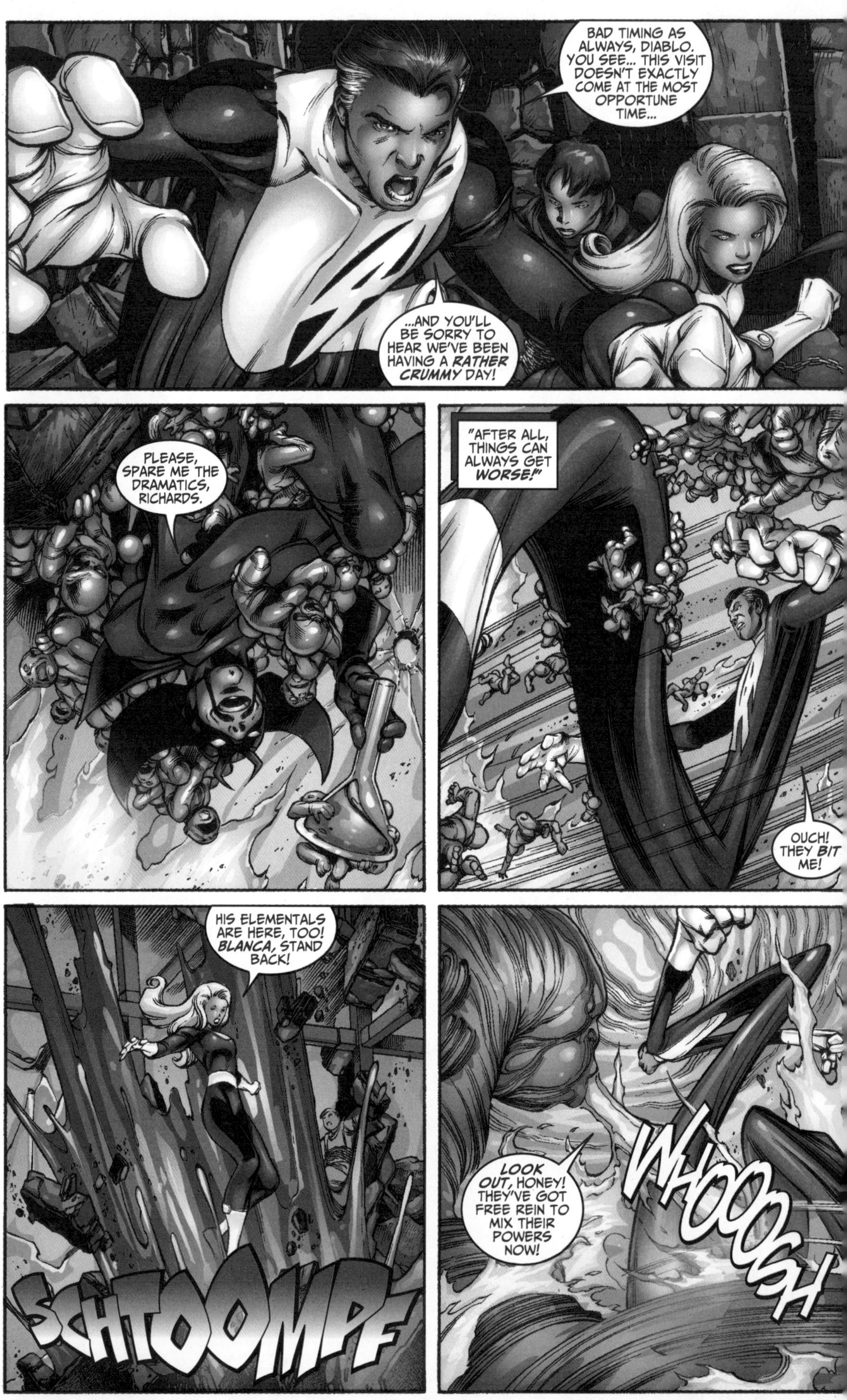
BAD TIMING AS ALWAYS, DIABLO. YOU SEE... THIS VISIT DOESN'T EXACTLY COME AT THE MOST OPPORTUNE TIME...
...AND YOU'LL BE SORRY TO HEAR WE'VE BEEN HAVING A *RATHER CRUMMY* DAY!
PLEASE, SPARE ME THE DRAMATICS, RICHARDS.
"AFTER ALL, THINGS CAN ALWAYS GET *WORSE!*"
OUCH! THEY *BIT* ME!
HIS ELEMENTALS ARE HERE, TOO! *BLANCA*, STAND BACK!
SCHTOOMPF
LOOK OUT, HONEY! THEY'VE GOT FREE REIN TO MIX THEIR POWERS NOW!
WHOOOSH

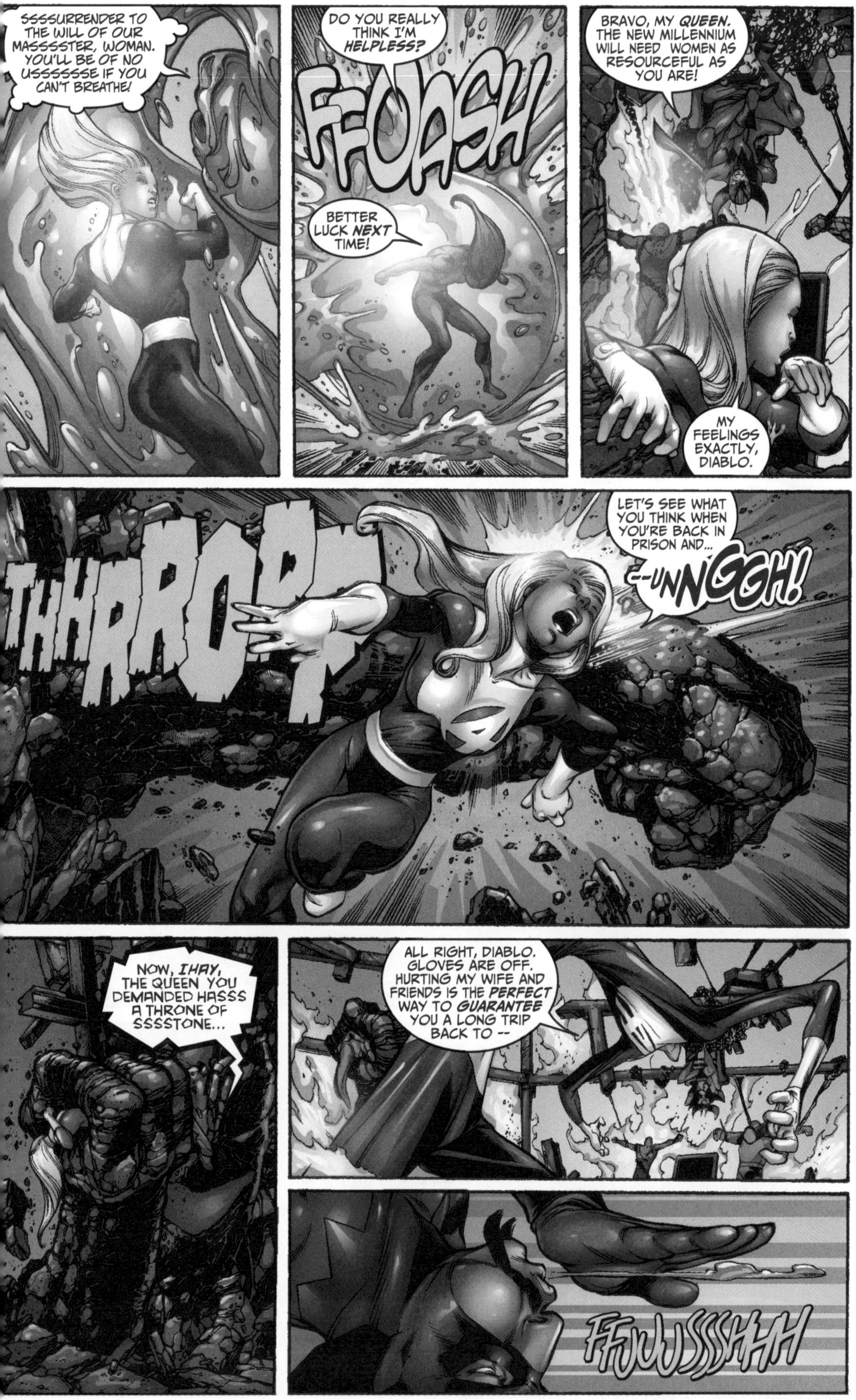
SSSSURRENDER TO THE WILL OF OUR MASSSSTER, WOMAN. YOU'LL BE OF NO USSSSSSE IF YOU CAN'T BREATHE!
DO YOU REALLY THINK I'M HELPLESS?
FFOASH
BETTER LUCK NEXT TIME!
BRAVO, MY QUEEN. THE NEW MILLENNIUM WILL NEED WOMEN AS RESOURCEFUL AS YOU ARE!
MY FEELINGS EXACTLY, DIABLO.
THHROOM
LET'S SEE WHAT YOU THINK WHEN YOU'RE BACK IN PRISON AND...
--UNNGGH!
NOW, IHAY, THE QUEEN YOU DEMANDED HASSS A THRONE OF SSSSTONE...
ALL RIGHT, DIABLO. GLOVES ARE OFF. HURTING MY WIFE AND FRIENDS IS THE PERFECT WAY TO GUARANTEE YOU A LONG TRIP BACK TO --
FFUUUSSSHHH

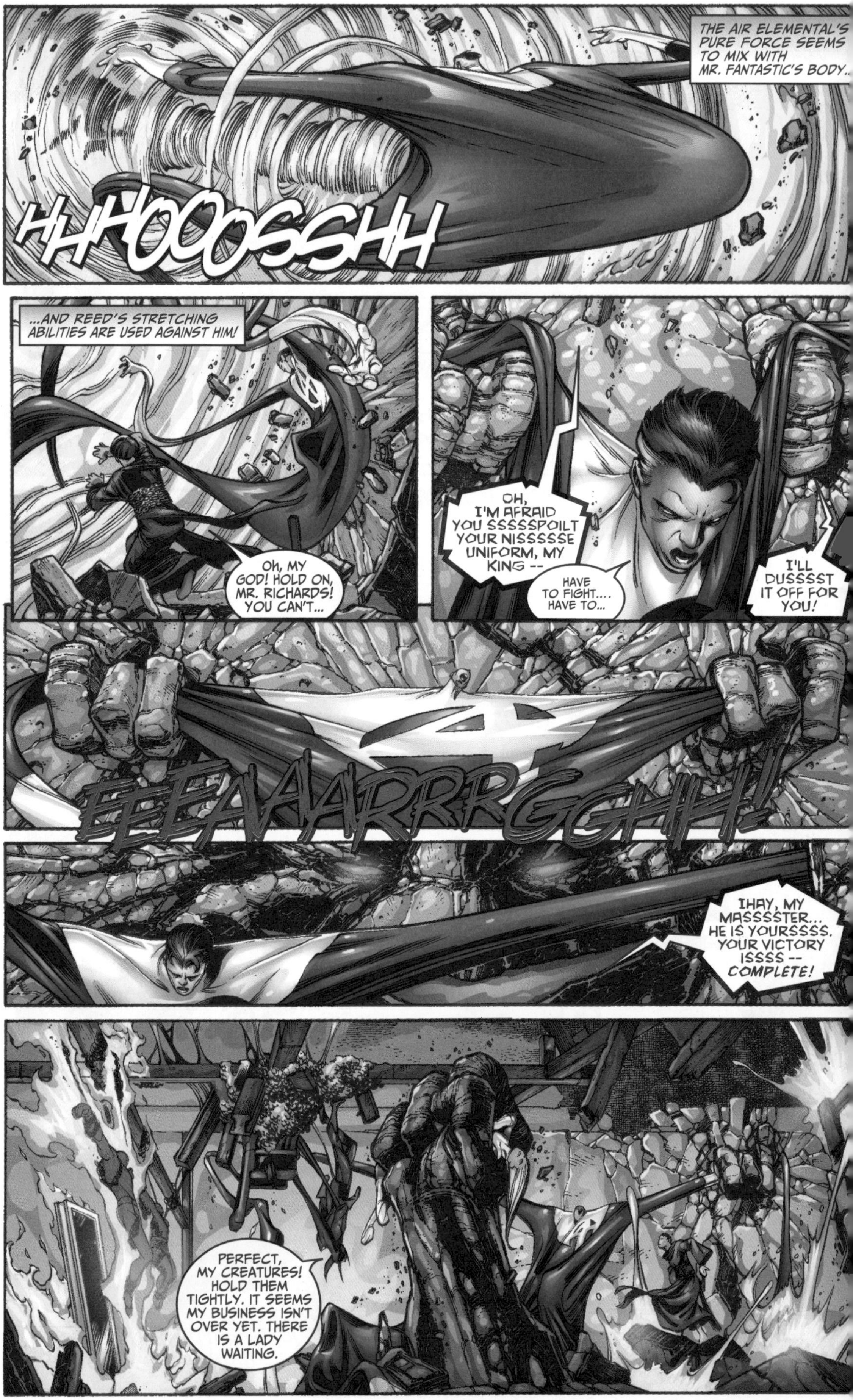
THE AIR ELEMENTAL'S PURE FORCE SEEMS TO MIX WITH MR. FANTASTIC'S BODY...
HHHOOOSSHH
...AND REED'S STRETCHING ABILITIES ARE USED AGAINST HIM!
Oh, MY GOD! HOLD ON, MR. RICHARDS! YOU CAN'T...
OH, I'M AFRAID YOU SSSSSPOILT YOUR NISSSSSE UNIFORM, MY KING --
HAVE TO FIGHT.... HAVE TO...
I'LL DUSSSST IT OFF FOR YOU!
EEEAAARRRGGHH!!
IHAY, MY MASSSSTER... HE IS YOURSSSS. YOUR VICTORY ISSSS -- COMPLETE!
PERFECT, MY CREATURES! HOLD THEM TIGHTLY. IT SEEMS MY BUSINESS ISN'T OVER YET. THERE IS A LADY WAITING.

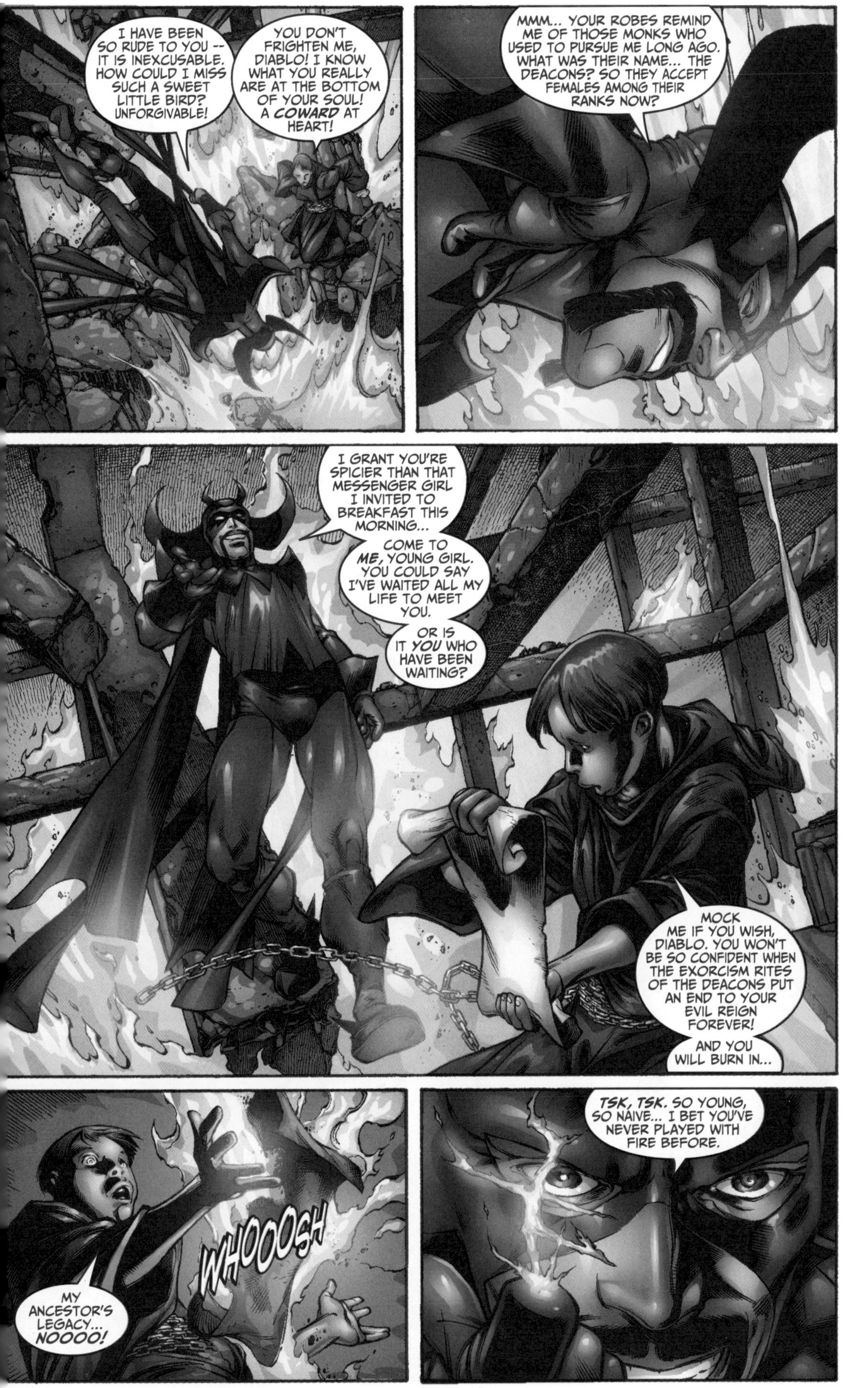
I HAVE BEEN SO RUDE TO YOU -- IT IS INEXCUSABLE. HOW COULD I MISS SUCH A SWEET LITTLE BIRD? UNFORGIVABLE!
YOU DON'T FRIGHTEN ME, DIABLO! I KNOW WHAT YOU REALLY ARE AT THE BOTTOM OF YOUR SOUL! A *COWARD* AT HEART!
MMM... YOUR ROBES REMIND ME OF THOSE MONKS WHO USED TO PURSUE ME LONG AGO. WHAT WAS THEIR NAME... THE DEACONS? SO THEY ACCEPT FEMALES AMONG THEIR RANKS NOW?
I GRANT YOU'RE SPICIER THAN THAT MESSENGER GIRL I INVITED TO BREAKFAST THIS MORNING...
COME TO *ME*, YOUNG GIRL. YOU COULD SAY I'VE WAITED ALL MY LIFE TO MEET YOU.
OR IS IT *YOU* WHO HAVE BEEN WAITING?
MOCK ME IF YOU WISH, DIABLO. YOU WON'T BE SO CONFIDENT WHEN THE EXORCISM RITES OF THE DEACONS PUT AN END TO YOUR EVIL REIGN FOREVER!
AND YOU WILL BURN IN...
WHOOOSH
MY ANCESTOR'S LEGACY... *NOOOO!*
TSK, TSK. SO YOUNG, SO NAIVE... I BET YOU'VE NEVER PLAYED WITH FIRE BEFORE.

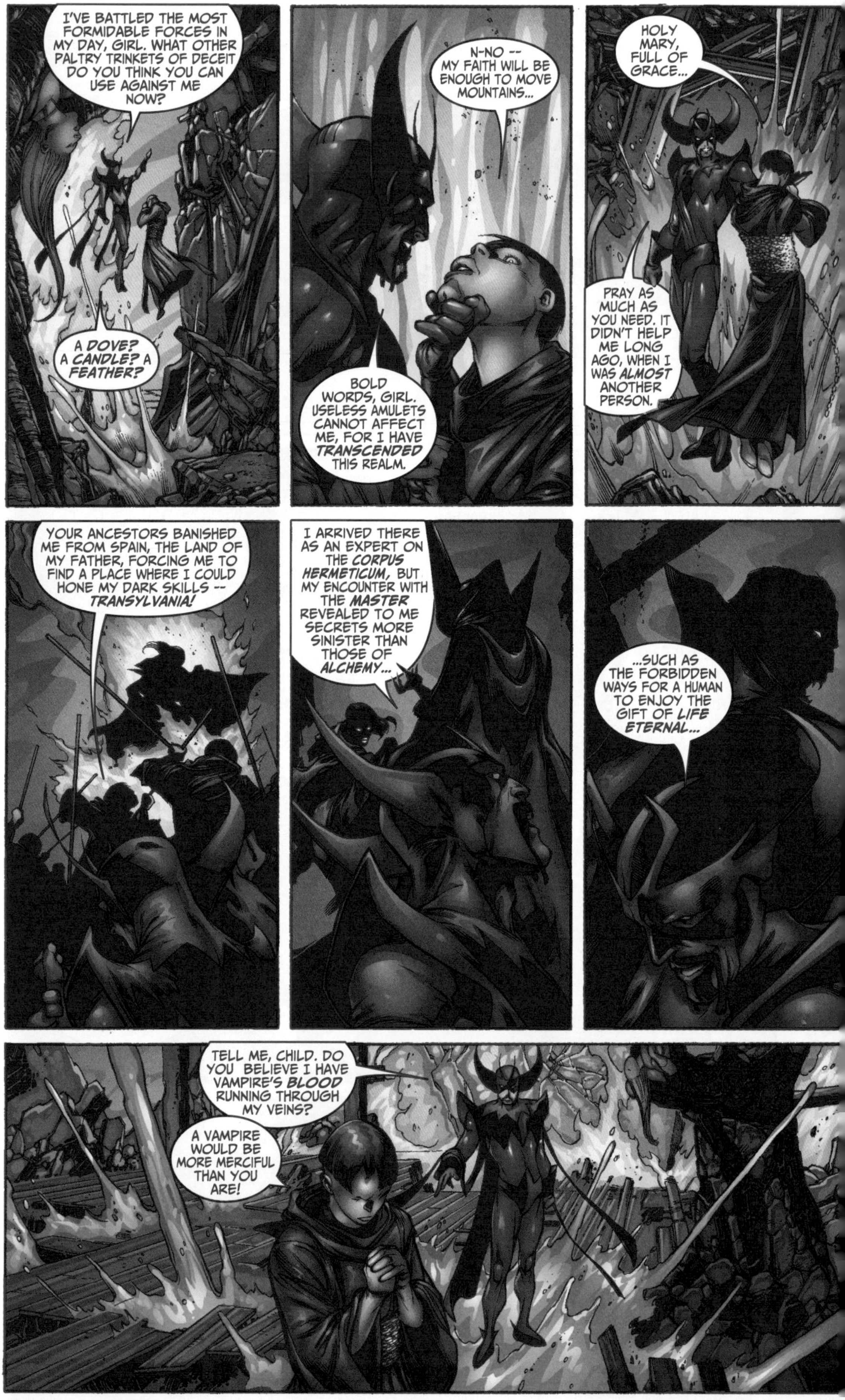
I'VE BATTLED THE MOST FORMIDABLE FORCES IN MY DAY, GIRL. WHAT OTHER PALTRY TRINKETS OF DECEIT DO YOU THINK YOU CAN USE AGAINST ME NOW?
A DOVE? A CANDLE? A FEATHER?
N-NO -- MY FAITH WILL BE ENOUGH TO MOVE MOUNTAINS...
BOLD WORDS, GIRL. USELESS AMULETS CANNOT AFFECT ME, FOR I HAVE TRANSCENDED THIS REALM.
HOLY MARY, FULL OF GRACE...
PRAY AS MUCH AS YOU NEED. IT DIDN'T HELP ME LONG AGO, WHEN I WAS ALMOST ANOTHER PERSON.
YOUR ANCESTORS BANISHED ME FROM SPAIN, THE LAND OF MY FATHER, FORCING ME TO FIND A PLACE WHERE I COULD HONE MY DARK SKILLS -- TRANSYLVANIA!
I ARRIVED THERE AS AN EXPERT ON THE CORPUS HERMETICUM, BUT MY ENCOUNTER WITH THE MASTER REVEALED TO ME SECRETS MORE SINISTER THAN THOSE OF ALCHEMY...
...SUCH AS THE FORBIDDEN WAYS FOR A HUMAN TO ENJOY THE GIFT OF LIFE ETERNAL...
TELL ME, CHILD. DO YOU BELIEVE I HAVE VAMPIRE'S BLOOD RUNNING THROUGH MY VEINS?
A VAMPIRE WOULD BE MORE MERCIFUL THAN YOU ARE!

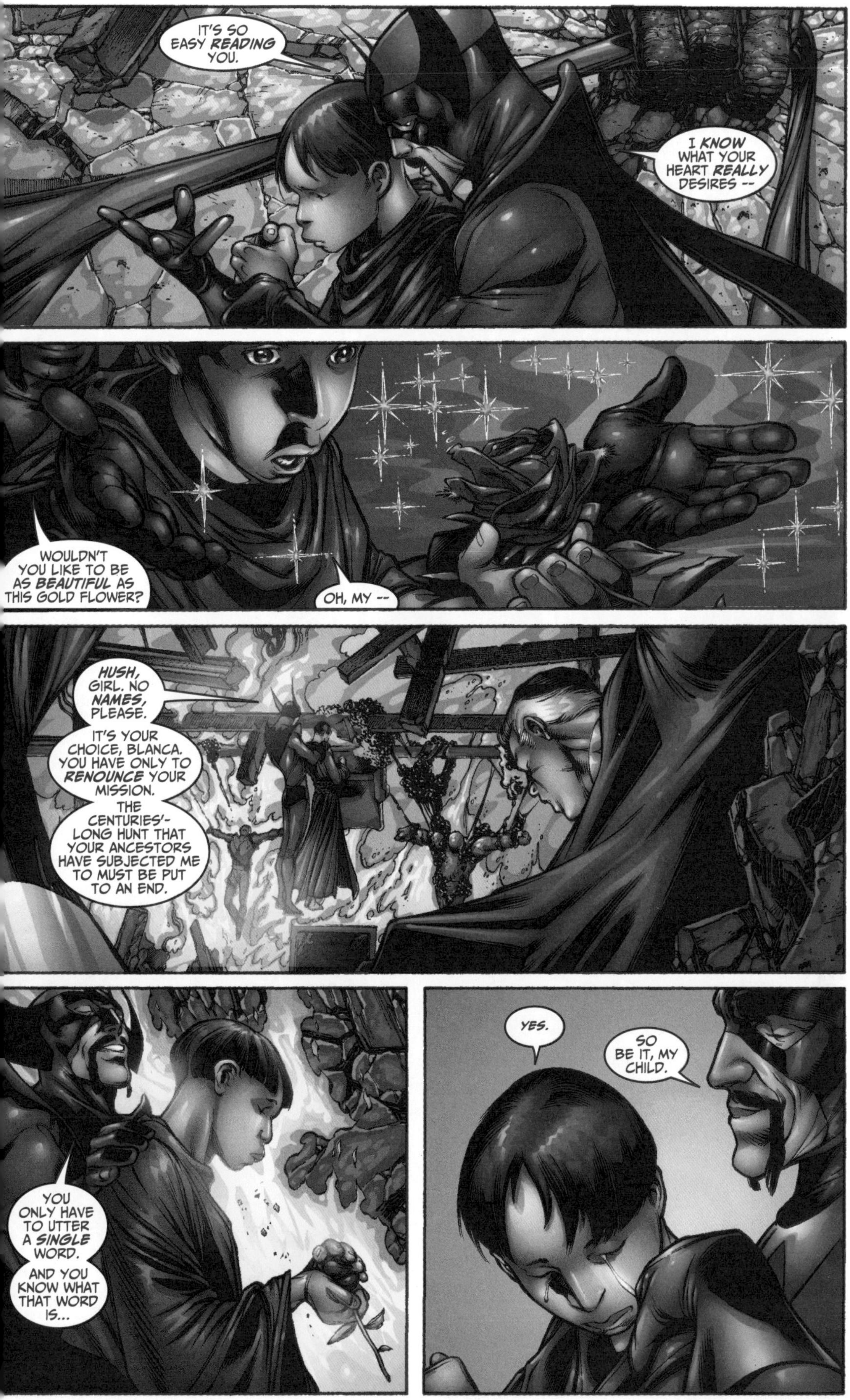
IT'S SO EASY READING YOU.
I KNOW WHAT YOUR HEART REALLY DESIRES --
WOULDN'T YOU LIKE TO BE AS BEAUTIFUL AS THIS GOLD FLOWER?
OH, MY --
HUSH, GIRL. NO NAMES, PLEASE.
IT'S YOUR CHOICE, BLANCA. YOU HAVE ONLY TO RENOUNCE YOUR MISSION.
THE CENTURIES'-LONG HUNT THAT YOUR ANCESTORS HAVE SUBJECTED ME TO MUST BE PUT TO AN END.
YOU ONLY HAVE TO UTTER A SINGLE WORD.
AND YOU KNOW WHAT THAT WORD IS...
YES.
SO BE IT, MY CHILD.

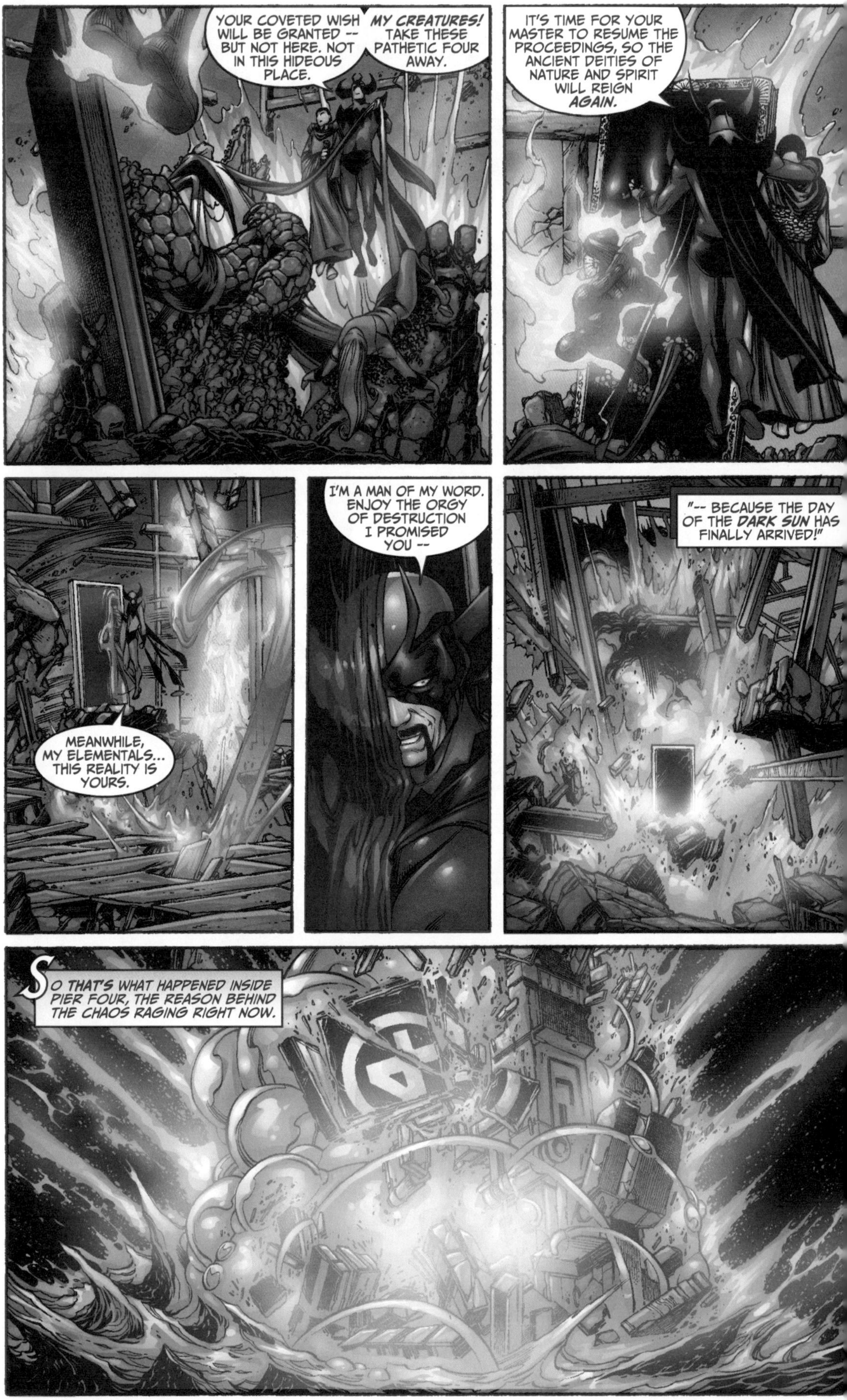
YOUR COVETED WISH WILL BE GRANTED -- BUT NOT HERE. NOT IN THIS HIDEOUS PLACE.
MY CREATURES! TAKE THESE PATHETIC FOUR AWAY.
IT'S TIME FOR YOUR MASTER TO RESUME THE PROCEEDINGS, SO THE ANCIENT DEITIES OF NATURE AND SPIRIT WILL REIGN AGAIN.
MEANWHILE, MY ELEMENTALS... THIS REALITY IS YOURS.
I'M A MAN OF MY WORD. ENJOY THE ORGY OF DESTRUCTION I PROMISED YOU --
"-- BECAUSE THE DAY OF THE DARK SUN HAS FINALLY ARRIVED!"
SO THAT'S WHAT HAPPENED INSIDE PIER FOUR, THE REASON BEHIND THE CHAOS RAGING RIGHT NOW.

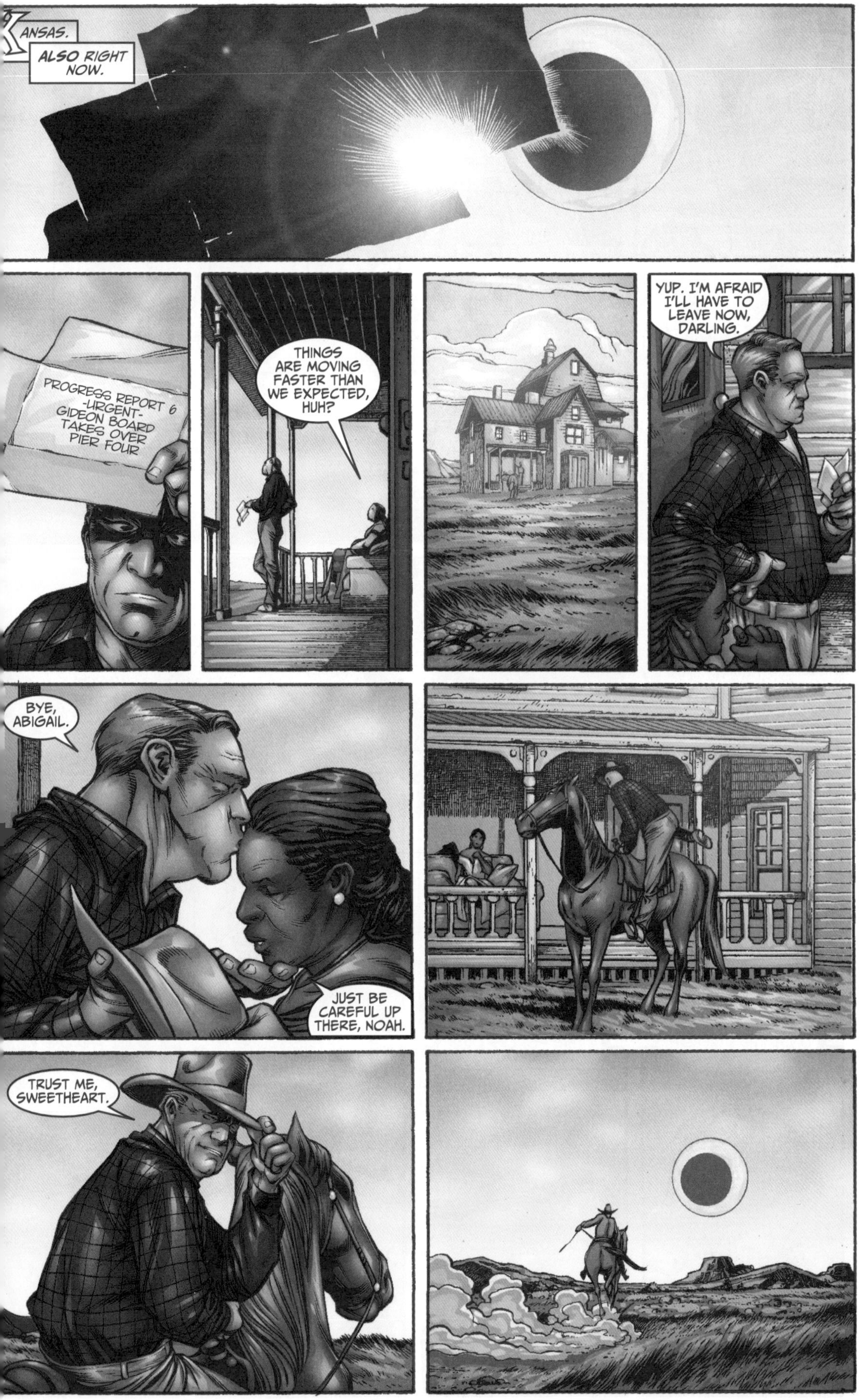
KANSAS.
ALSO RIGHT NOW.
PROGRESS REPORT 6 -URGENT- GIDEON BOARD TAKES OVER PIER FOUR
THINGS ARE MOVING FASTER THAN WE EXPECTED, HUH?
YUP. I'M AFRAID I'LL HAVE TO LEAVE NOW, DARLING.
BYE, ABIGAIL.
JUST BE CAREFUL UP THERE, NOAH.
TRUST ME, SWEETHEART.

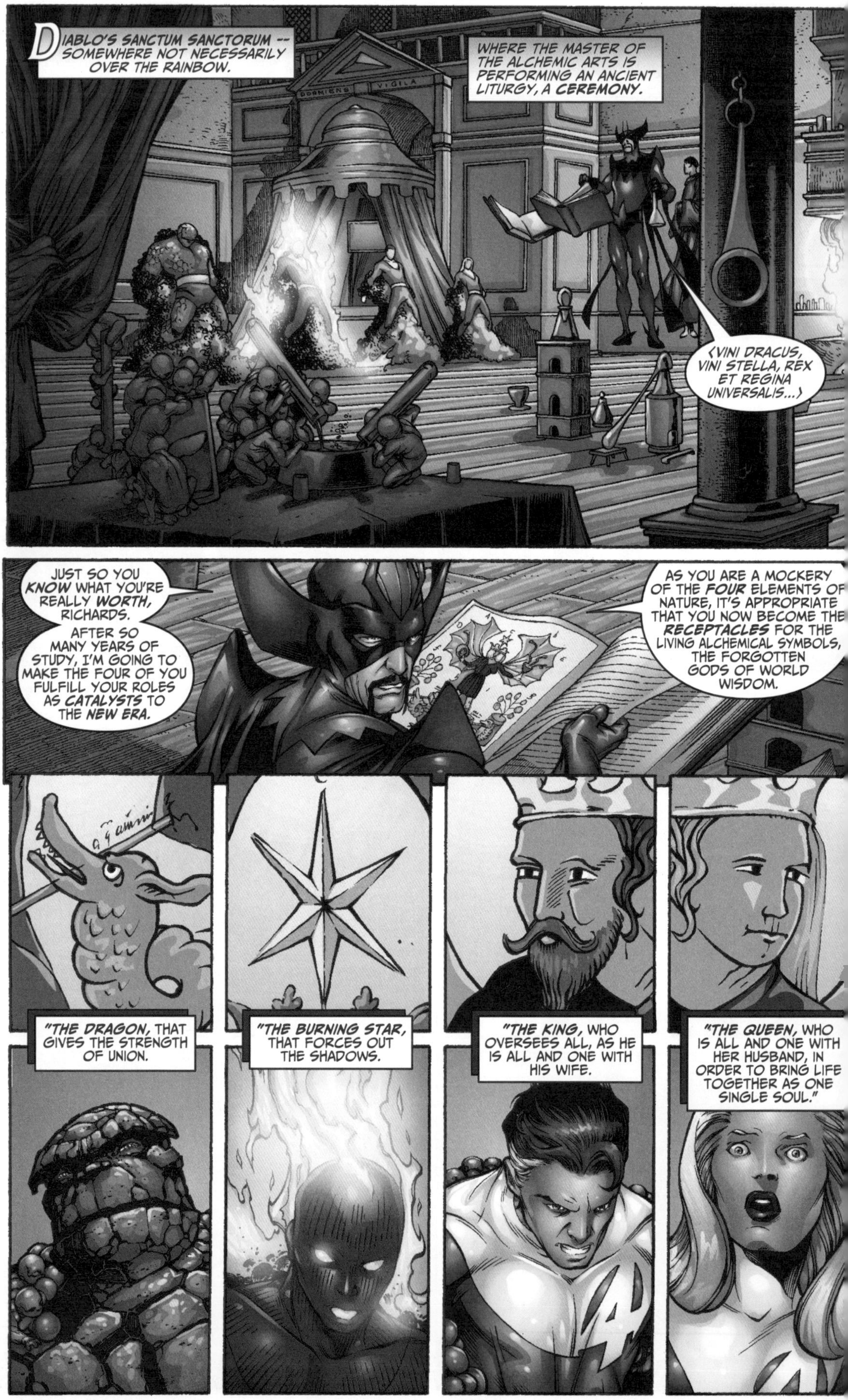
DIABLO'S SANCTUM SANCTORUM -- SOMEWHERE NOT NECESSARILY OVER THE RAINBOW.
WHERE THE MASTER OF THE ALCHEMIC ARTS IS PERFORMING AN ANCIENT LITURGY, A CEREMONY.
DORMIENS VIGILA
<VINI DRACUS, VINI STELLA, REX ET REGINA UNIVERSALIS...>
JUST SO YOU KNOW WHAT YOU'RE REALLY WORTH, RICHARDS.
AFTER SO MANY YEARS OF STUDY, I'M GOING TO MAKE THE FOUR OF YOU FULFILL YOUR ROLES AS CATALYSTS TO THE NEW ERA.
AS YOU ARE A MOCKERY OF THE FOUR ELEMENTS OF NATURE, IT'S APPROPRIATE THAT YOU NOW BECOME THE RECEPTACLES FOR THE LIVING ALCHEMICAL SYMBOLS, THE FORGOTTEN GODS OF WORLD WISDOM.
"THE DRAGON, THAT GIVES THE STRENGTH OF UNION.
"THE BURNING STAR, THAT FORCES OUT THE SHADOWS.
"THE KING, WHO OVERSEES ALL, AS HE IS ALL AND ONE WITH HIS WIFE.
"THE QUEEN, WHO IS ALL AND ONE WITH HER HUSBAND, IN ORDER TO BRING LIFE TOGETHER AS ONE SINGLE SOUL."

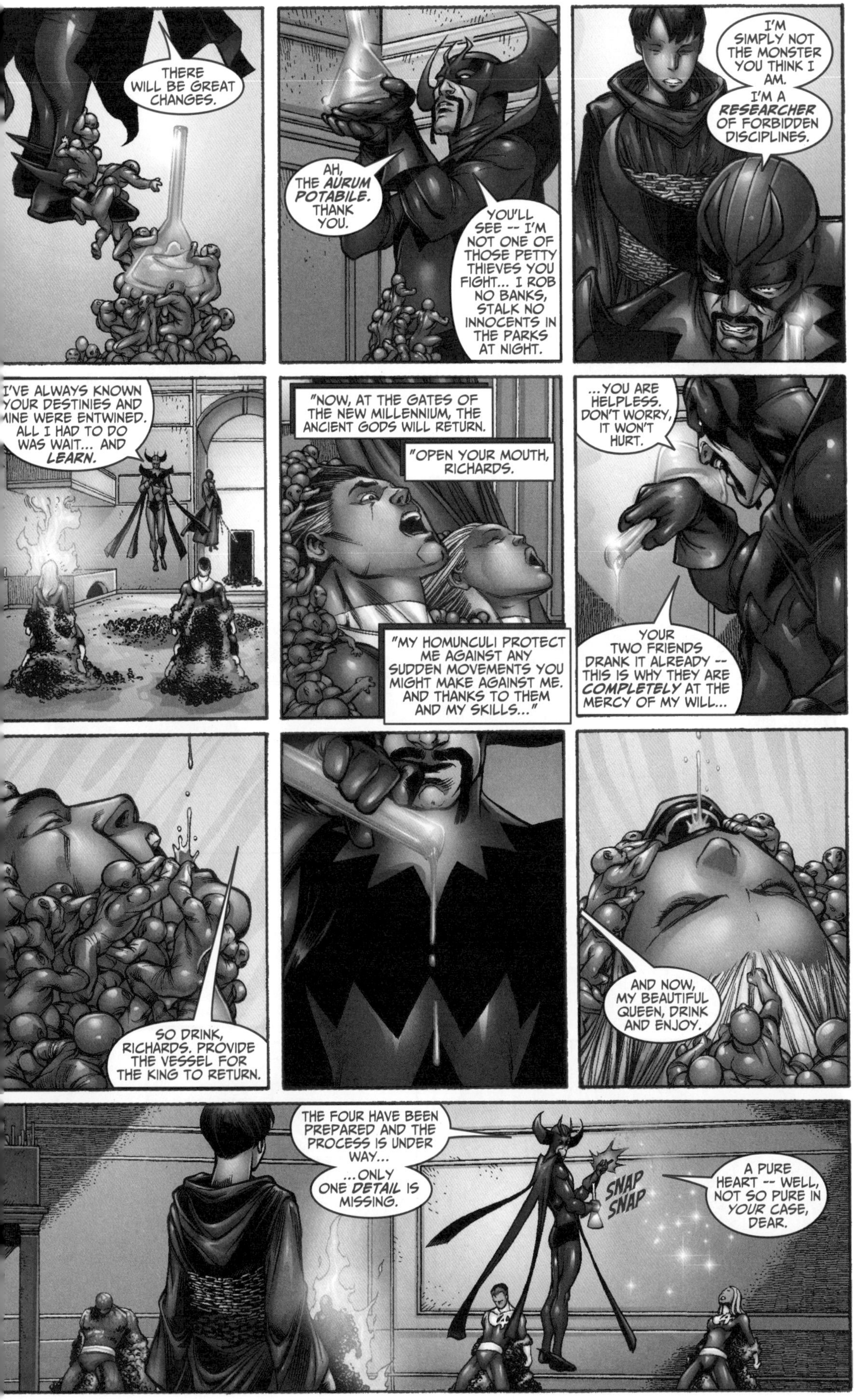
THERE WILL BE GREAT CHANGES.
AH, THE *AURUM POTABILE.* THANK YOU.
YOU'LL SEE -- I'M NOT ONE OF THOSE PETTY THIEVES YOU FIGHT... I ROB NO BANKS, STALK NO INNOCENTS IN THE PARKS AT NIGHT.
I'M SIMPLY NOT THE MONSTER YOU THINK I AM.
I'M A *RESEARCHER* OF FORBIDDEN DISCIPLINES.
I'VE ALWAYS KNOWN YOUR DESTINIES AND MINE WERE ENTWINED. ALL I HAD TO DO WAS WAIT... AND *LEARN.*
"NOW, AT THE GATES OF THE NEW MILLENNIUM, THE ANCIENT GODS WILL RETURN.
"OPEN YOUR MOUTH, RICHARDS.
"MY HOMUNCULI PROTECT ME AGAINST ANY SUDDEN MOVEMENTS YOU MIGHT MAKE AGAINST ME. AND THANKS TO THEM AND MY SKILLS..."
...YOU ARE HELPLESS. DON'T WORRY, IT WON'T HURT.
YOUR TWO FRIENDS DRANK IT ALREADY -- THIS IS WHY THEY ARE *COMPLETELY* AT THE MERCY OF MY WILL...
SO DRINK, RICHARDS. PROVIDE THE VESSEL FOR THE KING TO RETURN.
AND NOW, MY BEAUTIFUL QUEEN, DRINK AND ENJOY.
THE FOUR HAVE BEEN PREPARED AND THE PROCESS IS UNDER WAY...
...ONLY ONE *DETAIL* IS MISSING.
SNAP SNAP
A PURE HEART -- WELL, NOT SO PURE IN *YOUR CASE,* DEAR.

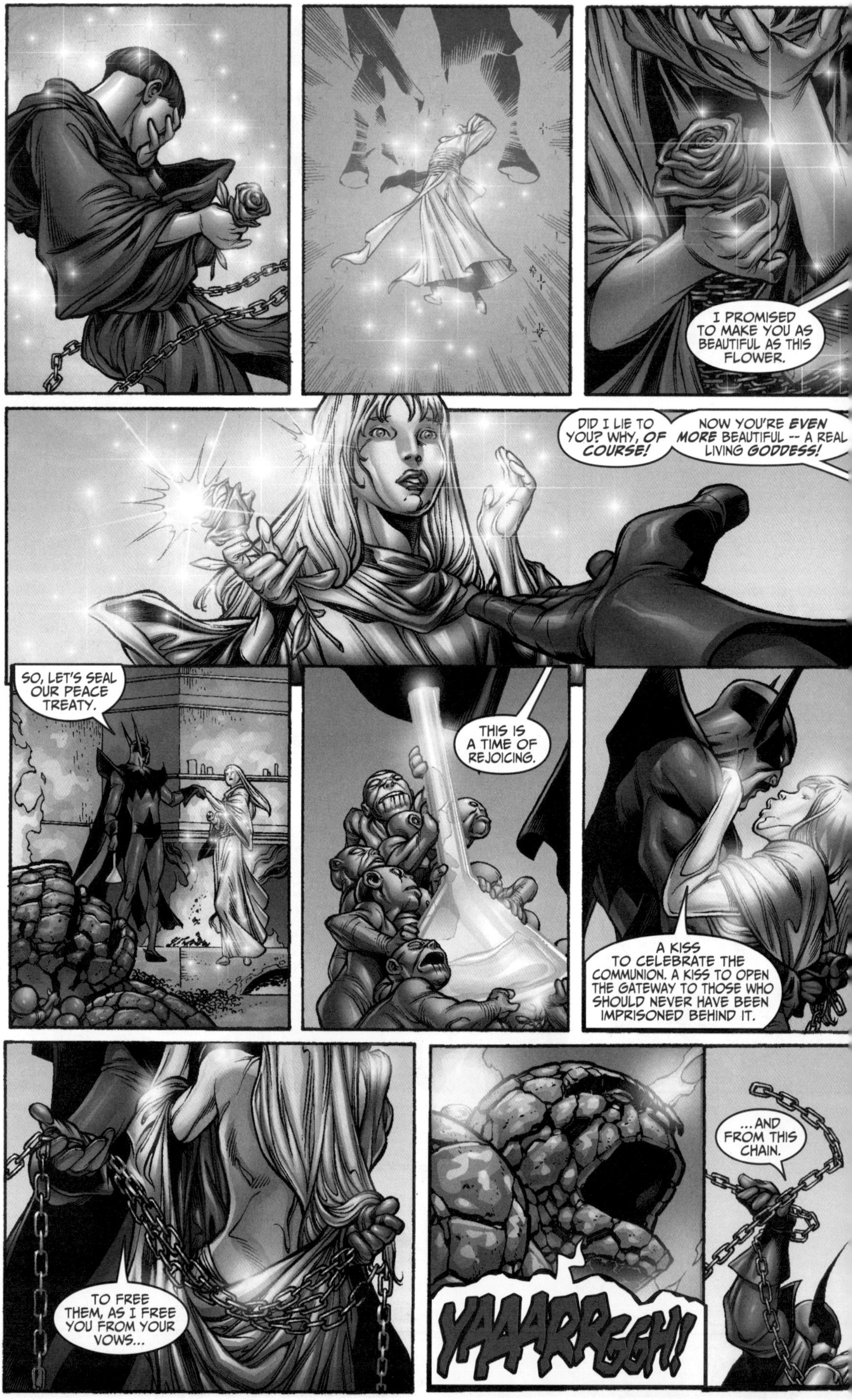
I PROMISED TO MAKE YOU AS BEAUTIFUL AS THIS FLOWER.
DID I LIE TO YOU? WHY, OF COURSE!
NOW YOU'RE EVEN MORE BEAUTIFUL -- A REAL LIVING GODDESS!
SO, LET'S SEAL OUR PEACE TREATY.
THIS IS A TIME OF REJOICING.
A KISS TO CELEBRATE THE COMMUNION. A KISS TO OPEN THE GATEWAY TO THOSE WHO SHOULD NEVER HAVE BEEN IMPRISONED BEHIND IT.
TO FREE THEM, AS I FREE YOU FROM YOUR VOWS...
YAAARRGGH!
...AND FROM THIS CHAIN.

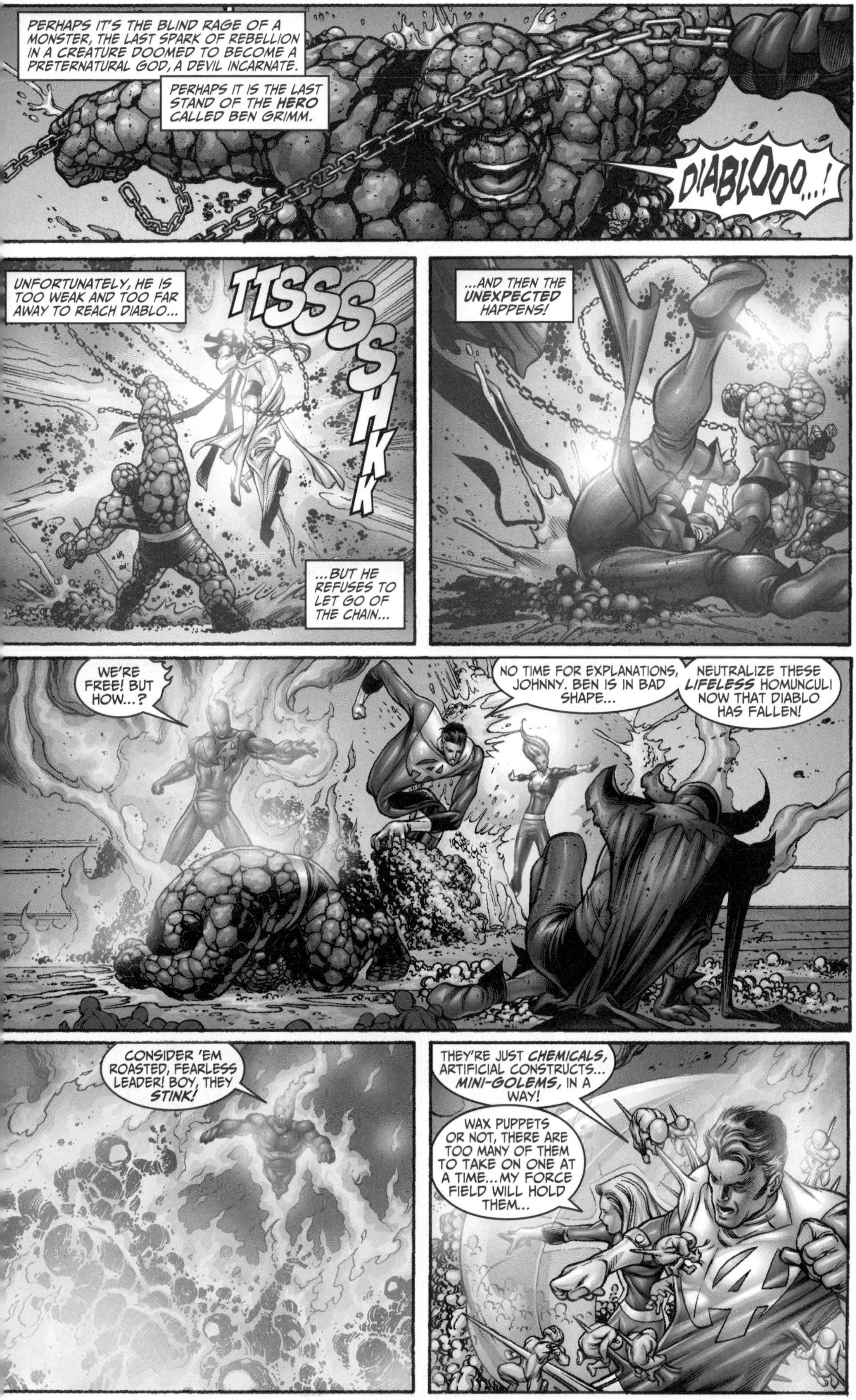
PERHAPS IT'S THE BLIND RAGE OF A MONSTER, THE LAST SPARK OF REBELLION IN A CREATURE DOOMED TO BECOME A PRETERNATURAL GOD, A DEVIL INCARNATE.
PERHAPS IT IS THE LAST STAND OF THE HERO CALLED BEN GRIMM.
DIABLOOO...!
UNFORTUNATELY, HE IS TOO WEAK AND TOO FAR AWAY TO REACH DIABLO...
TTSSSSHKK
...BUT HE REFUSES TO LET GO OF THE CHAIN...
...AND THEN THE UNEXPECTED HAPPENS!
WE'RE FREE! BUT HOW...?
NO TIME FOR EXPLANATIONS, JOHNNY. BEN IS IN BAD SHAPE...
NEUTRALIZE THESE LIFELESS HOMUNCULI NOW THAT DIABLO HAS FALLEN!
CONSIDER 'EM ROASTED, FEARLESS LEADER! BOY, THEY STINK!
THEY'RE JUST CHEMICALS, ARTIFICIAL CONSTRUCTS... MINI-GOLEMS, IN A WAY!
WAX PUPPETS OR NOT, THERE ARE TOO MANY OF THEM TO TAKE ON ONE AT A TIME... MY FORCE FIELD WILL HOLD THEM...

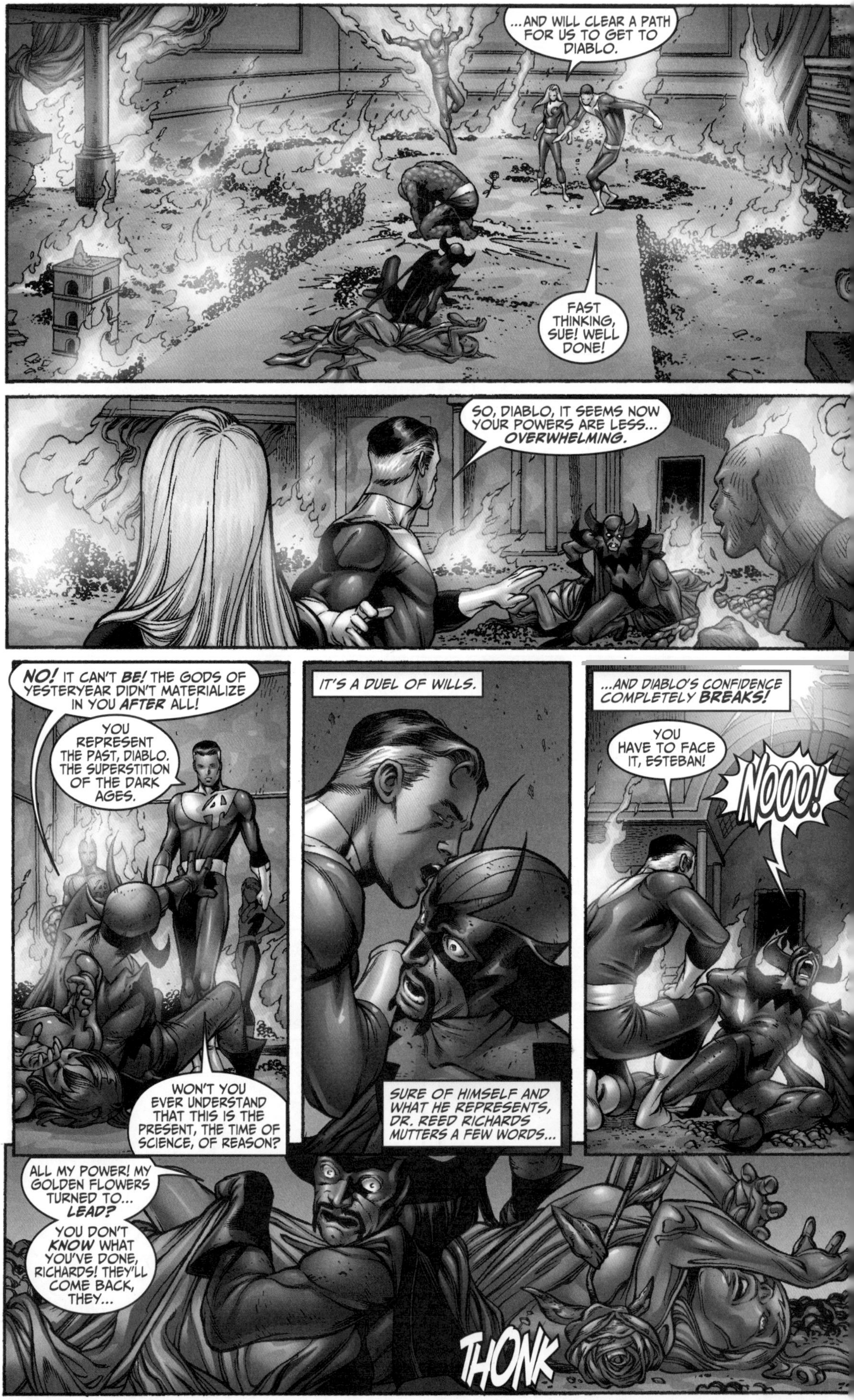

...AND WILL CLEAR A PATH FOR US TO GET TO DIABLO.
FAST THINKING, SUE! WELL DONE!
SO, DIABLO, IT SEEMS NOW YOUR POWERS ARE LESS... OVERWHELMING.
NO! IT CAN'T BE! THE GODS OF YESTERYEAR DIDN'T MATERIALIZE IN YOU AFTER ALL!
YOU REPRESENT THE PAST, DIABLO. THE SUPERSTITION OF THE DARK AGES.
WON'T YOU EVER UNDERSTAND THAT THIS IS THE PRESENT, THE TIME OF SCIENCE, OF REASON?
IT'S A DUEL OF WILLS.
SURE OF HIMSELF AND WHAT HE REPRESENTS, DR. REED RICHARDS MUTTERS A FEW WORDS...
...AND DIABLO'S CONFIDENCE COMPLETELY BREAKS!
YOU HAVE TO FACE IT, ESTEBAN!
NOOO!
ALL MY POWER! MY GOLDEN FLOWERS TURNED TO... LEAD?
YOU DON'T KNOW WHAT YOU'VE DONE, RICHARDS! THEY'LL COME BACK, THEY...
THONK

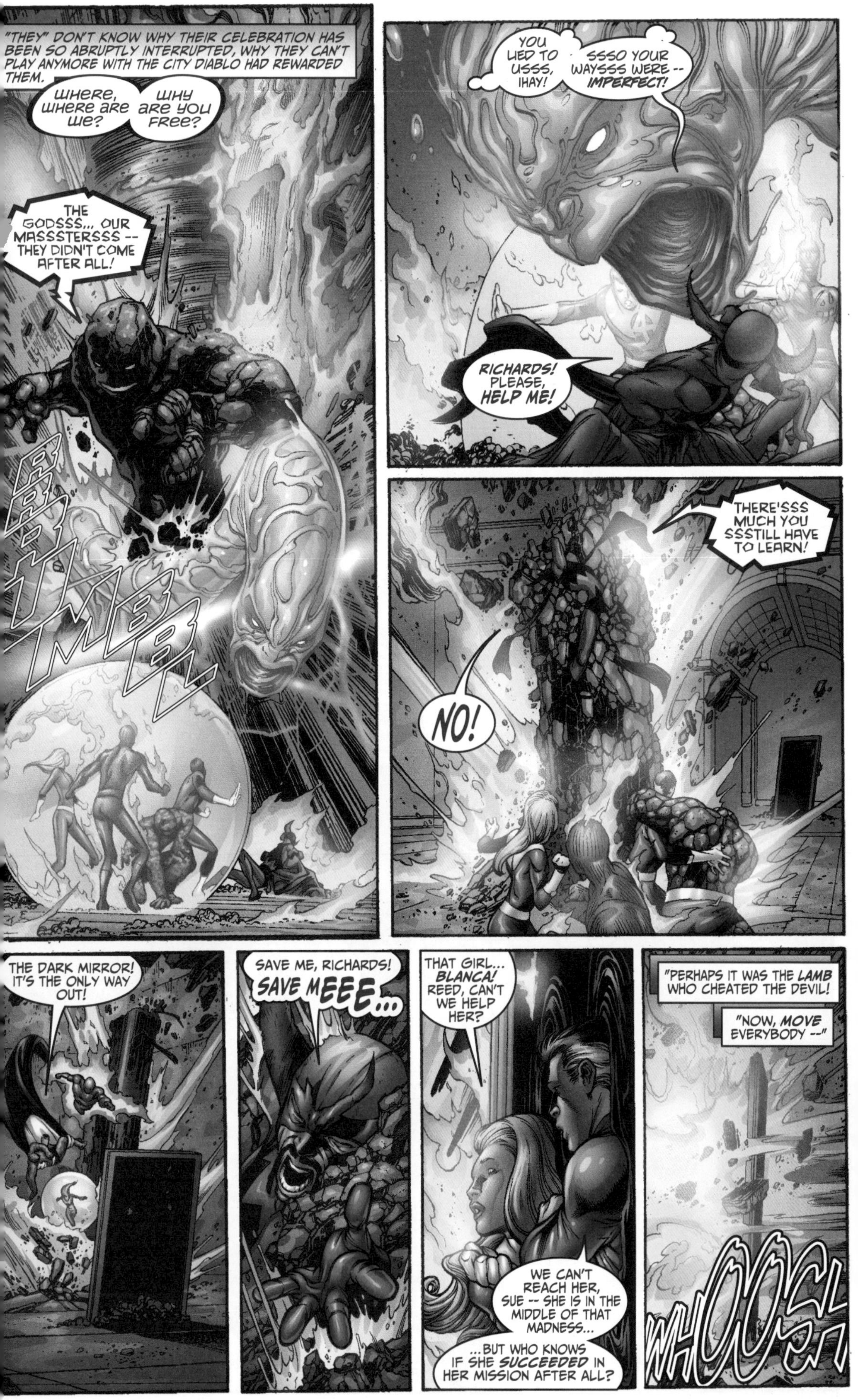
"THEY" DON'T KNOW WHY THEIR CELEBRATION HAS BEEN SO ABRUPTLY INTERRUPTED, WHY THEY CAN'T PLAY ANYMORE WITH THE CITY DIABLO HAD REWARDED THEM.
WHERE, WHERE ARE WE?
WHY ARE YOU FREE?
THE GODSSS... OUR MASSSTERSSS -- THEY DIDN'T COME AFTER ALL!
RRRUMBBL
YOU LIED TO USSS, IHAY!
SSSO YOUR WAYSSS WERE -- IMPERFECT!
RICHARDS! PLEASE, HELP ME!
THERE'SSS MUCH YOU SSSTILL HAVE TO LEARN!
NO!
THE DARK MIRROR! IT'S THE ONLY WAY OUT!
SAVE ME, RICHARDS! SAVE MEEE...
THAT GIRL... BLANCA! REED, CAN'T WE HELP HER?
WE CAN'T REACH HER, SUE -- SHE IS IN THE MIDDLE OF THAT MADNESS...
...BUT WHO KNOWS IF SHE SUCCEEDED IN HER MISSION AFTER ALL?
"PERHAPS IT WAS THE LAMB WHO CHEATED THE DEVIL!
"NOW, MOVE EVERYBODY --"
WHOOSH

CLANNK

-- FAST!

EASY, FELLAS! WE'RE FINALLY -- -- HOME?

BEN... ARE YOU *OKAY*, BIG GUY?

I'VE SEEN BETTER DAYS, STRETCH. THERE'S SUMTHIN' IN MY THROAT --

-- THAT DARN "*AURUS POTABILUS*" I WUZ FORCED TA DRINK.

I WOULD PREFER *HOT CHOCOLATE*, THOUGH. HEY, WHAT JUST HAPPENED HERE?

PTUH!

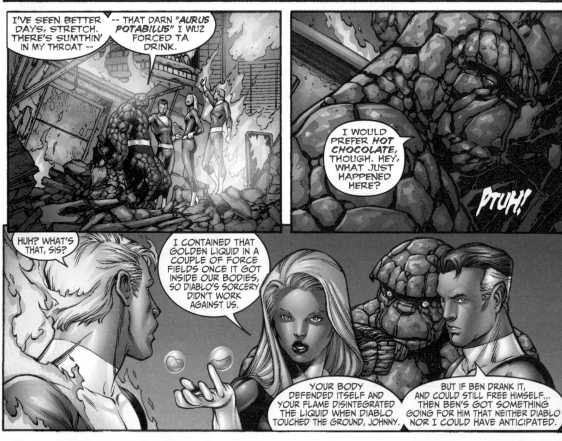

HUH? WHAT'S THAT, SIS?

I CONTAINED THAT GOLDEN LIQUID IN A COUPLE OF FORCE FIELDS ONCE IT GOT INSIDE OUR BODIES, SO DIABLO'S SORCERY DIDN'T WORK AGAINST US.

YOUR BODY DEFENDED ITSELF AND YOUR FLAME DISINTEGRATED THE LIQUID WHEN DIABLO TOUCHED THE GROUND, JOHNNY.

BUT IF BEN DRANK IT, AND COULD STILL FREE HIMSELF... THEN BEN'S GOT SOMETHING GOING FOR HIM THAT NEITHER DIABLO NOR I COULD HAVE ANTICIPATED.

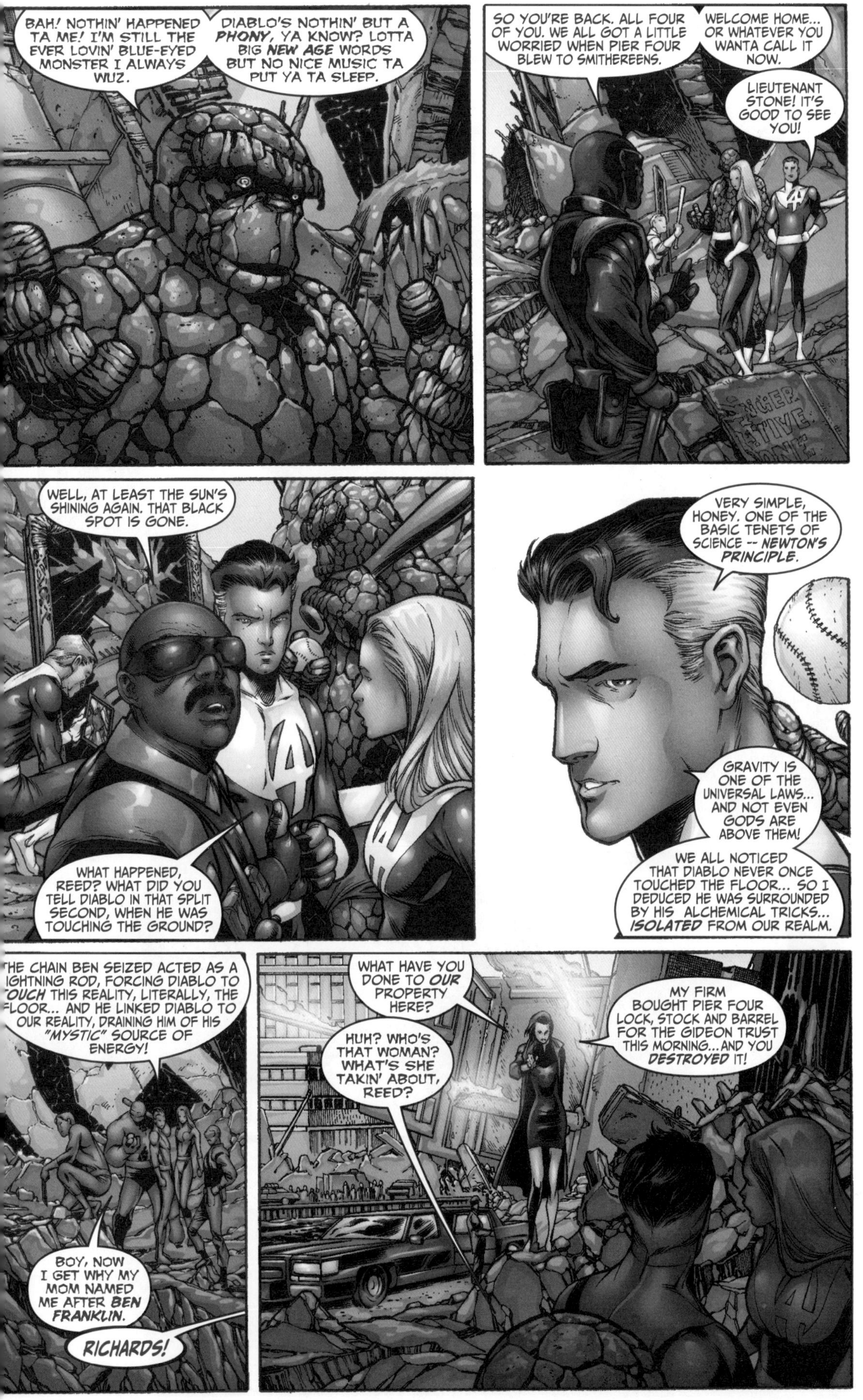
BAH! NOTHIN' HAPPENED TA ME! I'M STILL THE EVER LOVIN' BLUE-EYED MONSTER I ALWAYS WUZ.
DIABLO'S NOTHIN' BUT A PHONY, YA KNOW? LOTTA BIG NEW AGE WORDS BUT NO NICE MUSIC TA PUT YA TA SLEEP.
SO YOU'RE BACK. ALL FOUR OF YOU. WE ALL GOT A LITTLE WORRIED WHEN PIER FOUR BLEW TO SMITHEREENS.
WELCOME HOME... OR WHATEVER YOU WANTA CALL IT NOW.
LIEUTENANT STONE! IT'S GOOD TO SEE YOU!
WELL, AT LEAST THE SUN'S SHINING AGAIN. THAT BLACK SPOT IS GONE.
WHAT HAPPENED, REED? WHAT DID YOU TELL DIABLO IN THAT SPLIT SECOND, WHEN HE WAS TOUCHING THE GROUND?
VERY SIMPLE, HONEY. ONE OF THE BASIC TENETS OF SCIENCE -- NEWTON'S PRINCIPLE.
GRAVITY IS ONE OF THE UNIVERSAL LAWS... AND NOT EVEN GODS ARE ABOVE THEM!
WE ALL NOTICED THAT DIABLO NEVER ONCE TOUCHED THE FLOOR... SO I DEDUCED HE WAS SURROUNDED BY HIS ALCHEMICAL TRICKS... ISOLATED FROM OUR REALM.
THE CHAIN BEN SEIZED ACTED AS A IGHTNING ROD, FORCING DIABLO TO OUCH THIS REALITY, LITERALLY, THE FLOOR... AND HE LINKED DIABLO TO OUR REALITY, DRAINING HIM OF HIS "MYSTIC" SOURCE OF ENERGY!
BOY, NOW I GET WHY MY MOM NAMED ME AFTER BEN FRANKLIN.
RICHARDS!
WHAT HAVE YOU DONE TO OUR PROPERTY HERE?
HUH? WHO'S THAT WOMAN? WHAT'S SHE TAKIN' ABOUT, REED?
MY FIRM BOUGHT PIER FOUR LOCK, STOCK AND BARREL FOR THE GIDEON TRUST THIS MORNING... AND YOU DESTROYED IT!

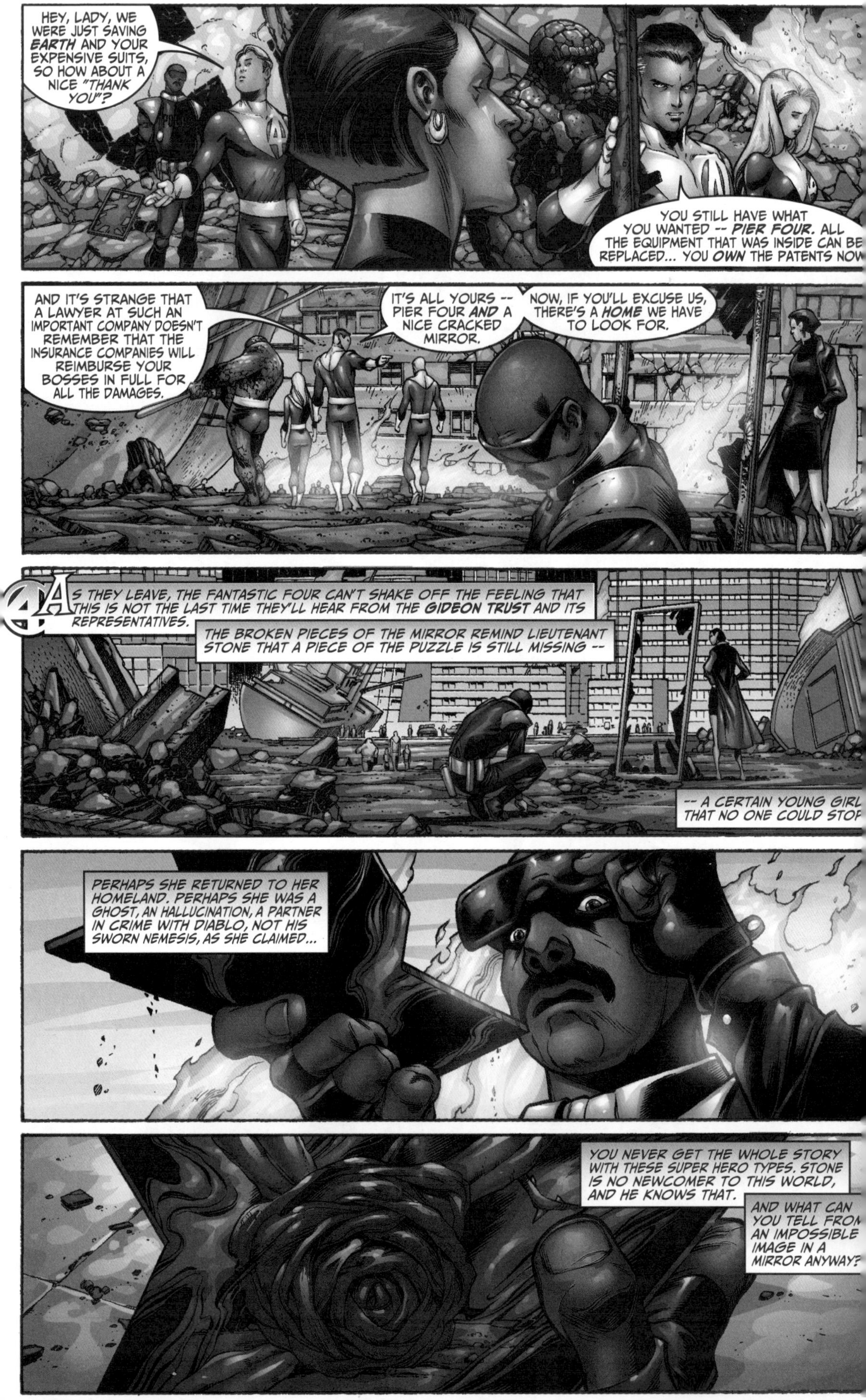
HEY, LADY, WE WERE JUST SAVING EARTH AND YOUR EXPENSIVE SUITS, SO HOW ABOUT A NICE "THANK YOU"?
YOU STILL HAVE WHAT YOU WANTED -- PIER FOUR. ALL THE EQUIPMENT THAT WAS INSIDE CAN BE REPLACED... YOU OWN THE PATENTS NOW
AND IT'S STRANGE THAT A LAWYER AT SUCH AN IMPORTANT COMPANY DOESN'T REMEMBER THAT THE INSURANCE COMPANIES WILL REIMBURSE YOUR BOSSES IN FULL FOR ALL THE DAMAGES.
IT'S ALL YOURS -- PIER FOUR AND A NICE CRACKED MIRROR.
NOW, IF YOU'LL EXCUSE US, THERE'S A HOME WE HAVE TO LOOK FOR.
AS THEY LEAVE, THE FANTASTIC FOUR CAN'T SHAKE OFF THE FEELING THAT THIS IS NOT THE LAST TIME THEY'LL HEAR FROM THE GIDEON TRUST AND ITS REPRESENTATIVES.
THE BROKEN PIECES OF THE MIRROR REMIND LIEUTENANT STONE THAT A PIECE OF THE PUZZLE IS STILL MISSING --
-- A CERTAIN YOUNG GIRL THAT NO ONE COULD STOP
PERHAPS SHE RETURNED TO HER HOMELAND. PERHAPS SHE WAS A GHOST, AN HALLUCINATION, A PARTNER IN CRIME WITH DIABLO, NOT HIS SWORN NEMESIS, AS SHE CLAIMED...
YOU NEVER GET THE WHOLE STORY WITH THESE SUPER HERO TYPES. STONE IS NO NEWCOMER TO THIS WORLD, AND HE KNOWS THAT.
AND WHAT CAN YOU TELL FROM AN IMPOSSIBLE IMAGE IN A MIRROR ANYWAY?

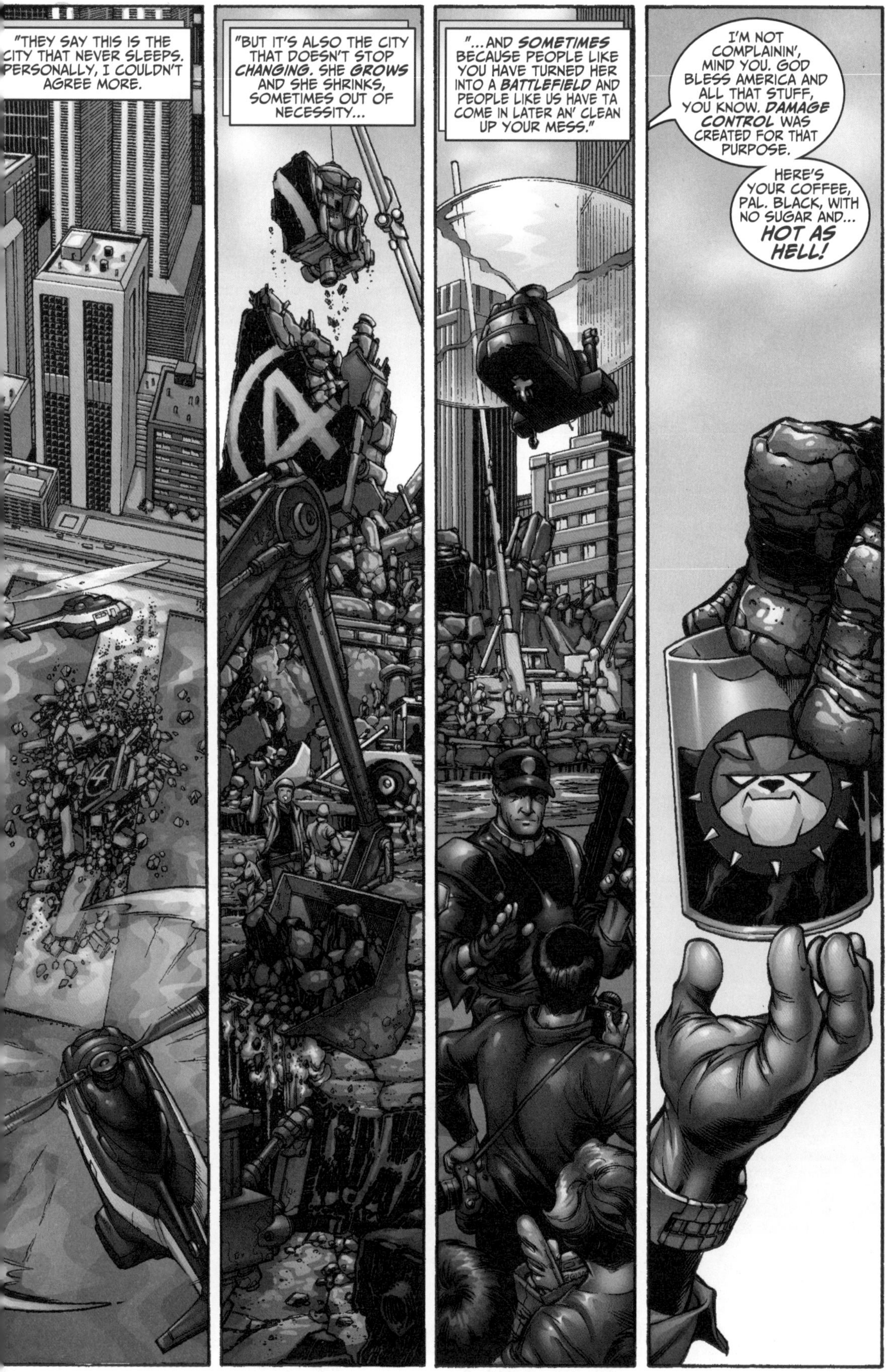
"THEY SAY THIS IS THE CITY THAT NEVER SLEEPS. PERSONALLY, I COULDN'T AGREE MORE.
"BUT IT'S ALSO THE CITY THAT DOESN'T STOP CHANGING. SHE GROWS AND SHE SHRINKS, SOMETIMES OUT OF NECESSITY...
"...AND SOMETIMES BECAUSE PEOPLE LIKE YOU HAVE TURNED HER INTO A BATTLEFIELD AND PEOPLE LIKE US HAVE TA COME IN LATER AN' CLEAN UP YOUR MESS."
I'M NOT COMPLAININ', MIND YOU. GOD BLESS AMERICA AND ALL THAT STUFF, YOU KNOW. DAMAGE CONTROL WAS CREATED FOR THAT PURPOSE.
HERE'S YOUR COFFEE, PAL. BLACK, WITH NO SUGAR AND... HOT AS HELL!

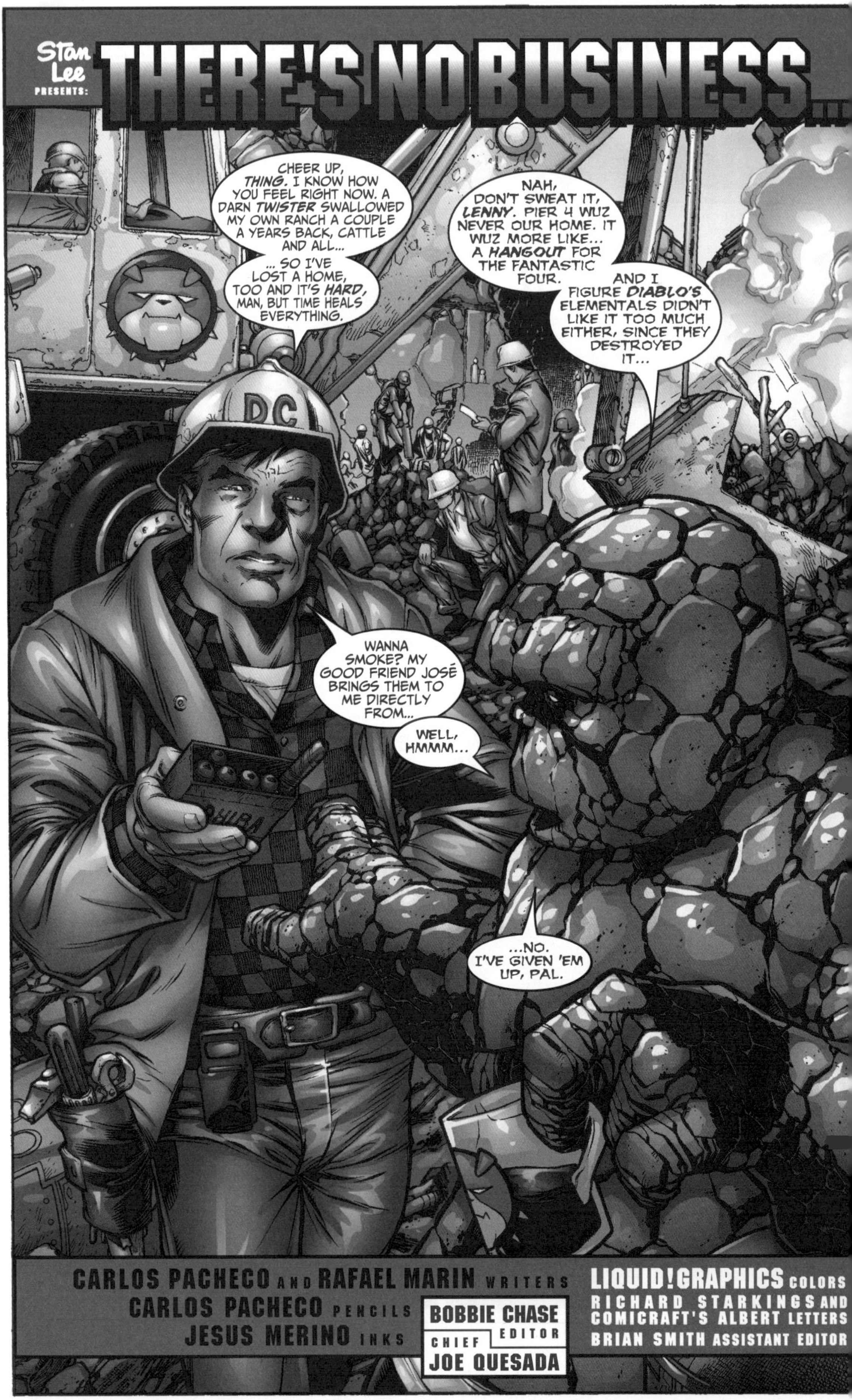
Stan Lee PRESENTS:
THERE'S NO BUSINESS...
CHEER UP, THING. I KNOW HOW YOU FEEL RIGHT NOW. A DARN TWISTER SWALLOWED MY OWN RANCH A COUPLE A YEARS BACK, CATTLE AND ALL...
... SO I'VE LOST A HOME, TOO AND IT'S HARD, MAN, BUT TIME HEALS EVERYTHING.
NAH, DON'T SWEAT IT, LENNY. PIER 4 WUZ NEVER OUR HOME. IT WUZ MORE LIKE... A HANGOUT FOR THE FANTASTIC FOUR.
AND I FIGURE DIABLO'S ELEMENTALS DIDN'T LIKE IT TOO MUCH EITHER, SINCE THEY DESTROYED IT...
DC
WANNA SMOKE? MY GOOD FRIEND JOSÉ BRINGS THEM TO ME DIRECTLY FROM...
WELL, HMMM...
...NO. I'VE GIVEN 'EM UP, PAL.
CARLOS PACHECO AND RAFAEL MARIN WRITERS
CARLOS PACHECO PENCILS
JESUS MERINO INKS
BOBBIE CHASE EDITOR
CHIEF JOE QUESADA
LIQUID!GRAPHICS COLORS
RICHARD STARKINGS AND COMICRAFT'S ALBERT LETTERS
BRIAN SMITH ASSISTANT EDITOR

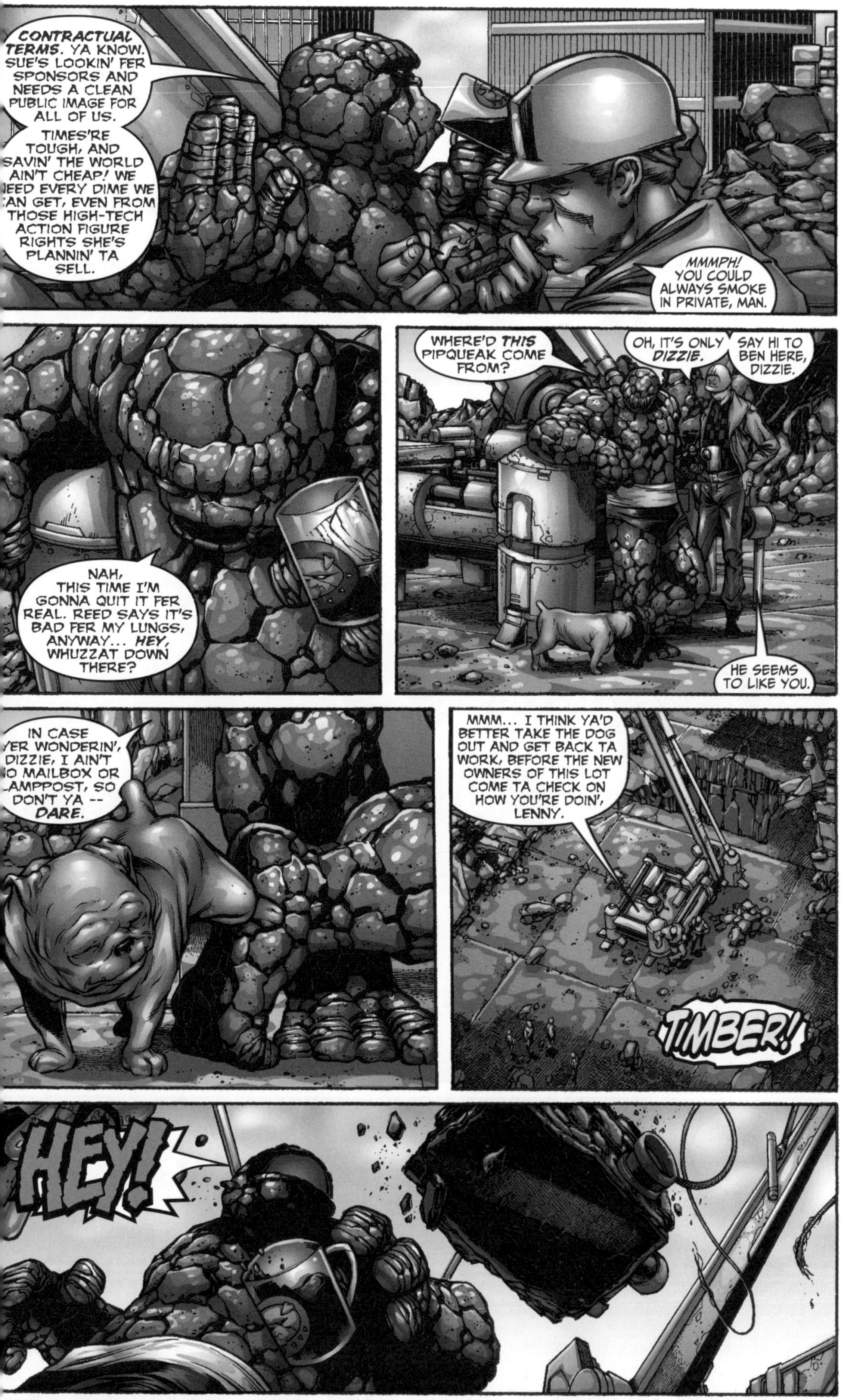
CONTRACTUAL TERMS. YA KNOW. SUE'S LOOKIN' FER SPONSORS AND NEEDS A CLEAN PUBLIC IMAGE FOR ALL OF US.
TIMES'RE TOUGH, AND SAVIN' THE WORLD AIN'T CHEAP! WE NEED EVERY DIME WE CAN GET, EVEN FROM THOSE HIGH-TECH ACTION FIGURE RIGHTS SHE'S PLANNIN' TA SELL.
MMMPH! YOU COULD ALWAYS SMOKE IN PRIVATE, MAN.
NAH, THIS TIME I'M GONNA QUIT IT FER REAL. REED SAYS IT'S BAD FER MY LUNGS, ANYWAY... HEY, WHUZZAT DOWN THERE?
WHERE'D THIS PIPQUEAK COME FROM?
OH, IT'S ONLY DIZZIE.
SAY HI TO BEN HERE, DIZZIE.
HE SEEMS TO LIKE YOU.
IN CASE YER WONDERIN', DIZZIE, I AIN'T NO MAILBOX OR LAMPPOST, SO DON'T YA -- DARE.
MMM... I THINK YA'D BETTER TAKE THE DOG OUT AND GET BACK TA WORK, BEFORE THE NEW OWNERS OF THIS LOT COME TA CHECK ON HOW YOU'RE DOIN', LENNY.
TIMBER!
HEY!

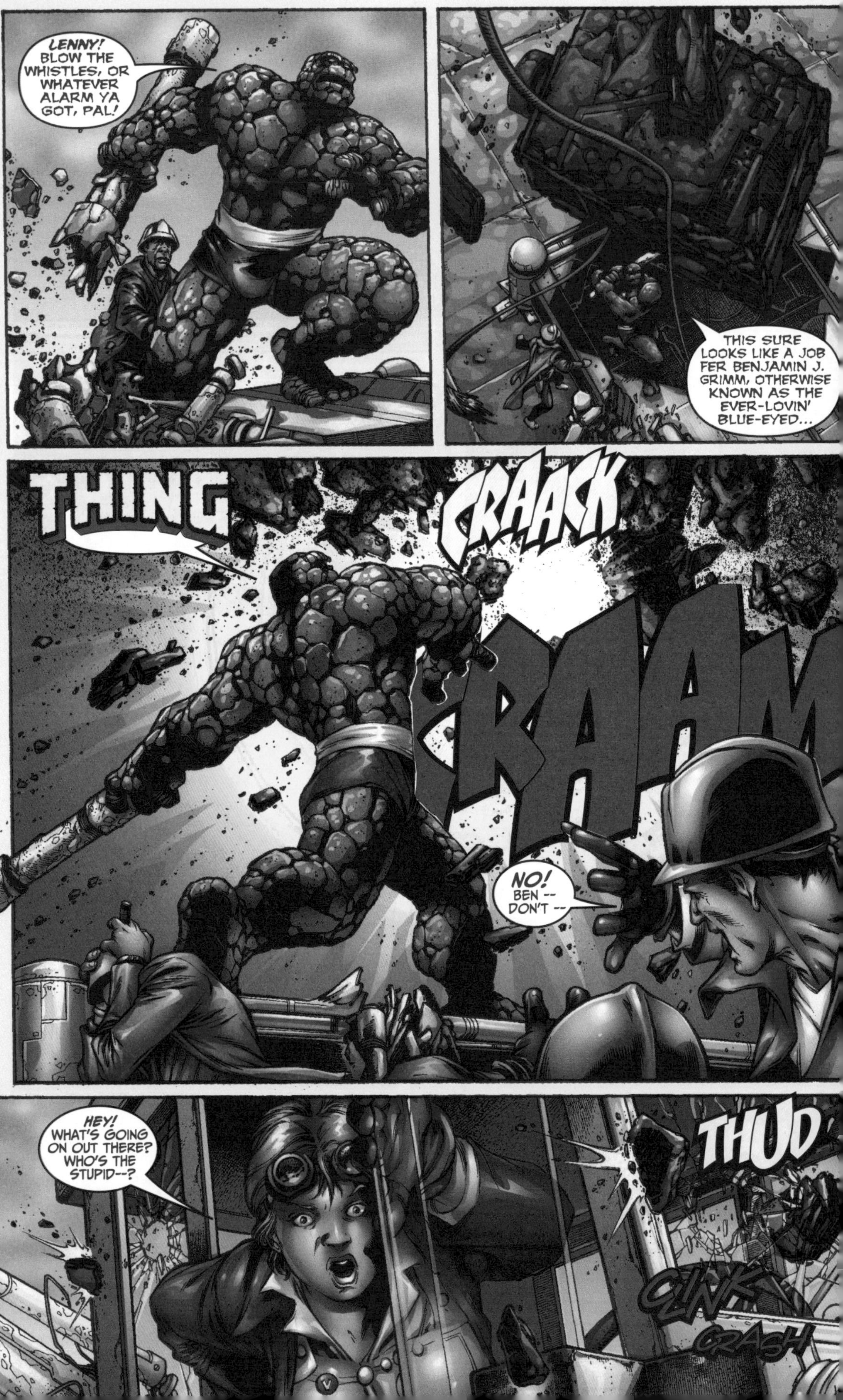
LENNY! BLOW THE WHISTLES, OR WHATEVER ALARM YA GOT, PAL!
THIS SURE LOOKS LIKE A JOB FER BENJAMIN J. GRIMM, OTHERWISE KNOWN AS THE EVER-LOVIN' BLUE-EYED...
THING
CRAACK
CRAAM
NO! BEN -- DON'T --
HEY! WHAT'S GOING ON OUT THERE? WHO'S THE STUPID--?
THUD
CLINK
CRASH

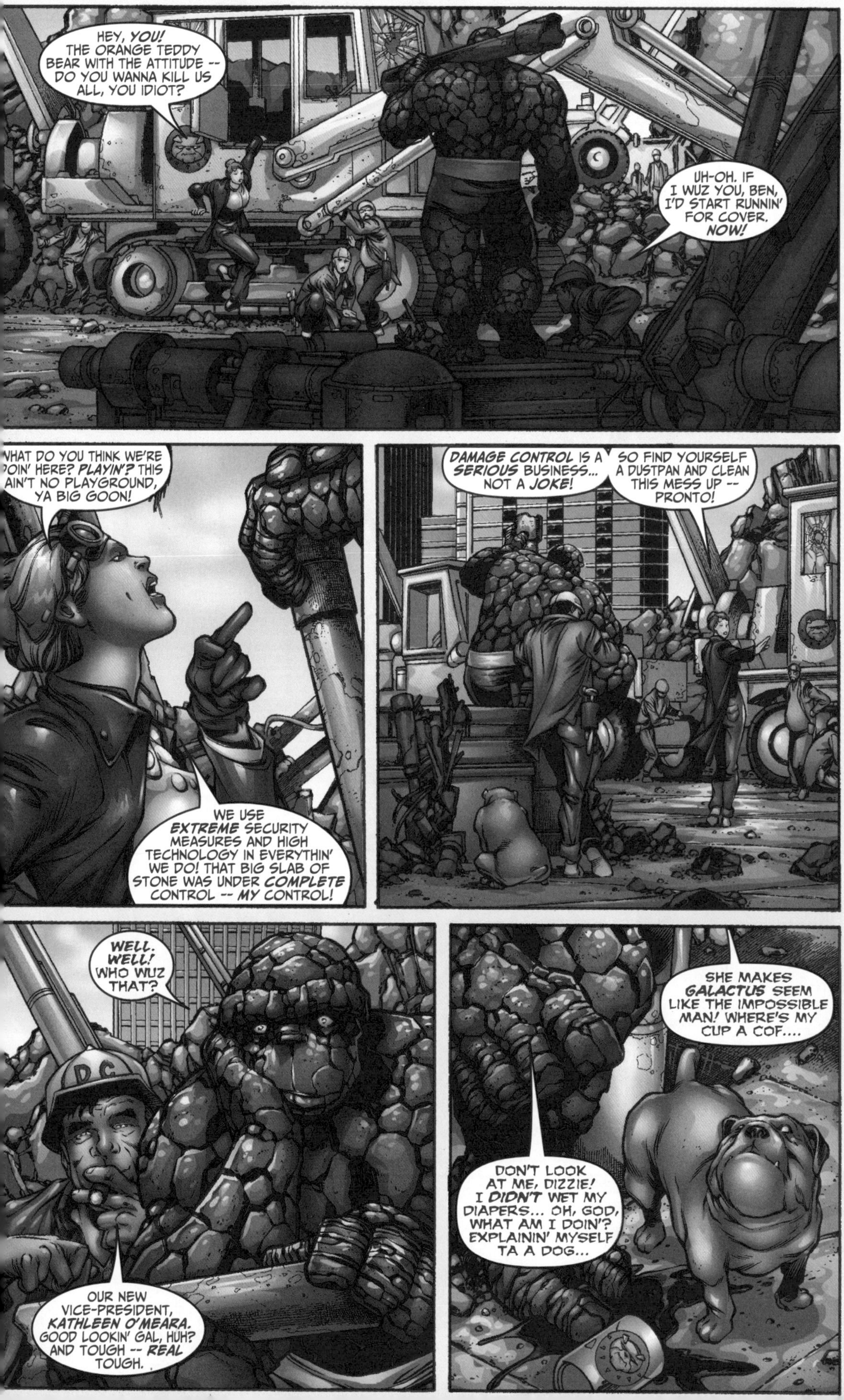
HEY, *YOU!* THE ORANGE TEDDY BEAR WITH THE ATTITUDE -- DO YOU WANNA KILL US ALL, YOU IDIOT?
UH-OH. IF I WUZ YOU, BEN, I'D START RUNNIN' FOR COVER. *NOW!*
WHAT DO YOU THINK WE'RE DOIN' HERE? *PLAYIN'?* THIS AIN'T NO PLAYGROUND, YA BIG GOON!
WE USE *EXTREME* SECURITY MEASURES AND HIGH TECHNOLOGY IN EVERYTHIN' WE DO! THAT BIG SLAB OF STONE WAS UNDER *COMPLETE* CONTROL -- *MY* CONTROL!
DAMAGE CONTROL IS A *SERIOUS* BUSINESS... NOT A *JOKE!*
SO FIND YOURSELF A DUSTPAN AND CLEAN THIS MESS UP -- PRONTO!
WELL. WELL! WHO WUZ THAT?
OUR NEW VICE-PRESIDENT, *KATHLEEN O'MEARA.* GOOD LOOKIN' GAL, HUH? AND TOUGH -- *REAL* TOUGH.
SHE MAKES *GALACTUS* SEEM LIKE THE IMPOSSIBLE MAN! WHERE'S MY CUP A COF....
DON'T LOOK AT ME, DIZZIE! I *DIDN'T* WET MY DIAPERS... OH, GOD, WHAT AM I DOIN'? EXPLAININ' MYSELF TA A DOG...

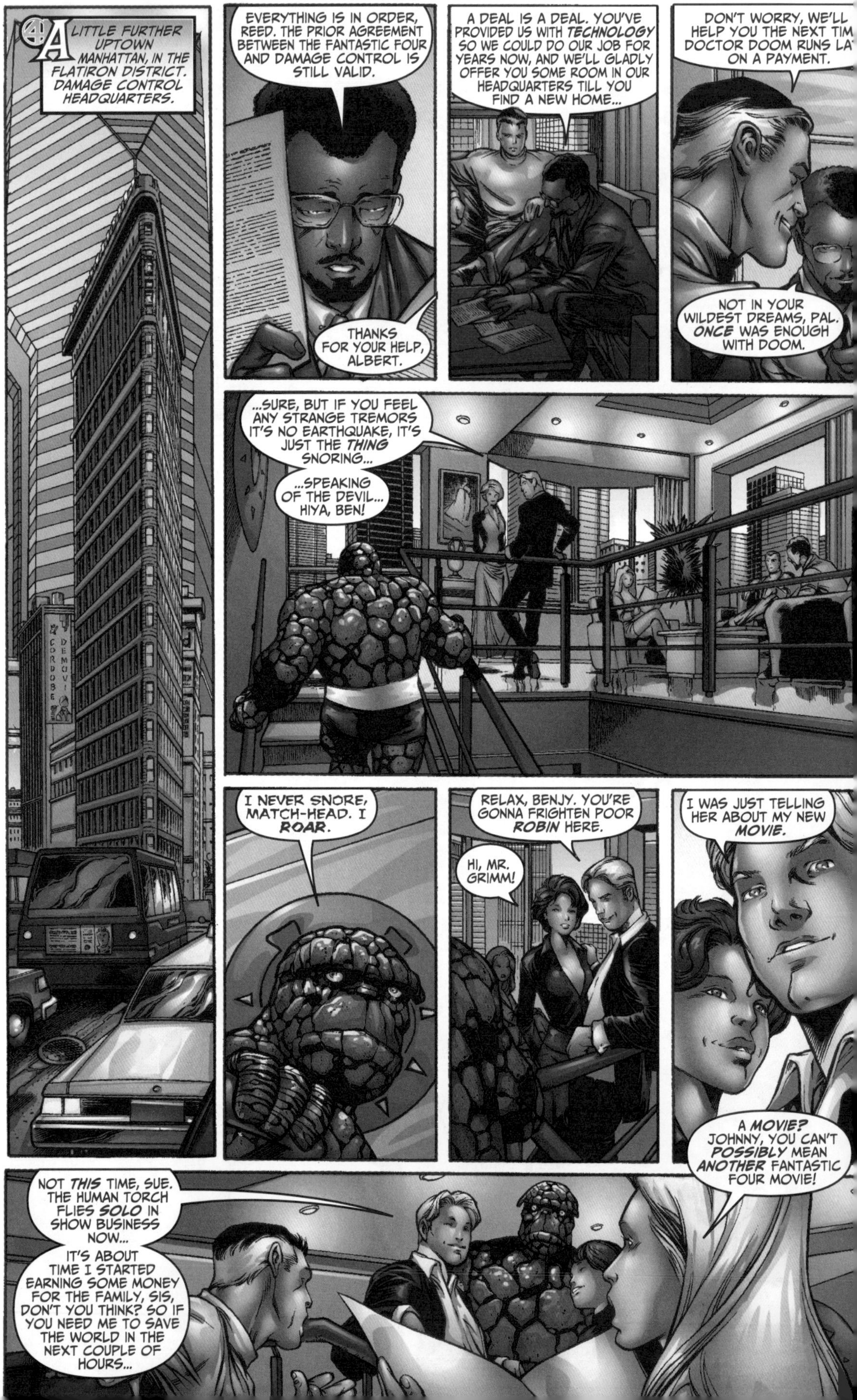
A LITTLE FURTHER UPTOWN MANHATTAN, IN THE FLATIRON DISTRICT. DAMAGE CONTROL HEADQUARTERS.
EVERYTHING IS IN ORDER, REED. THE PRIOR AGREEMENT BETWEEN THE FANTASTIC FOUR AND DAMAGE CONTROL IS STILL VALID.
THANKS FOR YOUR HELP, ALBERT.
A DEAL IS A DEAL. YOU'VE PROVIDED US WITH TECHNOLOGY SO WE COULD DO OUR JOB FOR YEARS NOW, AND WE'LL GLADLY OFFER YOU SOME ROOM IN OUR HEADQUARTERS TILL YOU FIND A NEW HOME...
DON'T WORRY, WE'LL HELP YOU THE NEXT TIM DOCTOR DOOM RUNS LA ON A PAYMENT.
NOT IN YOUR WILDEST DREAMS, PAL. ONCE WAS ENOUGH WITH DOOM.
...SURE, BUT IF YOU FEEL ANY STRANGE TREMORS IT'S NO EARTHQUAKE, IT'S JUST THE THING SNORING...
...SPEAKING OF THE DEVIL... HIYA, BEN!
I NEVER SNORE, MATCH-HEAD. I ROAR.
RELAX, BENJY. YOU'RE GONNA FRIGHTEN POOR ROBIN HERE.
HI, MR. GRIMM!
I WAS JUST TELLING HER ABOUT MY NEW MOVIE.
A MOVIE? JOHNNY, YOU CAN'T POSSIBLY MEAN ANOTHER FANTASTIC FOUR MOVIE!
NOT THIS TIME, SUE. THE HUMAN TORCH FLIES SOLO IN SHOW BUSINESS NOW...
IT'S ABOUT TIME I STARTED EARNING SOME MONEY FOR THE FAMILY, SIS, DON'T YOU THINK? SO IF YOU NEED ME TO SAVE THE WORLD IN THE NEXT COUPLE OF HOURS...

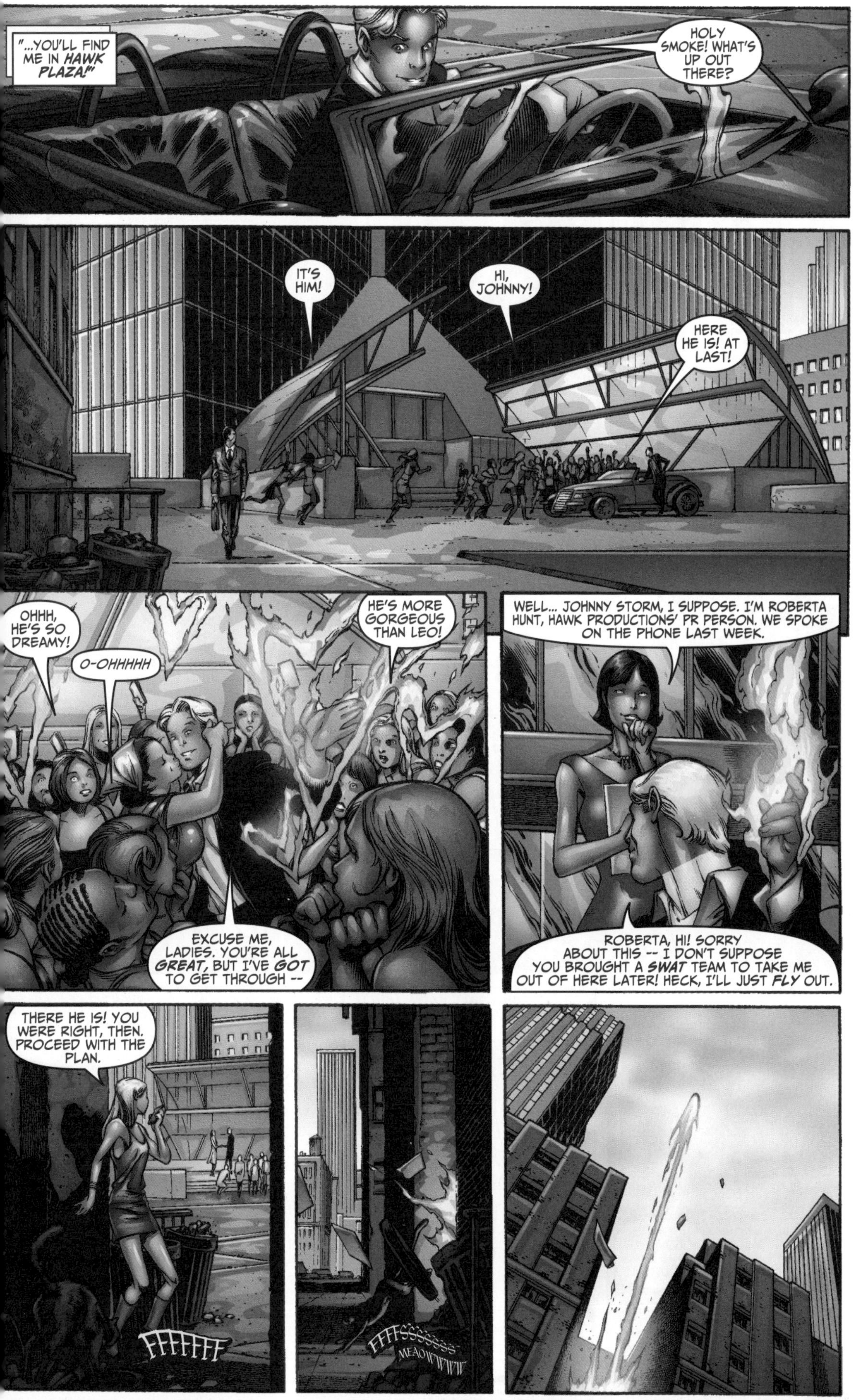
"...YOU'LL FIND ME IN HAWK PLAZA!"
HOLY SMOKE! WHAT'S UP OUT THERE?
IT'S HIM!
HI, JOHNNY!
HERE HE IS! AT LAST!
OHHH, HE'S SO DREAMY!
O-OHHHHH
HE'S MORE GORGEOUS THAN LEO!
EXCUSE ME, LADIES. YOU'RE ALL GREAT, BUT I'VE GOT TO GET THROUGH --
WELL... JOHNNY STORM, I SUPPOSE. I'M ROBERTA HUNT, HAWK PRODUCTIONS' PR PERSON. WE SPOKE ON THE PHONE LAST WEEK.
ROBERTA, HI! SORRY ABOUT THIS -- I DON'T SUPPOSE YOU BROUGHT A SWAT TEAM TO TAKE ME OUT OF HERE LATER! HECK, I'LL JUST FLY OUT.
THERE HE IS! YOU WERE RIGHT, THEN. PROCEED WITH THE PLAN.
FFFFFFF
FFFFSSSSSSSS
MEAOWWWW

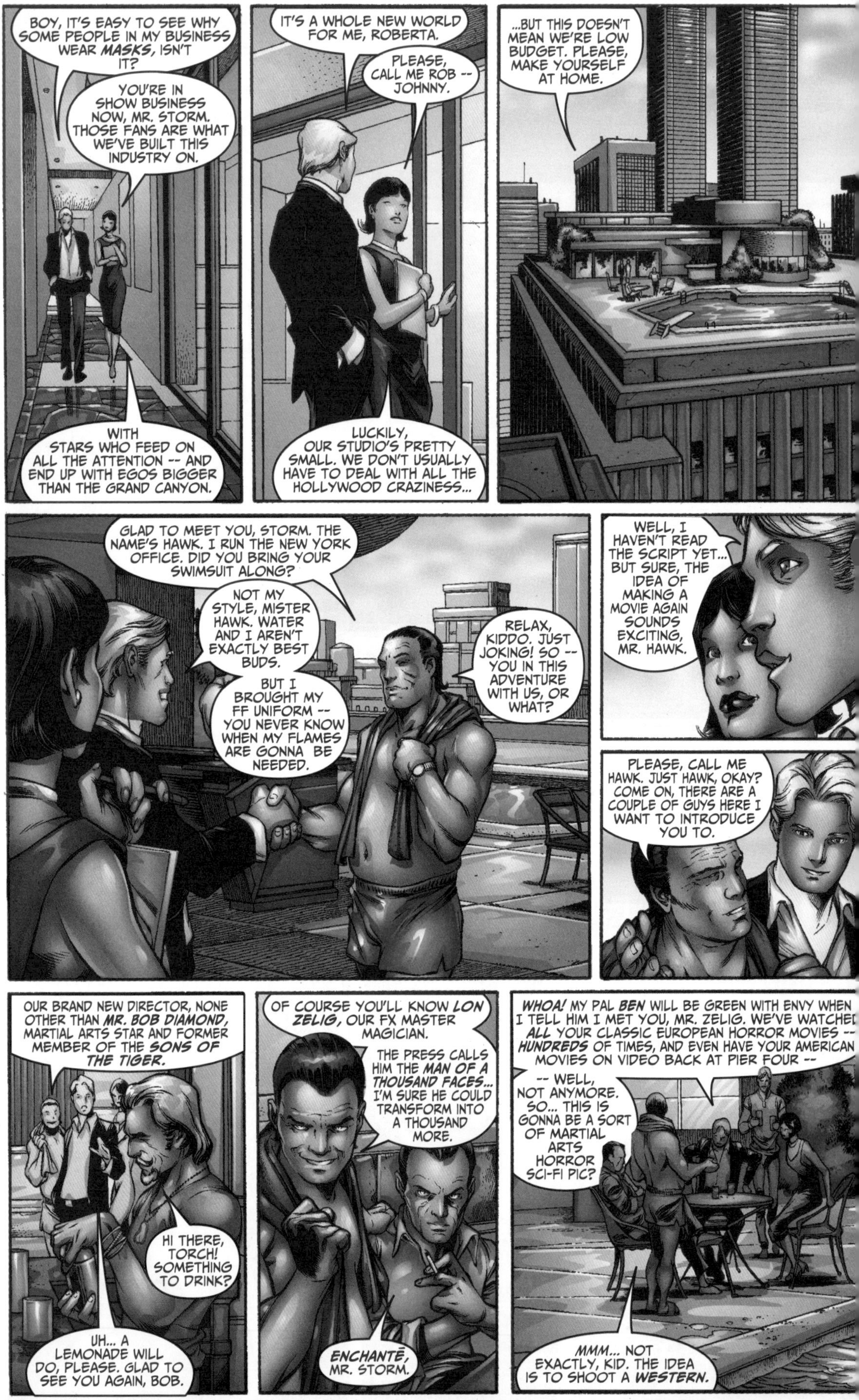
BOY, IT'S EASY TO SEE WHY SOME PEOPLE IN MY BUSINESS WEAR *MASKS,* ISN'T IT?
YOU'RE IN SHOW BUSINESS NOW, MR. STORM. THOSE FANS ARE WHAT WE'VE BUILT THIS INDUSTRY ON.
WITH STARS WHO FEED ON ALL THE ATTENTION -- AND END UP WITH EGOS BIGGER THAN THE GRAND CANYON.
IT'S A WHOLE NEW WORLD FOR ME, ROBERTA.
PLEASE, CALL ME ROB -- JOHNNY.
LUCKILY, OUR STUDIO'S PRETTY SMALL. WE DON'T USUALLY HAVE TO DEAL WITH ALL THE HOLLYWOOD CRAZINESS...
...BUT THIS DOESN'T MEAN WE'RE LOW BUDGET. PLEASE, MAKE YOURSELF AT HOME.
GLAD TO MEET YOU, STORM. THE NAME'S HAWK. I RUN THE NEW YORK OFFICE. DID YOU BRING YOUR SWIMSUIT ALONG?
NOT MY STYLE, MISTER HAWK. WATER AND I AREN'T EXACTLY BEST BUDS.
BUT I BROUGHT MY FF UNIFORM -- YOU NEVER KNOW WHEN MY FLAMES ARE GONNA BE NEEDED.
RELAX, KIDDO. JUST JOKING! SO -- YOU IN THIS ADVENTURE WITH US, OR WHAT?
WELL, I HAVEN'T READ THE SCRIPT YET... BUT SURE, THE IDEA OF MAKING A MOVIE AGAIN SOUNDS EXCITING, MR. HAWK.
PLEASE, CALL ME HAWK. JUST HAWK, OKAY? COME ON, THERE ARE A COUPLE OF GUYS HERE I WANT TO INTRODUCE YOU TO.
OUR BRAND NEW DIRECTOR, NONE OTHER THAN *MR. BOB DIAMOND,* MARTIAL ARTS STAR AND FORMER MEMBER OF THE *SONS OF THE TIGER.*
HI THERE, TORCH! SOMETHING TO DRINK?
UH... A LEMONADE WILL DO, PLEASE. GLAD TO SEE YOU AGAIN, BOB.
OF COURSE YOU'LL KNOW *LON ZELIG,* OUR FX MASTER MAGICIAN.
THE PRESS CALLS HIM THE *MAN OF A THOUSAND FACES...* I'M SURE HE COULD TRANSFORM INTO A THOUSAND MORE.
ENCHANTÉ, MR. STORM.
WHOA! MY PAL *BEN* WILL BE GREEN WITH ENVY WHEN I TELL HIM I MET YOU, MR. ZELIG. WE'VE WATCHED *ALL* YOUR CLASSIC EUROPEAN HORROR MOVIES -- *HUNDREDS* OF TIMES, AND EVEN HAVE YOUR AMERICAN MOVIES ON VIDEO BACK AT PIER FOUR --
-- WELL, NOT ANYMORE. SO... THIS IS GONNA BE A SORT OF MARTIAL ARTS HORROR SCI-FI PIC?
MMM... NOT EXACTLY, KID. THE IDEA IS TO SHOOT A *WESTERN.*

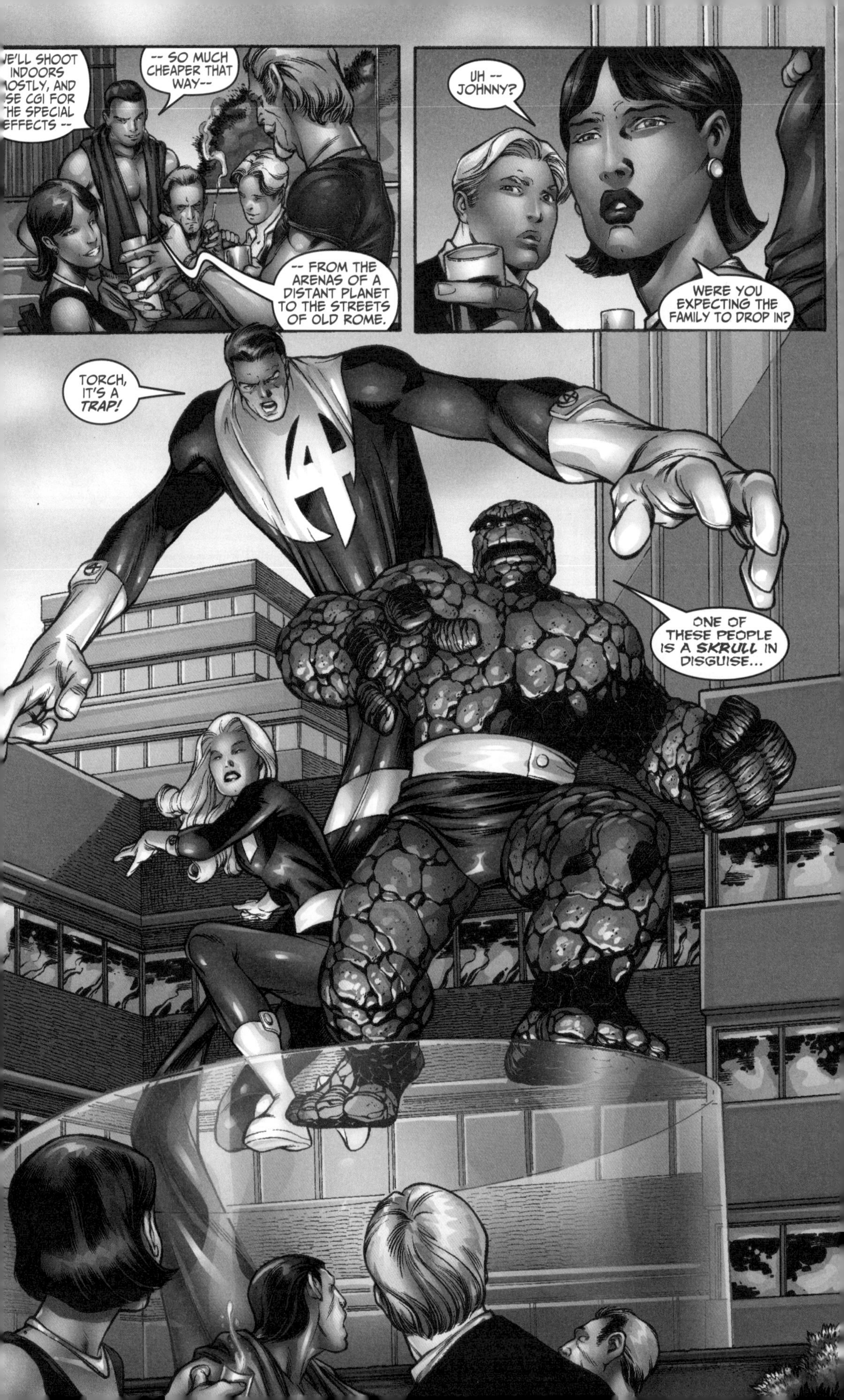

E'LL SHOOT INDOORS OSTLY, AND SE CGI FOR HE SPECIAL EFFECTS --
-- SO MUCH CHEAPER THAT WAY--
-- FROM THE ARENAS OF A DISTANT PLANET TO THE STREETS OF OLD ROME.
UH -- JOHNNY?
WERE YOU EXPECTING THE FAMILY TO DROP IN?
TORCH, IT'S A TRAP!
ONE OF THESE PEOPLE IS A SKRULL IN DISGUISE...

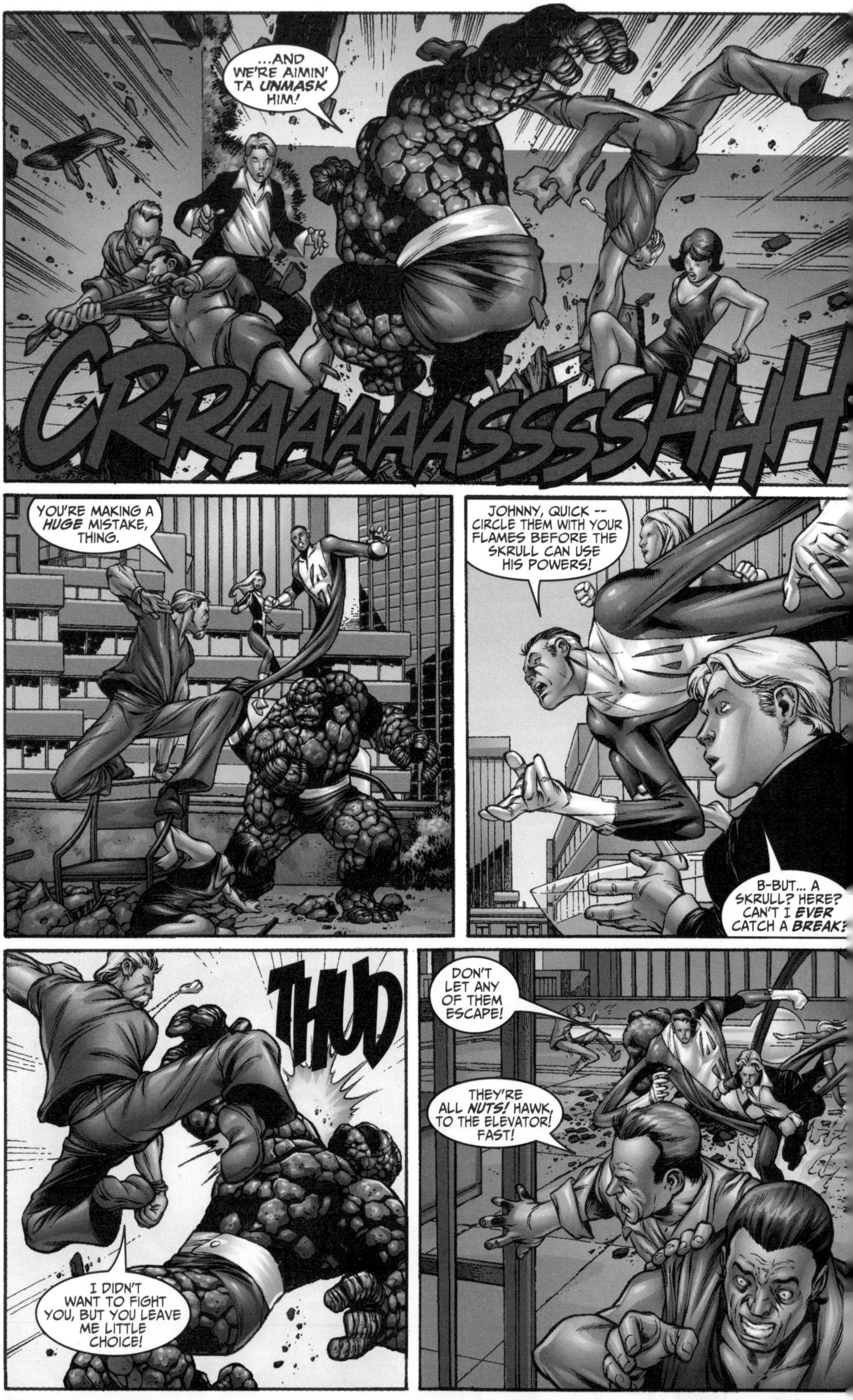
...AND WE'RE AIMIN' TA UNMASK HIM!
CRRAAAAASSSSHH
YOU'RE MAKING A HUGE MISTAKE, THING.
JOHNNY, QUICK -- CIRCLE THEM WITH YOUR FLAMES BEFORE THE SKRULL CAN USE HIS POWERS!
B-BUT... A SKRULL? HERE? CAN'T I EVER CATCH A BREAK?
THUD
I DIDN'T WANT TO FIGHT YOU, BUT YOU LEAVE ME LITTLE CHOICE!
DON'T LET ANY OF THEM ESCAPE!
THEY'RE ALL NUTS! HAWK, TO THE ELEVATOR! FAST!

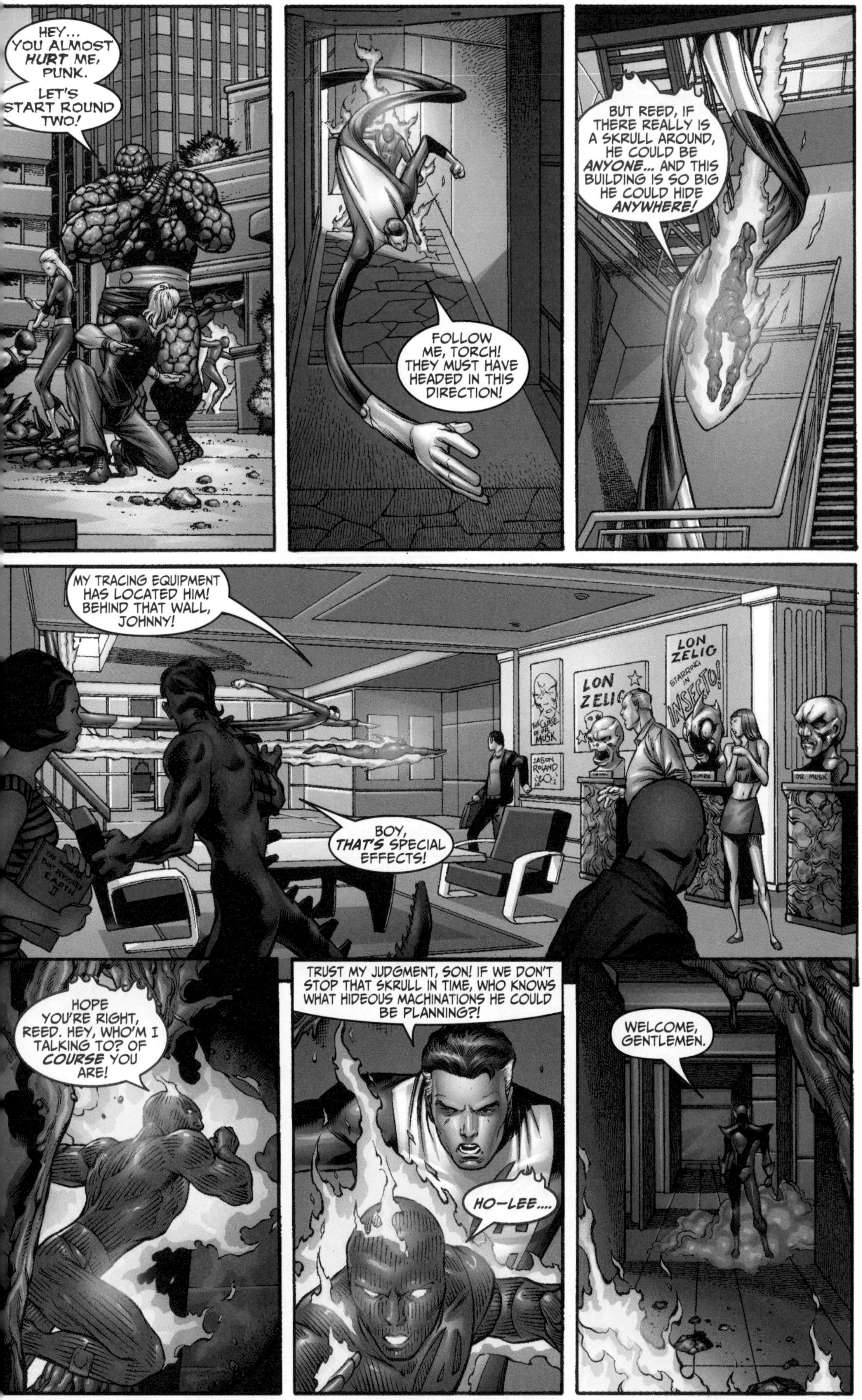
HEY... YOU ALMOST *HURT* ME, PUNK.
LET'S START ROUND TWO!
FOLLOW ME, TORCH! THEY MUST HAVE HEADED IN THIS DIRECTION!
BUT REED, IF THERE REALLY IS A SKRULL AROUND, HE COULD BE *ANYONE...* AND THIS BUILDING IS SO BIG HE COULD HIDE *ANYWHERE!*
MY TRACING EQUIPMENT HAS LOCATED HIM! BEHIND THAT WALL, JOHNNY!
LON ZELIG
LON ZELIG STARRING IN INSECTO!
BOY, *THAT'S* SPECIAL EFFECTS!
HOPE YOU'RE RIGHT, REED. HEY, WHO'M I TALKING TO? OF *COURSE* YOU ARE!
TRUST MY JUDGMENT, SON! IF WE DON'T STOP THAT SKRULL IN TIME, WHO KNOWS WHAT HIDEOUS MACHINATIONS HE COULD BE PLANNING?!
HO-LEE....
WELCOME, GENTLEMEN.

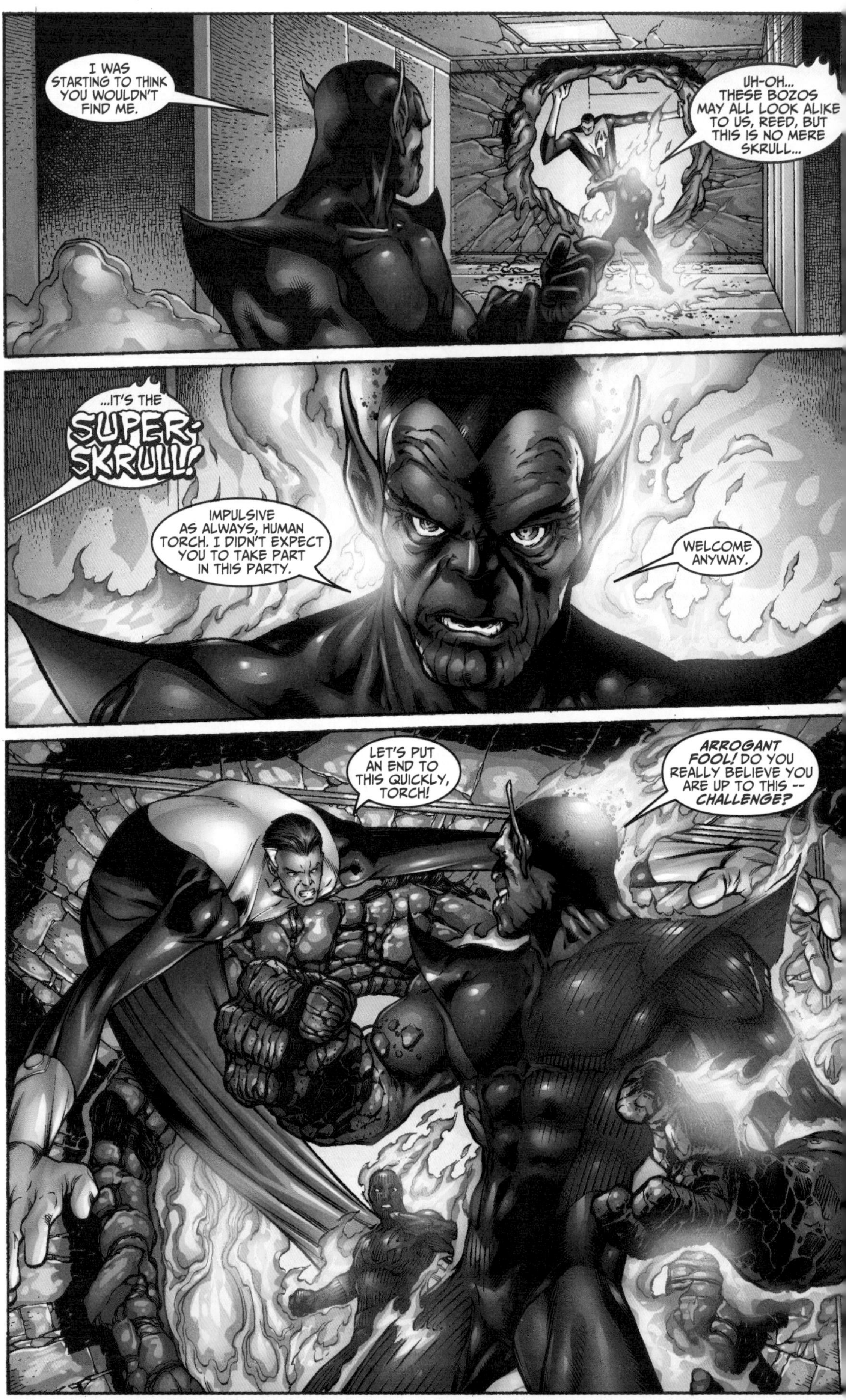
I WAS STARTING TO THINK YOU WOULDN'T FIND ME.
UH-OH... THESE BOZOS MAY ALL LOOK ALIKE TO US, REED, BUT THIS IS NO MERE SKRULL...
...IT'S THE SUPER-SKRULL!
IMPULSIVE AS ALWAYS, HUMAN TORCH. I DIDN'T EXPECT YOU TO TAKE PART IN THIS PARTY.
WELCOME ANYWAY.
LET'S PUT AN END TO THIS QUICKLY, TORCH!
ARROGANT FOOL! DO YOU REALLY BELIEVE YOU ARE UP TO THIS -- CHALLENGE?

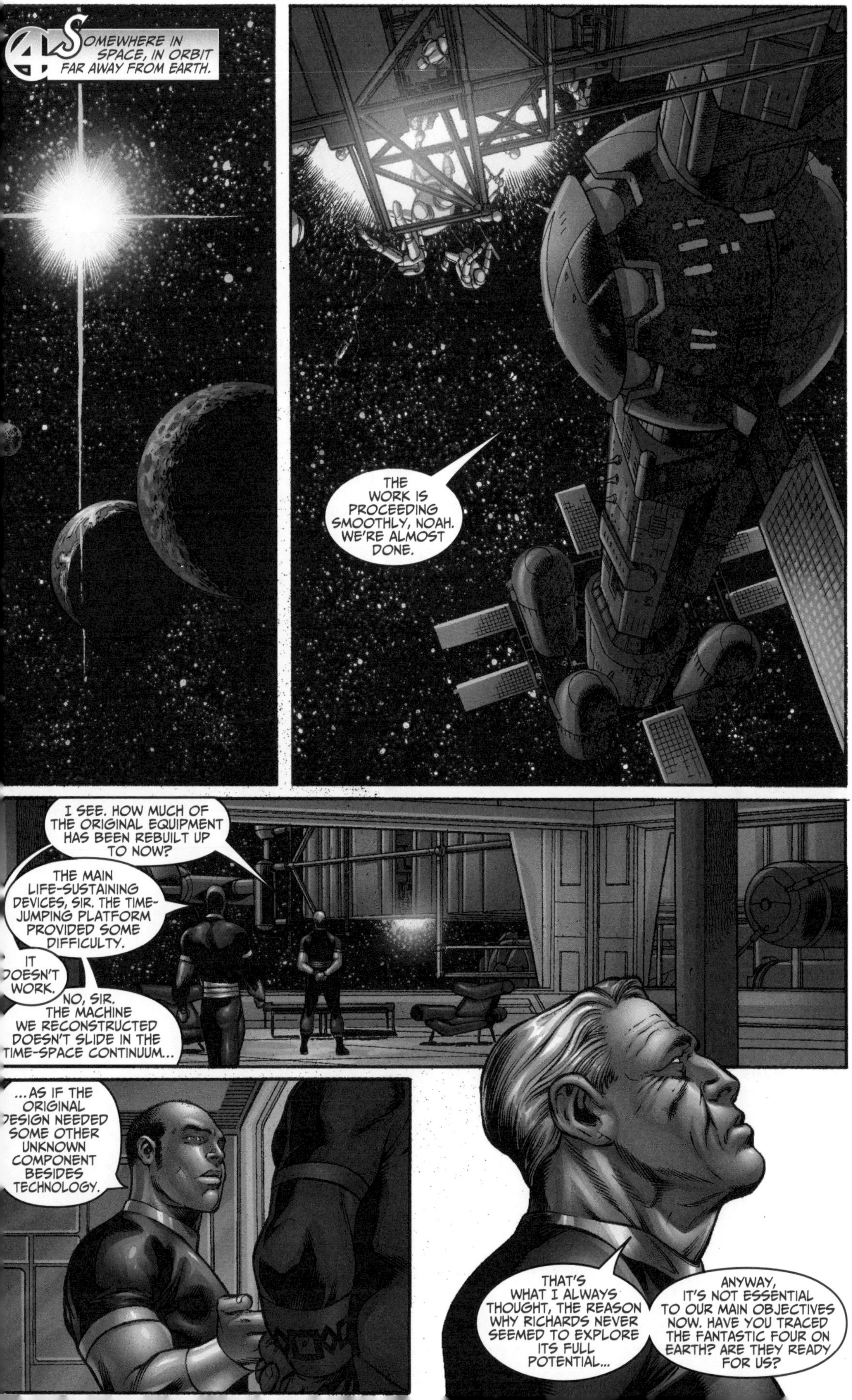
SOMEWHERE IN SPACE, IN ORBIT FAR AWAY FROM EARTH.
THE WORK IS PROCEEDING SMOOTHLY, NOAH. WE'RE ALMOST DONE.
I SEE. HOW MUCH OF THE ORIGINAL EQUIPMENT HAS BEEN REBUILT UP TO NOW?
THE MAIN LIFE-SUSTAINING DEVICES, SIR. THE TIME-JUMPING PLATFORM PROVIDED SOME DIFFICULTY.
IT DOESN'T WORK.
NO, SIR. THE MACHINE WE RECONSTRUCTED DOESN'T SLIDE IN THE TIME-SPACE CONTINUUM...
...AS IF THE ORIGINAL DESIGN NEEDED SOME OTHER UNKNOWN COMPONENT BESIDES TECHNOLOGY.
THAT'S WHAT I ALWAYS THOUGHT, THE REASON WHY RICHARDS NEVER SEEMED TO EXPLORE ITS FULL POTENTIAL...
ANYWAY, IT'S NOT ESSENTIAL TO OUR MAIN OBJECTIVES NOW. HAVE YOU TRACED THE FANTASTIC FOUR ON EARTH? ARE THEY READY FOR US?

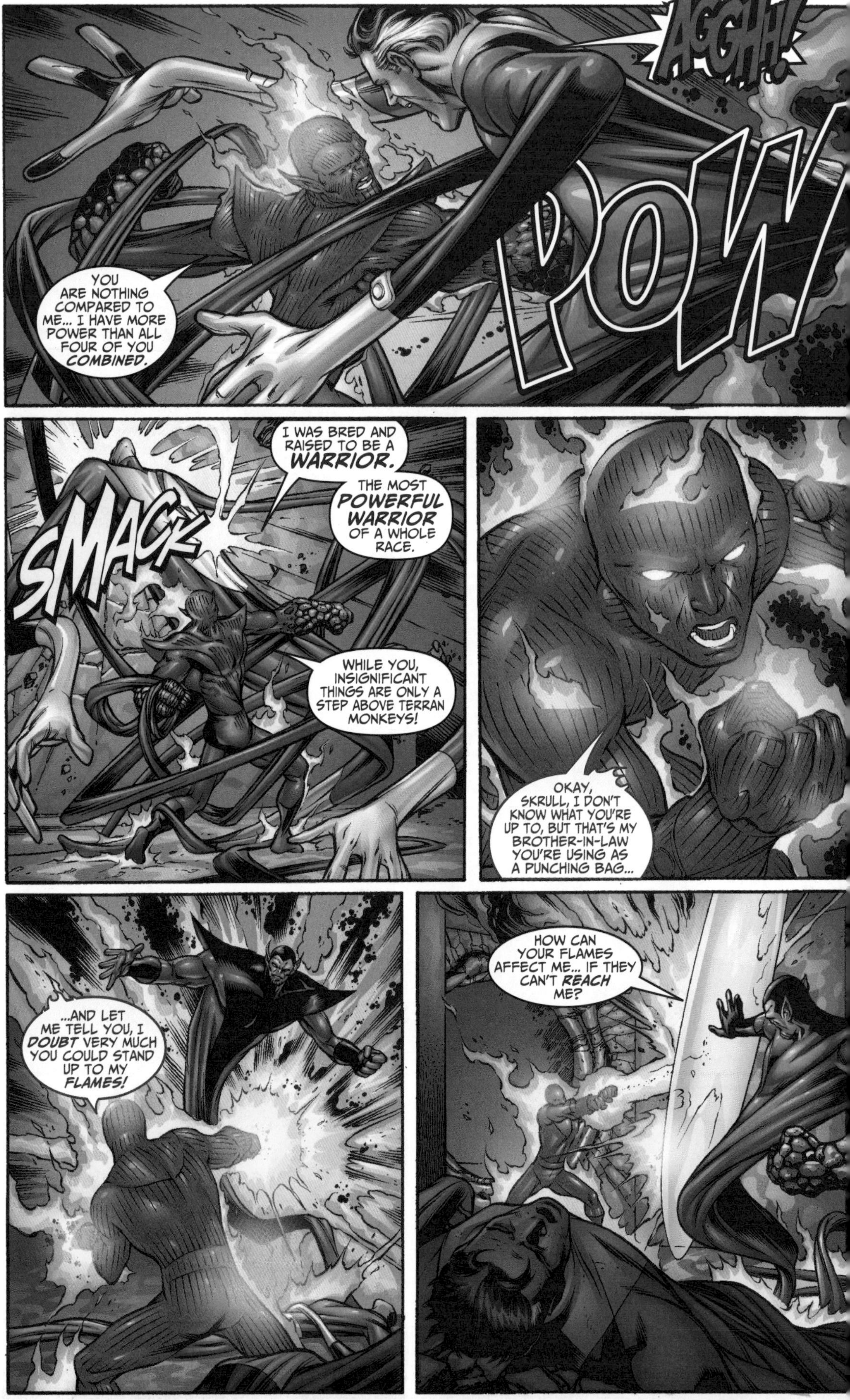
AGGHH!
POW
YOU ARE NOTHING COMPARED TO ME... I HAVE MORE POWER THAN ALL FOUR OF YOU COMBINED.
I WAS BRED AND RAISED TO BE A WARRIOR.
THE MOST POWERFUL WARRIOR OF A WHOLE RACE.
SMACK
WHILE YOU, INSIGNIFICANT THINGS ARE ONLY A STEP ABOVE TERRAN MONKEYS!
OKAY, SKRULL, I DON'T KNOW WHAT YOU'RE UP TO, BUT THAT'S MY BROTHER-IN-LAW YOU'RE USING AS A PUNCHING BAG...
...AND LET ME TELL YOU, I DOUBT VERY MUCH YOU COULD STAND UP TO MY FLAMES!
HOW CAN YOUR FLAMES AFFECT ME... IF THEY CAN'T REACH ME?

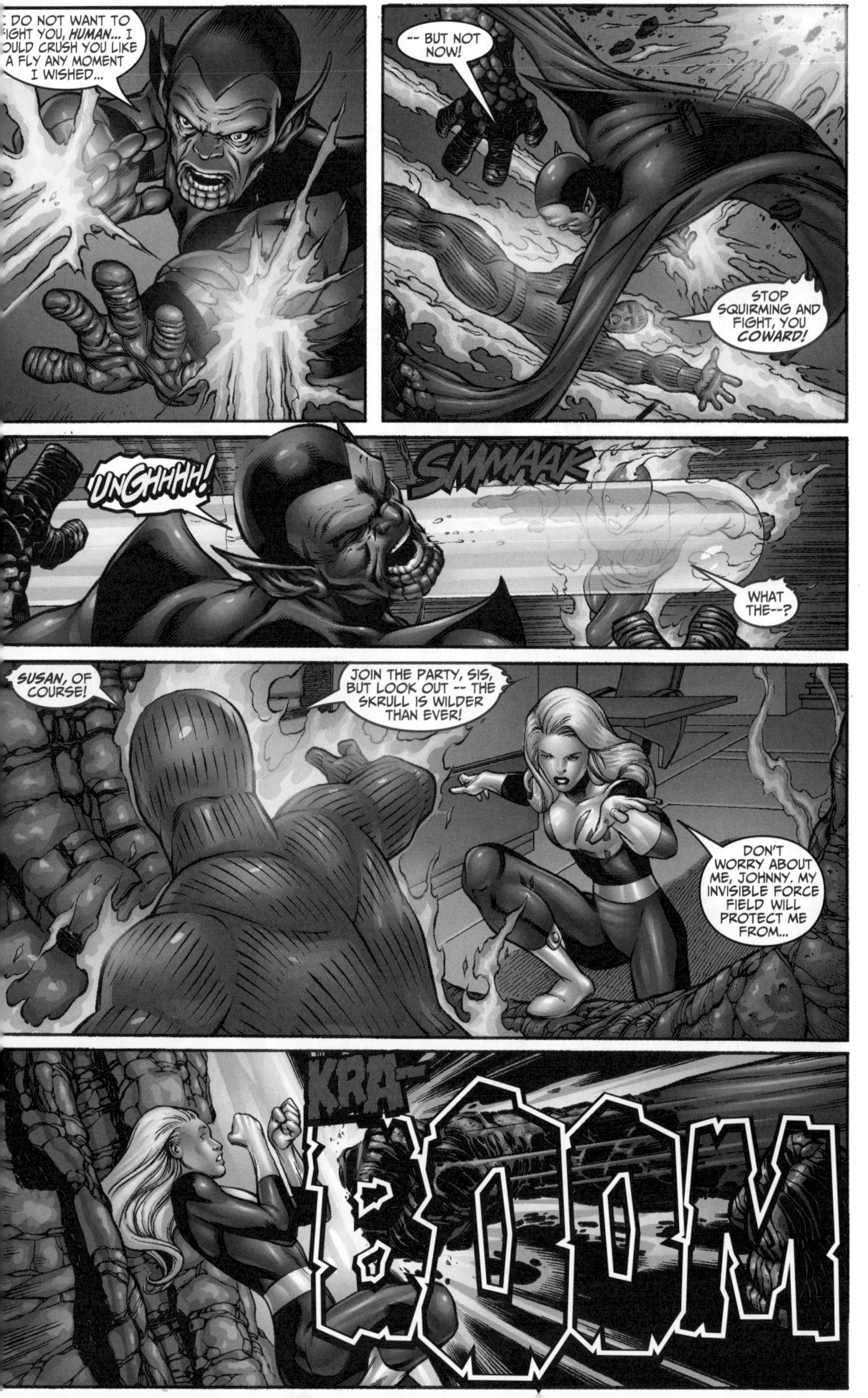

I DO NOT WANT TO FIGHT YOU, HUMAN... I COULD CRUSH YOU LIKE A FLY ANY MOMENT I WISHED...
-- BUT NOT NOW!
STOP SQUIRMING AND FIGHT, YOU COWARD!
UNGHHHH!
SMMAAK
WHAT THE--?
SUSAN, OF COURSE!
JOIN THE PARTY, SIS, BUT LOOK OUT -- THE SKRULL IS WILDER THAN EVER!
DON'T WORRY ABOUT ME, JOHNNY. MY INVISIBLE FORCE FIELD WILL PROTECT ME FROM...
KRA-BOOM

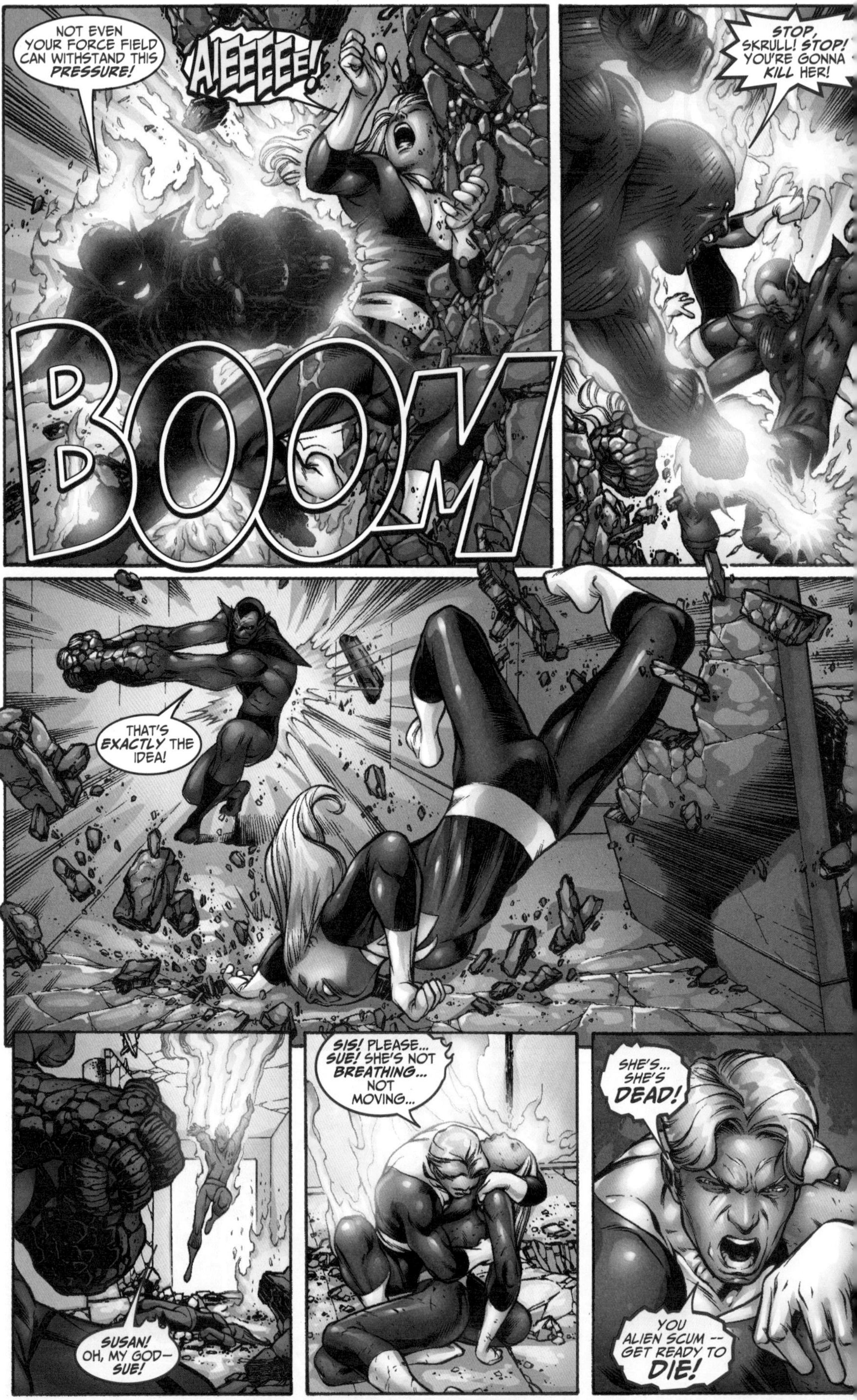
NOT EVEN YOUR FORCE FIELD CAN WITHSTAND THIS PRESSURE!
AIEEEEE!
BOOM
STOP, SKRULL! STOP! YOU'RE GONNA KILL HER!
THAT'S EXACTLY THE IDEA!
SUSAN! OH, MY GOD-- SUE!
SIS! PLEASE... SUE! SHE'S NOT BREATHING... NOT MOVING...
SHE'S... SHE'S DEAD!
YOU ALIEN SCUM -- GET READY TO DIE!

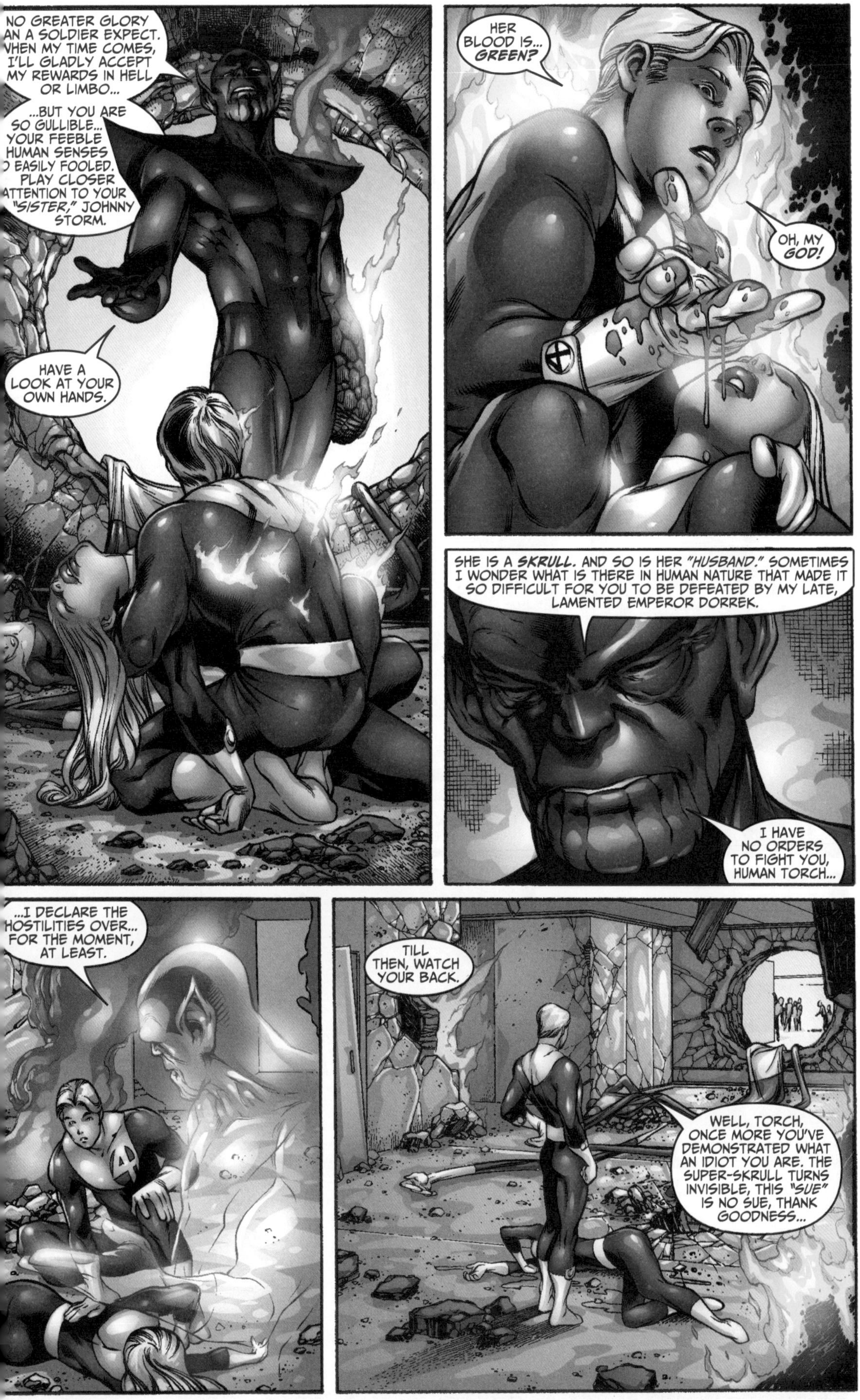
NO GREATER GLORY AN A SOLDIER EXPECT. VHEN MY TIME COMES, I'LL GLADLY ACCEPT MY REWARDS IN HELL OR LIMBO...
...BUT YOU ARE SO GULLIBLE... YOUR FEEBLE HUMAN SENSES O EASILY FOOLED. PLAY CLOSER ATTENTION TO YOUR "SISTER," JOHNNY STORM.
HAVE A LOOK AT YOUR OWN HANDS.
HER BLOOD IS... GREEN?
OH, MY GOD!
SHE IS A SKRULL. AND SO IS HER "HUSBAND." SOMETIMES I WONDER WHAT IS THERE IN HUMAN NATURE THAT MADE IT SO DIFFICULT FOR YOU TO BE DEFEATED BY MY LATE, LAMENTED EMPEROR DORREK.
I HAVE NO ORDERS TO FIGHT YOU, HUMAN TORCH...
...I DECLARE THE HOSTILITIES OVER... FOR THE MOMENT, AT LEAST.
TILL THEN, WATCH YOUR BACK.
WELL, TORCH, ONCE MORE YOU'VE DEMONSTRATED WHAT AN IDIOT YOU ARE. THE SUPER-SKRULL TURNS INVISIBLE, THIS "SUE" IS NO SUE, THANK GOODNESS...

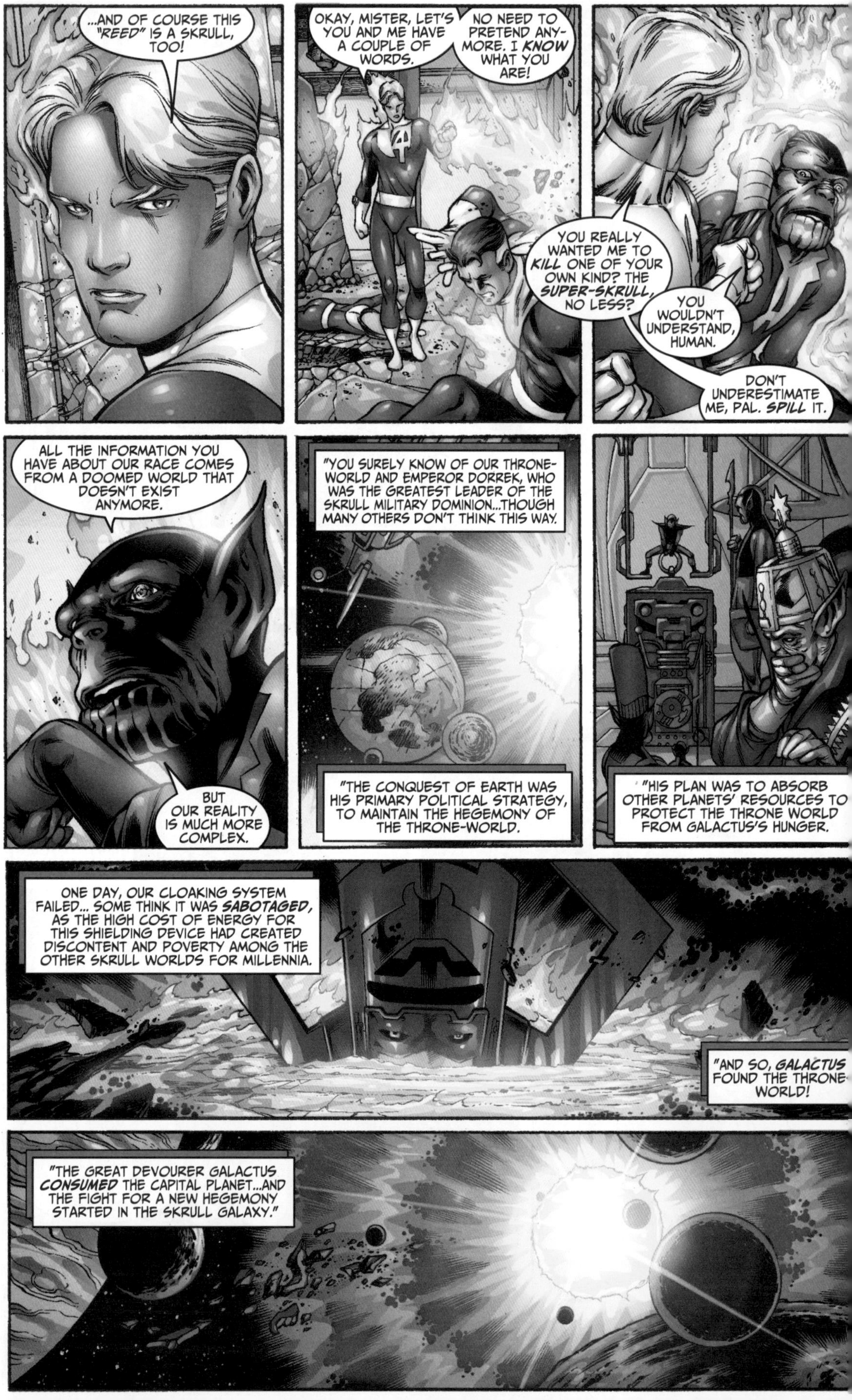
...AND OF COURSE THIS "REED" IS A SKRULL, TOO!
OKAY, MISTER, LET'S YOU AND ME HAVE A COUPLE OF WORDS.
NO NEED TO PRETEND ANY-MORE. I KNOW WHAT YOU ARE!
YOU REALLY WANTED ME TO KILL ONE OF YOUR OWN KIND? THE SUPER-SKRULL, NO LESS?
YOU WOULDN'T UNDERSTAND, HUMAN.
DON'T UNDERESTIMATE ME, PAL. SPILL IT.
ALL THE INFORMATION YOU HAVE ABOUT OUR RACE COMES FROM A DOOMED WORLD THAT DOESN'T EXIST ANYMORE.
BUT OUR REALITY IS MUCH MORE COMPLEX.
"YOU SURELY KNOW OF OUR THRONE-WORLD AND EMPEROR DORREK, WHO WAS THE GREATEST LEADER OF THE SKRULL MILITARY DOMINION...THOUGH MANY OTHERS DON'T THINK THIS WAY.
"THE CONQUEST OF EARTH WAS HIS PRIMARY POLITICAL STRATEGY, TO MAINTAIN THE HEGEMONY OF THE THRONE-WORLD.
"HIS PLAN WAS TO ABSORB OTHER PLANETS' RESOURCES TO PROTECT THE THRONE WORLD FROM GALACTUS'S HUNGER.
ONE DAY, OUR CLOAKING SYSTEM FAILED... SOME THINK IT WAS SABOTAGED, AS THE HIGH COST OF ENERGY FOR THIS SHIELDING DEVICE HAD CREATED DISCONTENT AND POVERTY AMONG THE OTHER SKRULL WORLDS FOR MILLENNIA.
"AND SO, GALACTUS FOUND THE THRONE-WORLD!
"THE GREAT DEVOURER GALACTUS CONSUMED THE CAPITAL PLANET...AND THE FIGHT FOR A NEW HEGEMONY STARTED IN THE SKRULL GALAXY."

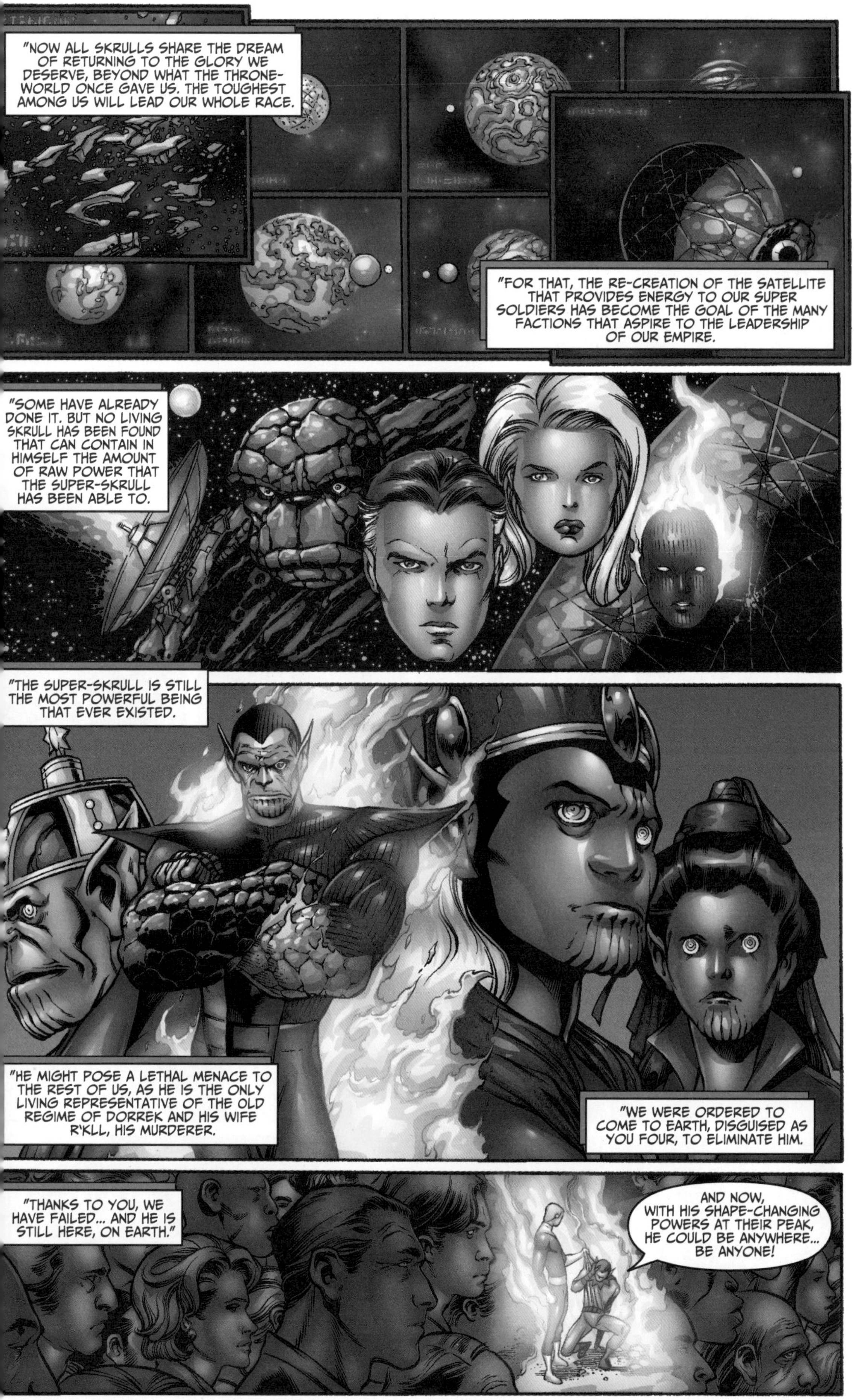
"NOW ALL SKRULLS SHARE THE DREAM OF RETURNING TO THE GLORY WE DESERVE, BEYOND WHAT THE THRONE-WORLD ONCE GAVE US. THE TOUGHEST AMONG US WILL LEAD OUR WHOLE RACE.
"FOR THAT, THE RE-CREATION OF THE SATELLITE THAT PROVIDES ENERGY TO OUR SUPER SOLDIERS HAS BECOME THE GOAL OF THE MANY FACTIONS THAT ASPIRE TO THE LEADERSHIP OF OUR EMPIRE.
"SOME HAVE ALREADY DONE IT. BUT NO LIVING SKRULL HAS BEEN FOUND THAT CAN CONTAIN IN HIMSELF THE AMOUNT OF RAW POWER THAT THE SUPER-SKRULL HAS BEEN ABLE TO.
"THE SUPER-SKRULL IS STILL THE MOST POWERFUL BEING THAT EVER EXISTED.
"HE MIGHT POSE A LETHAL MENACE TO THE REST OF US, AS HE IS THE ONLY LIVING REPRESENTATIVE OF THE OLD REGIME OF DORREK AND HIS WIFE R'KLL, HIS MURDERER.
"WE WERE ORDERED TO COME TO EARTH, DISGUISED AS YOU FOUR, TO ELIMINATE HIM.
"THANKS TO YOU, WE HAVE FAILED... AND HE IS STILL HERE, ON EARTH."
AND NOW, WITH HIS SHAPE-CHANGING POWERS AT THEIR PEAK, HE COULD BE ANYWHERE... BE ANYONE!

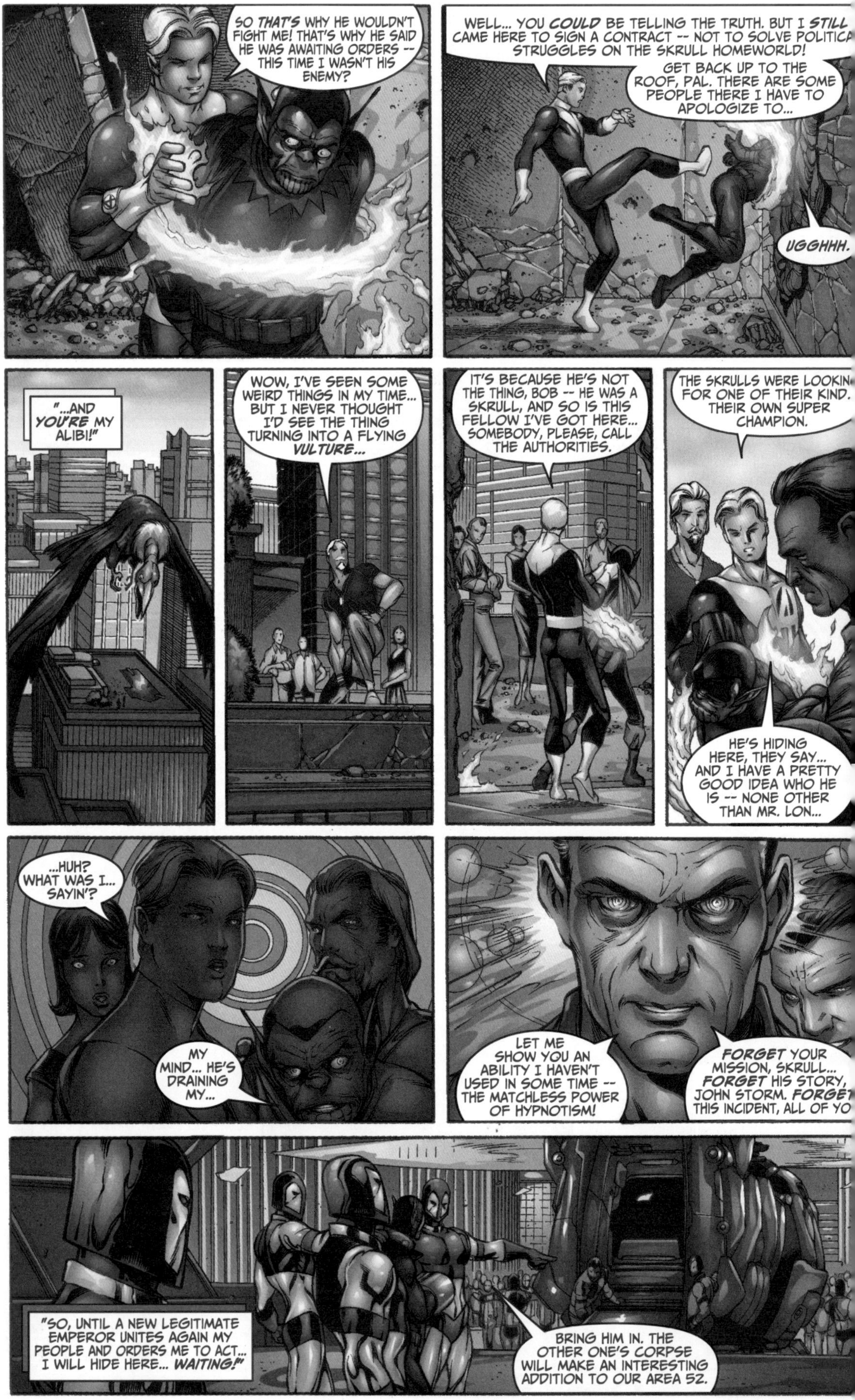
SO THAT'S WHY HE WOULDN'T FIGHT ME! THAT'S WHY HE SAID HE WAS AWAITING ORDERS -- THIS TIME I WASN'T HIS ENEMY?
WELL... YOU COULD BE TELLING THE TRUTH. BUT I STILL CAME HERE TO SIGN A CONTRACT -- NOT TO SOLVE POLITICA STRUGGLES ON THE SKRULL HOMEWORLD!
GET BACK UP TO THE ROOF, PAL. THERE ARE SOME PEOPLE THERE I HAVE TO APOLOGIZE TO...
UGGHHH.
"...AND YOU'RE MY ALIBI!"
WOW, I'VE SEEN SOME WEIRD THINGS IN MY TIME... BUT I NEVER THOUGHT I'D SEE THE THING TURNING INTO A FLYING VULTURE...
IT'S BECAUSE HE'S NOT THE THING, BOB -- HE WAS A SKRULL, AND SO IS THIS FELLOW I'VE GOT HERE... SOMEBODY, PLEASE, CALL THE AUTHORITIES.
THE SKRULLS WERE LOOKIN FOR ONE OF THEIR KIND. THEIR OWN SUPER CHAMPION.
HE'S HIDING HERE, THEY SAY... AND I HAVE A PRETTY GOOD IDEA WHO HE IS -- NONE OTHER THAN MR. LON...
...HUH? WHAT WAS I... SAYIN'?
MY MIND... HE'S DRAINING MY...
LET ME SHOW YOU AN ABILITY I HAVEN'T USED IN SOME TIME -- THE MATCHLESS POWER OF HYPNOTISM!
FORGET YOUR MISSION, SKRULL... FORGET HIS STORY, JOHN STORM. FORGET THIS INCIDENT, ALL OF YO
"SO, UNTIL A NEW LEGITIMATE EMPEROR UNITES AGAIN MY PEOPLE AND ORDERS ME TO ACT... I WILL HIDE HERE... WAITING!"
BRING HIM IN. THE OTHER ONE'S CORPSE WILL MAKE AN INTERESTING ADDITION TO OUR AREA 52.

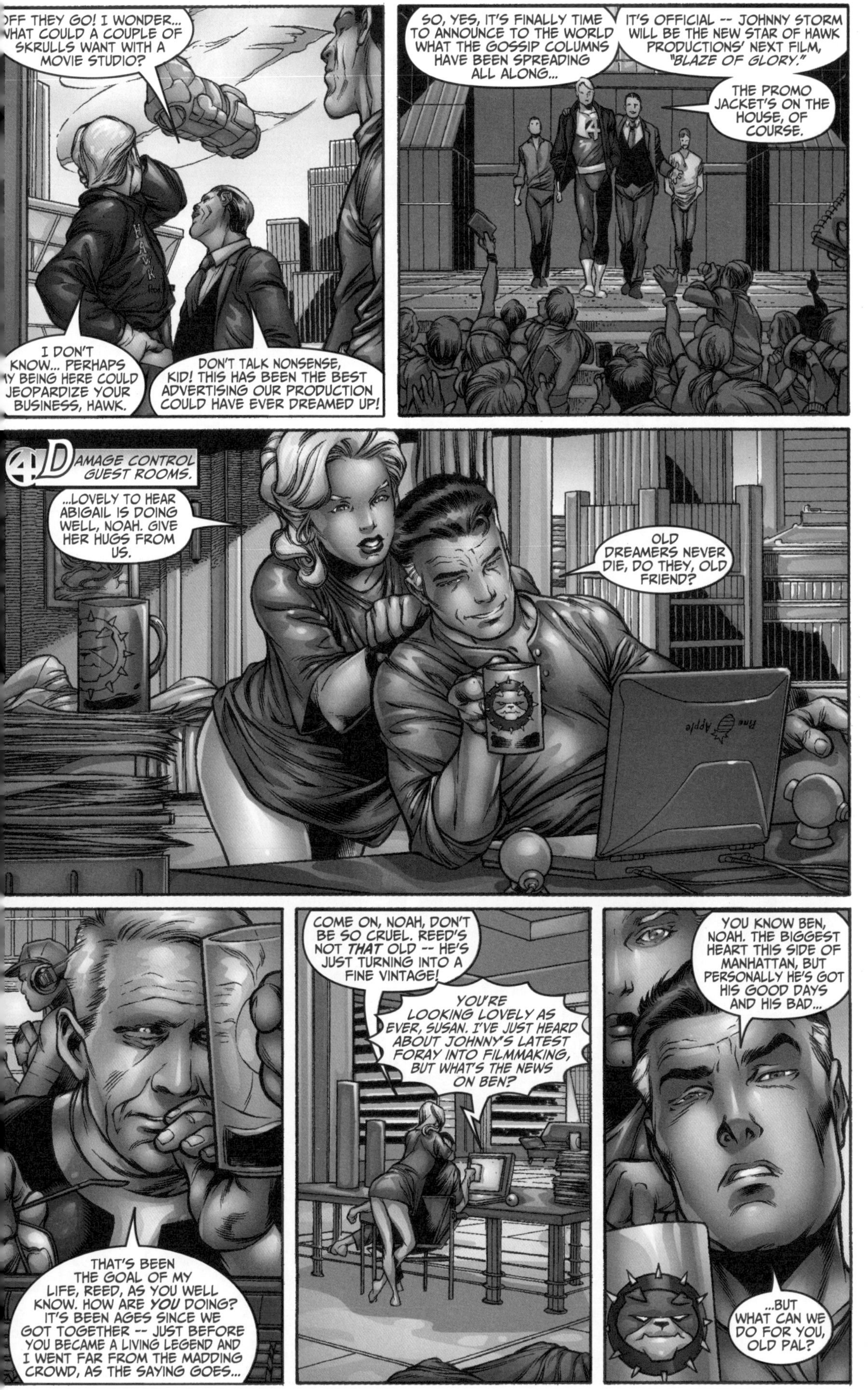
OFF THEY GO! I WONDER... WHAT COULD A COUPLE OF SKRULLS WANT WITH A MOVIE STUDIO?
I DON'T KNOW... PERHAPS MY BEING HERE COULD JEOPARDIZE YOUR BUSINESS, HAWK.
DON'T TALK NONSENSE, KID! THIS HAS BEEN THE BEST ADVERTISING OUR PRODUCTION COULD HAVE EVER DREAMED UP!
SO, YES, IT'S FINALLY TIME TO ANNOUNCE TO THE WORLD WHAT THE GOSSIP COLUMNS HAVE BEEN SPREADING ALL ALONG...
IT'S OFFICIAL -- JOHNNY STORM WILL BE THE NEW STAR OF HAWK PRODUCTIONS' NEXT FILM, "BLAZE OF GLORY."
THE PROMO JACKET'S ON THE HOUSE, OF COURSE.
DAMAGE CONTROL GUEST ROOMS.
...LOVELY TO HEAR ABIGAIL IS DOING WELL, NOAH. GIVE HER HUGS FROM US.
OLD DREAMERS NEVER DIE, DO THEY, OLD FRIEND?
THAT'S BEEN THE GOAL OF MY LIFE, REED, AS YOU WELL KNOW. HOW ARE YOU DOING? IT'S BEEN AGES SINCE WE GOT TOGETHER -- JUST BEFORE YOU BECAME A LIVING LEGEND AND I WENT FAR FROM THE MADDING CROWD, AS THE SAYING GOES...
COME ON, NOAH, DON'T BE SO CRUEL. REED'S NOT THAT OLD -- HE'S JUST TURNING INTO A FINE VINTAGE!
YOU'RE LOOKING LOVELY AS EVER, SUSAN. I'VE JUST HEARD ABOUT JOHNNY'S LATEST FORAY INTO FILMMAKING, BUT WHAT'S THE NEWS ON BEN?
YOU KNOW BEN, NOAH. THE BIGGEST HEART THIS SIDE OF MANHATTAN, BUT PERSONALLY HE'S GOT HIS GOOD DAYS AND HIS BAD...
...BUT WHAT CAN WE DO FOR YOU, OLD PAL?

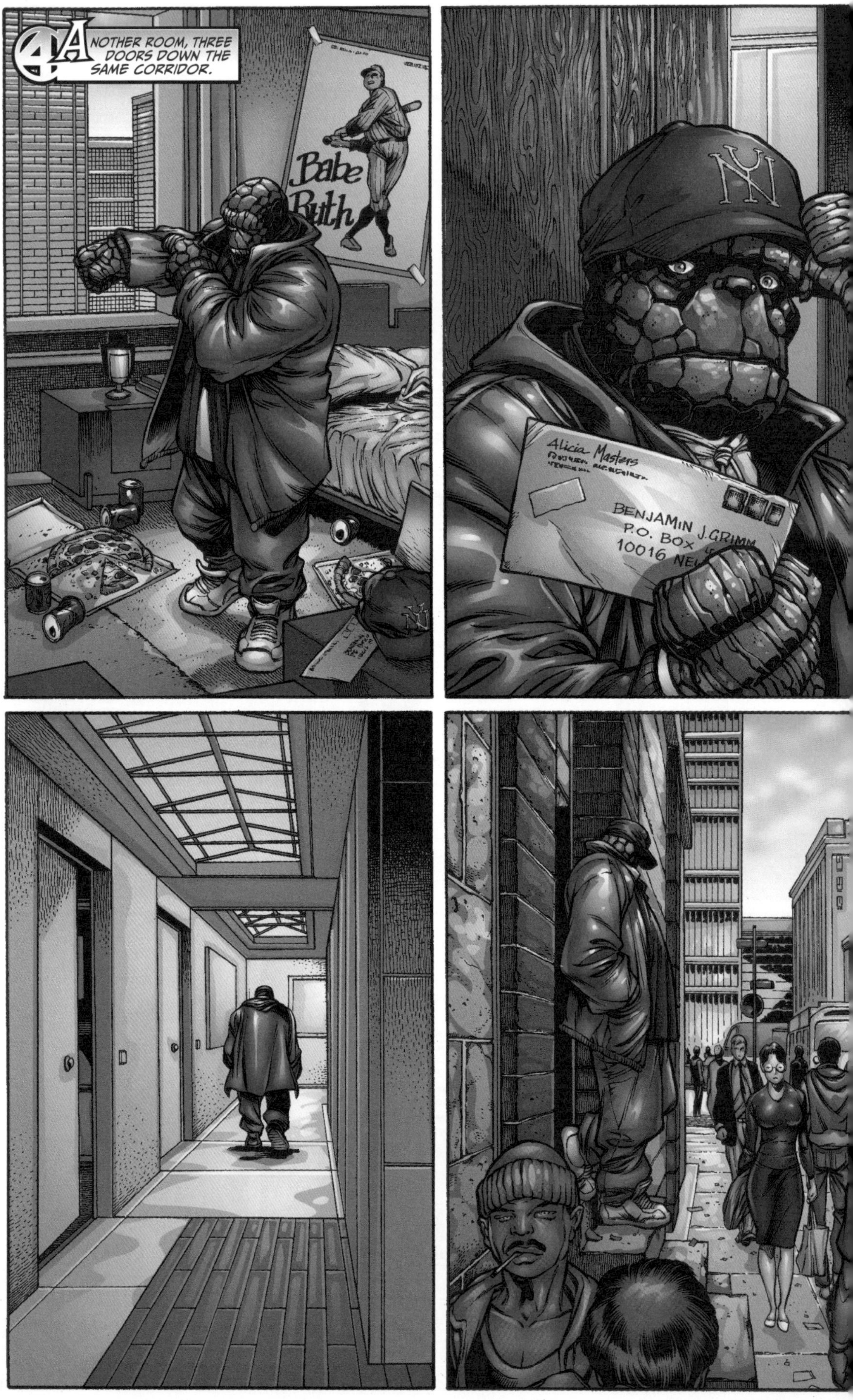
ANOTHER ROOM, THREE DOORS DOWN THE SAME CORRIDOR.
Babe Ruth
Alicia Masters
BENJAMIN J.GRIMM
P.O. BOX
10016

FLESH AND STONE
LITTLEFIELD, KANSAS.
DID YOU GET A NEW CAR?
CARLOS "The Prince" PACHECO Artist & Co-Plotter
RAFAEL "The Magic" MARIN Co-Plotter
JESUS "Mercury" MERINO Inks
LIQUID! "Soulful" GRAPHICS Colors
RICHARD "Silk" STARKINGS & COMICRAFT's 2nd Tiger, ALBERT Letters
BRIAN "Da Brain" SMITH Assistant Editor
BOBBIE "Da Bomb" CHASE Editor
and JOE "Da Boss" QUESADA Chief
EXTEND A WARM WELCOME ABOARD TO:
JEPH "Loudmouth" LOEB Wordsmith

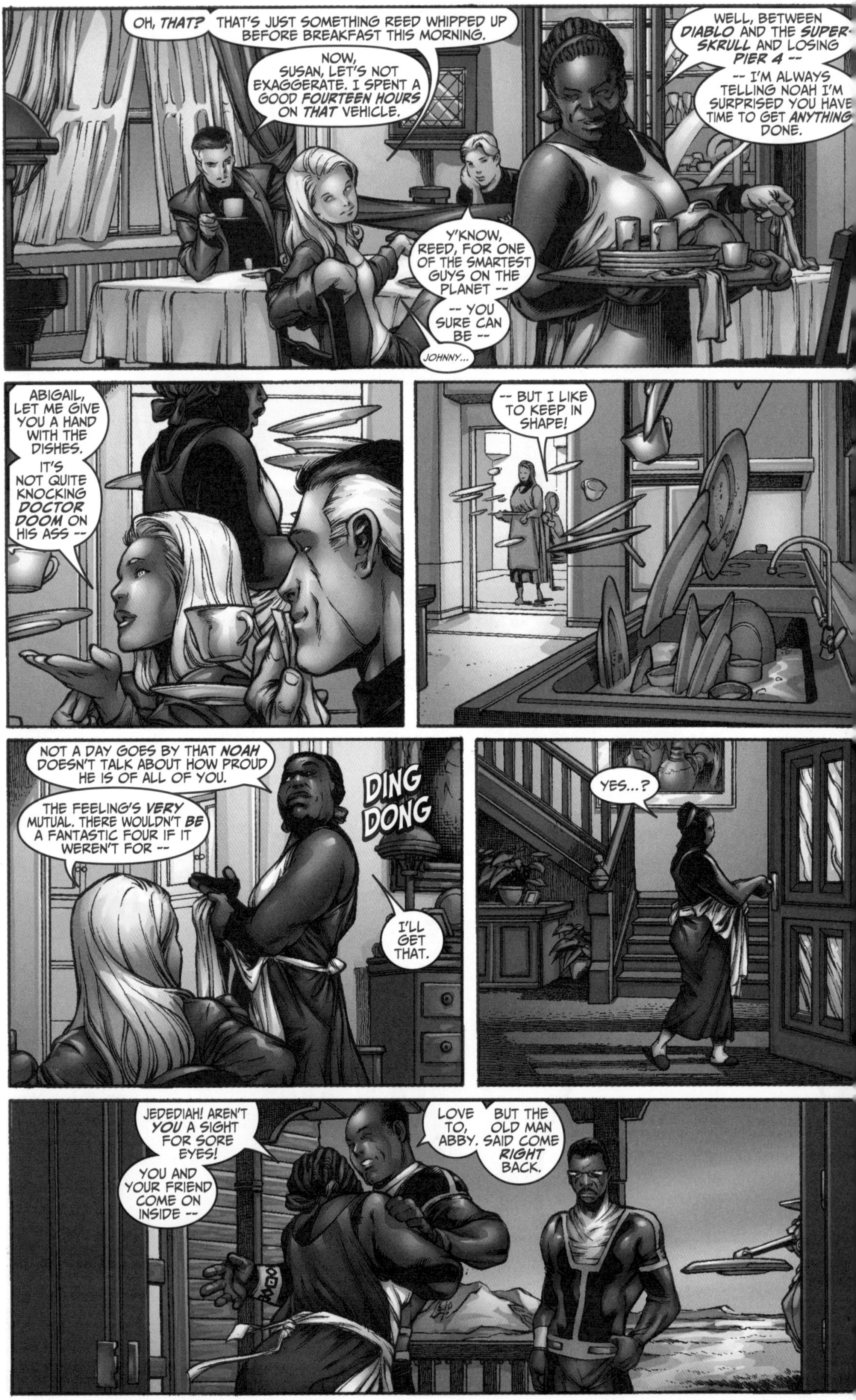
OH, THAT?
THAT'S JUST SOMETHING REED WHIPPED UP BEFORE BREAKFAST THIS MORNING.
NOW, SUSAN, LET'S NOT EXAGGERATE. I SPENT A GOOD FOURTEEN HOURS ON THAT VEHICLE.
WELL, BETWEEN DIABLO AND THE SUPER-SKRULL AND LOSING PIER 4 --
-- I'M ALWAYS TELLING NOAH I'M SURPRISED YOU HAVE TIME TO GET ANYTHING DONE.
Y'KNOW, REED, FOR ONE OF THE SMARTEST GUYS ON THE PLANET --
-- YOU SURE CAN BE --
JOHNNY...
ABIGAIL, LET ME GIVE YOU A HAND WITH THE DISHES.
IT'S NOT QUITE KNOCKING DOCTOR DOOM ON HIS ASS --
-- BUT I LIKE TO KEEP IN SHAPE!
NOT A DAY GOES BY THAT NOAH DOESN'T TALK ABOUT HOW PROUD HE IS OF ALL OF YOU.
THE FEELING'S VERY MUTUAL. THERE WOULDN'T BE A FANTASTIC FOUR IF IT WEREN'T FOR --
DING DONG
I'LL GET THAT.
YES...?
JEDEDIAH! AREN'T YOU A SIGHT FOR SORE EYES!
YOU AND YOUR FRIEND COME ON INSIDE --
LOVE TO, ABBY.
BUT THE OLD MAN SAID COME RIGHT BACK.

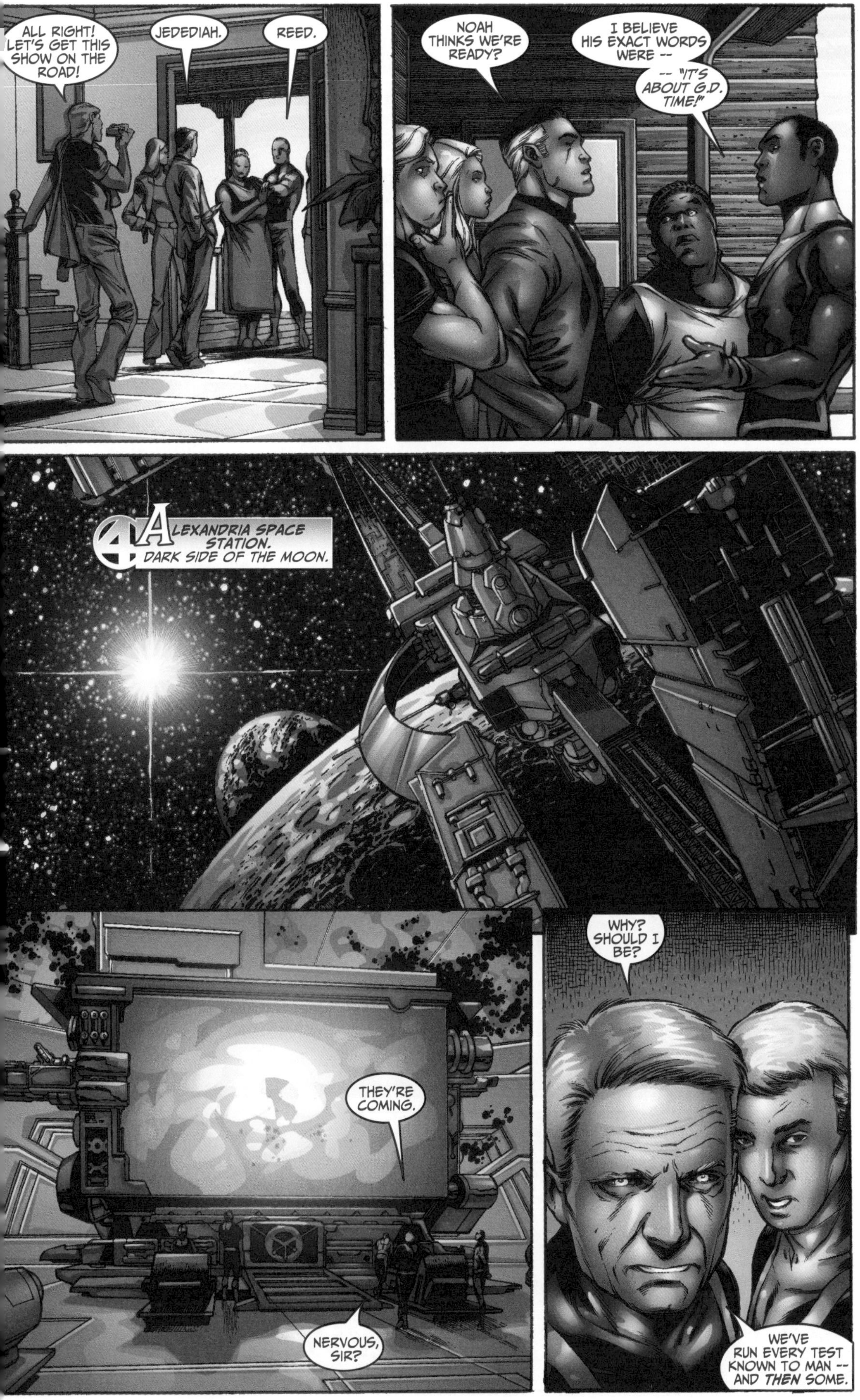
ALL RIGHT! LET'S GET THIS SHOW ON THE ROAD!
JEDEDIAH.
REED.
NOAH THINKS WE'RE READY?
I BELIEVE HIS EXACT WORDS WERE --
-- "IT'S ABOUT G.D. TIME!"
ALEXANDRIA SPACE STATION. DARK SIDE OF THE MOON.
THEY'RE COMING.
NERVOUS, SIR?
WHY? SHOULD I BE?
WE'VE RUN EVERY TEST KNOWN TO MAN -- AND THEN SOME.

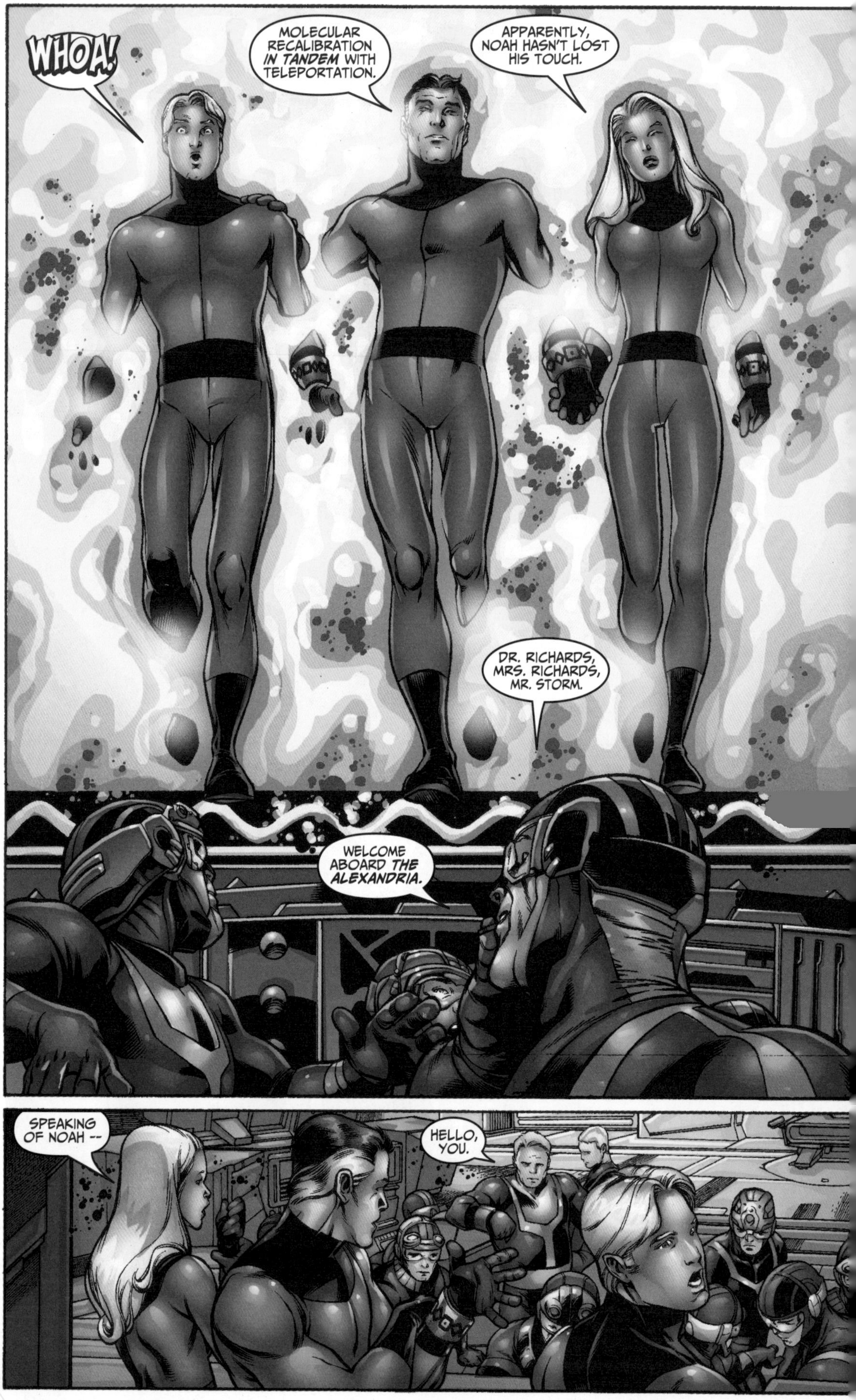
WHOA!
MOLECULAR RECALIBRATION *IN TANDEM* WITH TELEPORTATION.
APPARENTLY, NOAH HASN'T LOST HIS TOUCH.
DR. RICHARDS, MRS. RICHARDS, MR. STORM.
WELCOME ABOARD *THE ALEXANDRIA.*
SPEAKING OF NOAH --
HELLO, YOU.

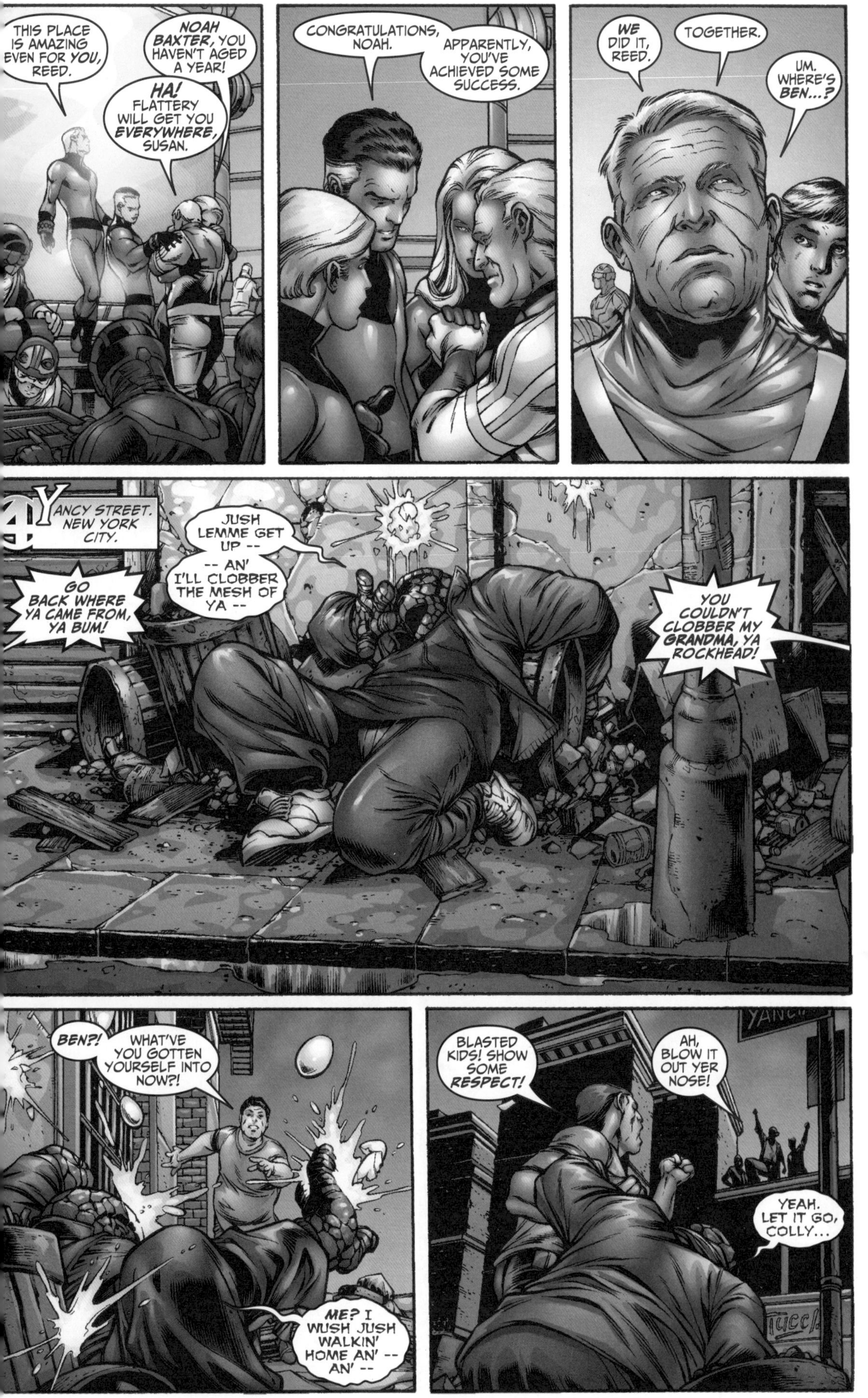

THIS PLACE IS AMAZING EVEN FOR YOU, REED.
NOAH BAXTER, YOU HAVEN'T AGED A YEAR!
HA! FLATTERY WILL GET YOU EVERYWHERE, SUSAN.
CONGRATULATIONS, NOAH.
APPARENTLY, YOU'VE ACHIEVED SOME SUCCESS.
WE DID IT, REED.
TOGETHER.
UM. WHERE'S BEN...?
YANCY STREET. NEW YORK CITY.
JUSH LEMME GET UP --
-- AN' I'LL CLOBBER THE MESH OF YA --
GO BACK WHERE YA CAME FROM, YA BUM!
YOU COULDN'T CLOBBER MY GRANDMA, YA ROCKHEAD!
BEN?!
WHAT'VE YOU GOTTEN YOURSELF INTO NOW?!
ME? I WUSH JUSH WALKIN' HOME AN' -- AN' --
BLASTED KIDS! SHOW SOME RESPECT!
AH, BLOW IT OUT YER NOSE!
YEAH. LET IT GO, COLLY...

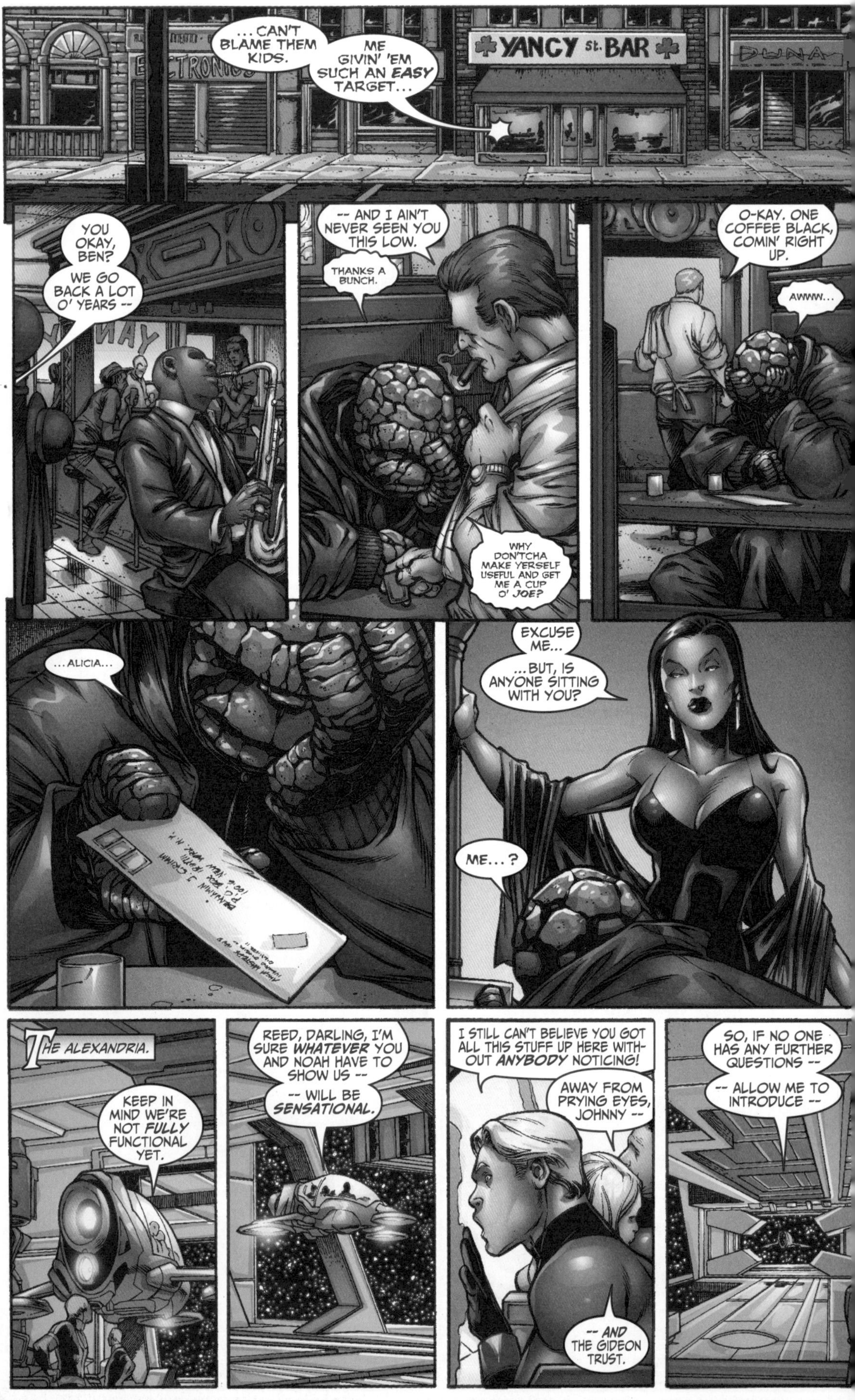

ELECTRONICS
...CAN'T BLAME THEM KIDS.
ME GIVIN' 'EM SUCH AN EASY TARGET...
YANCY St. BAR
YOU OKAY, BEN?
WE GO BACK A LOT O' YEARS --
-- AND I AIN'T NEVER SEEN YOU THIS LOW.
THANKS A BUNCH.
WHY DON'TCHA MAKE YERSELF USEFUL AND GET ME A CUP O' JOE?
O-KAY. ONE COFFEE BLACK, COMIN' RIGHT UP.
AWWW...
...ALICIA...
EXCUSE ME...
...BUT, IS ANYONE SITTING WITH YOU?
ME...?
THE ALEXANDRIA.
KEEP IN MIND WE'RE NOT FULLY FUNCTIONAL YET.
REED, DARLING, I'M SURE WHATEVER YOU AND NOAH HAVE TO SHOW US --
-- WILL BE SENSATIONAL.
I STILL CAN'T BELIEVE YOU GOT ALL THIS STUFF UP HERE WITHOUT ANYBODY NOTICING!
AWAY FROM PRYING EYES, JOHNNY --
SO, IF NO ONE HAS ANY FURTHER QUESTIONS --
-- ALLOW ME TO INTRODUCE --
-- AND THE GIDEON TRUST.

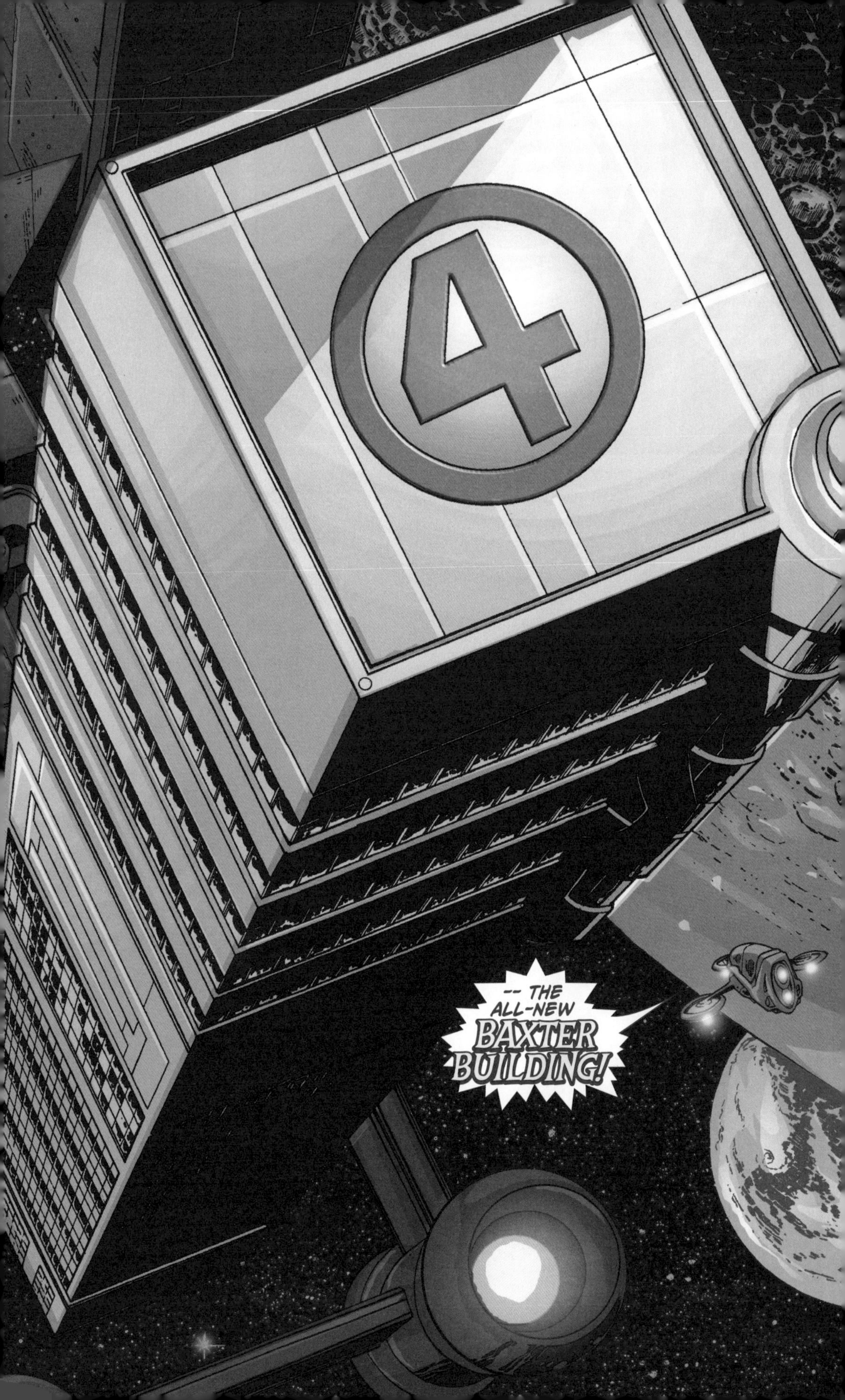
-- THE ALL-NEW BAXTER BUILDING!

WELL, EVERYONE?

WE'RE KEEPIN' IT, RIGHT?

WORKING FROM *OUTER SPACE* -- NOW *THAT'S* COOL.

REED, IT'S *EVERYTHING* YOU PROMISED AND MORE.

ER... NOT EXACTLY, JOHNNY.

BUT, WE'RE PRETTY SURE YOU'LL LIKE WHAT WE HAVE IN MIND.

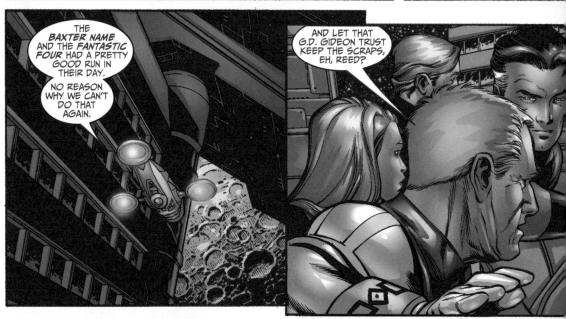

THE *BAXTER NAME* AND THE *FANTASTIC FOUR* HAD A PRETTY GOOD RUN IN THEIR DAY.

NO REASON WHY WE CAN'T DO THAT AGAIN.

AND LET THAT G.D. GIDEON TRUST KEEP THE SCRAPS, EH, REED?

NOT IN SO MANY WORDS, NOAH, BUT I THINK THIS IS THE BEST COURSE OF ACTION.

THE GIDEON TRUST NOW OWNS WHAT'S LEFT OF PIER FOUR *AND* MY MOST CURRENT PATENTS.

THEY WENT THROUGH A LOT OF TROUBLE TO GET THEM.

WHAT REMAINS TO BE SEEN IS --

-- WHY?

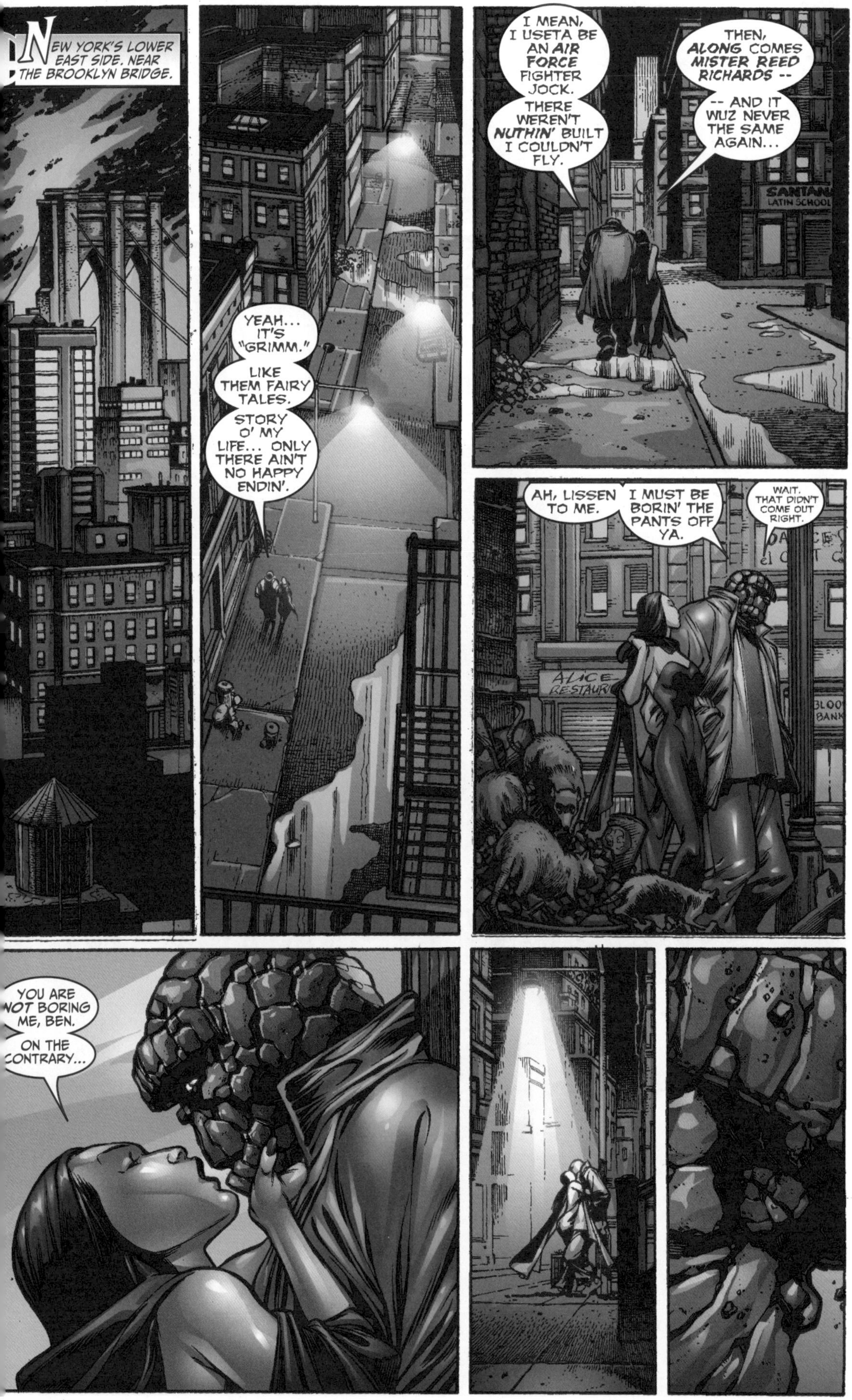
NEW YORK'S LOWER EAST SIDE. NEAR THE BROOKLYN BRIDGE.
YEAH... IT'S "GRIMM."
LIKE THEM FAIRY TALES.
STORY O' MY LIFE... ONLY THERE AIN'T NO HAPPY ENDIN'.
I MEAN, I USETA BE AN AIR FORCE FIGHTER JOCK.
THERE WEREN'T NUTHIN' BUILT I COULDN'T FLY.
THEN, ALONG COMES MISTER REED RICHARDS --
-- AND IT WUZ NEVER THE SAME AGAIN...
SANTANA
LATIN SCHOOL
AH, LISSEN TO ME.
I MUST BE BORIN' THE PANTS OFF YA.
WAIT. THAT DIDN'T COME OUT RIGHT.
ALICE
RESTAUR
YOU ARE NOT BORING ME, BEN.
ON THE CONTRARY...

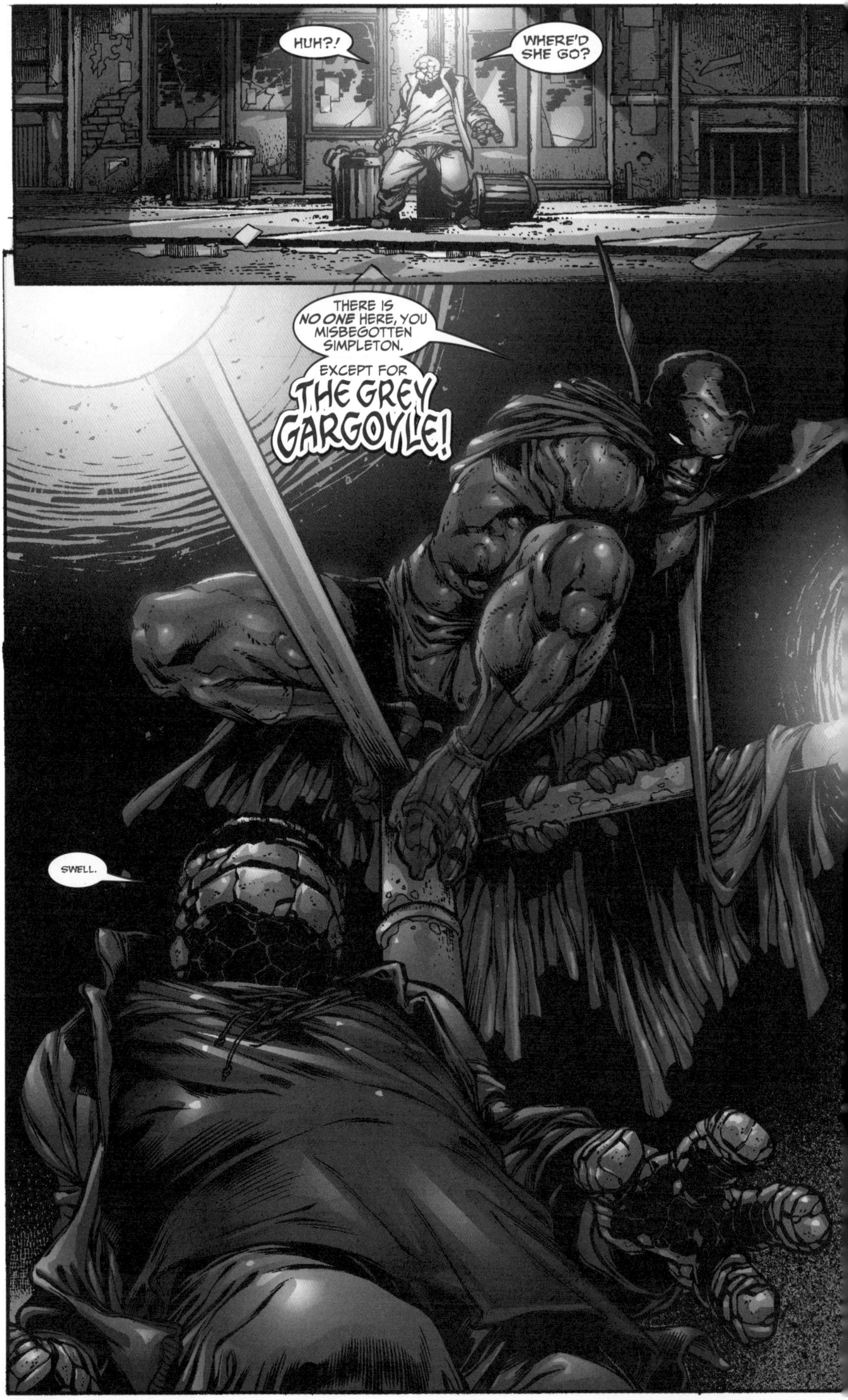
HUH?!
WHERE'D SHE GO?
THERE IS NO ONE HERE, YOU MISBEGOTTEN SIMPLETON.
EXCEPT FOR THE GREY GARGOYLE!
SWELL.

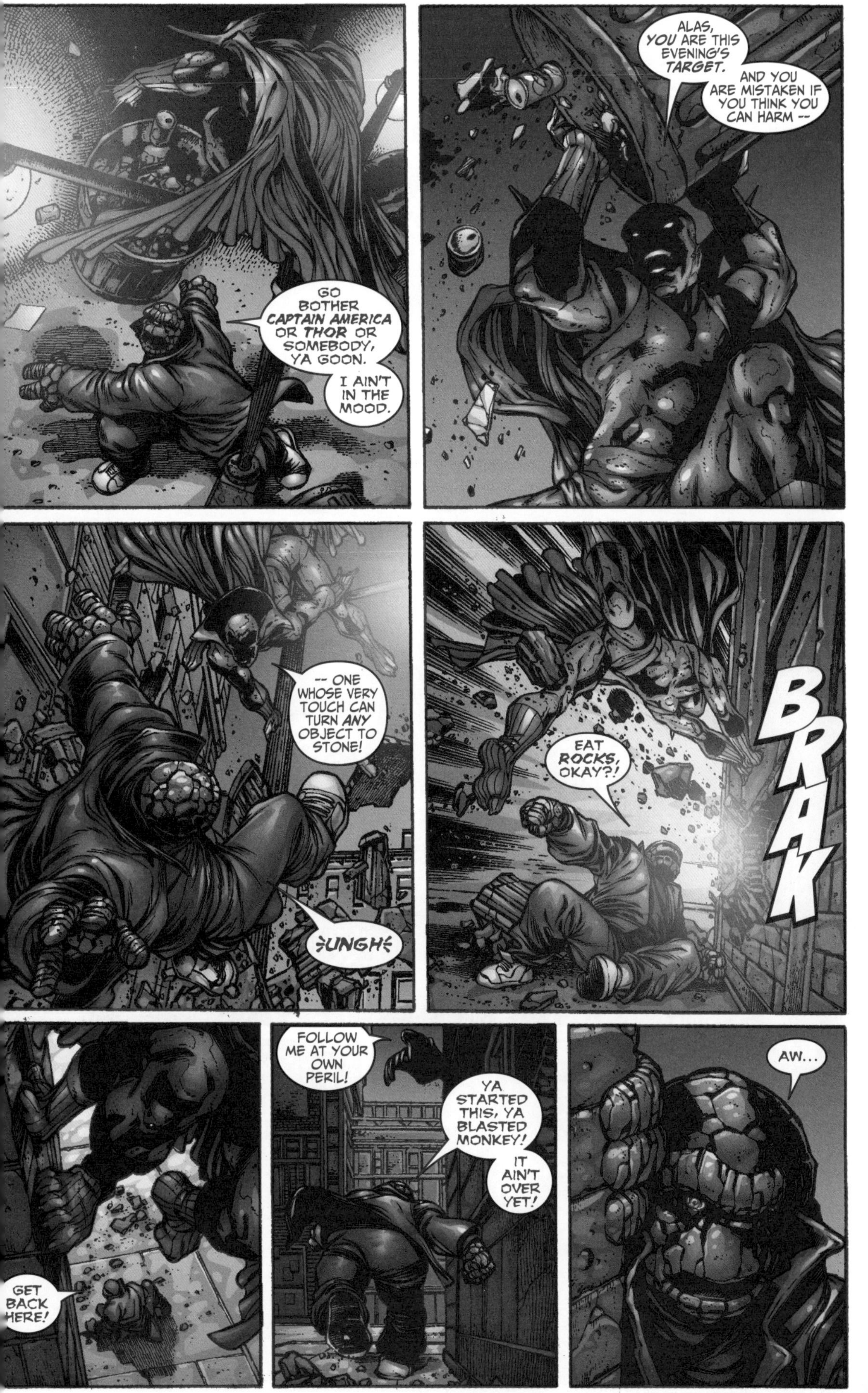
GO BOTHER CAPTAIN AMERICA OR THOR OR SOMEBODY, YA GOON.
I AIN'T IN THE MOOD.
ALAS, YOU ARE THIS EVENING'S TARGET.
AND YOU ARE MISTAKEN IF YOU THINK YOU CAN HARM --
-- ONE WHOSE VERY TOUCH CAN TURN ANY OBJECT TO STONE!
UNGH
EAT ROCKS, OKAY?!
BRAK
GET BACK HERE!
FOLLOW ME AT YOUR OWN PERIL!
YA STARTED THIS, YA BLASTED MONKEY!
IT AIN'T OVER YET!
AW...

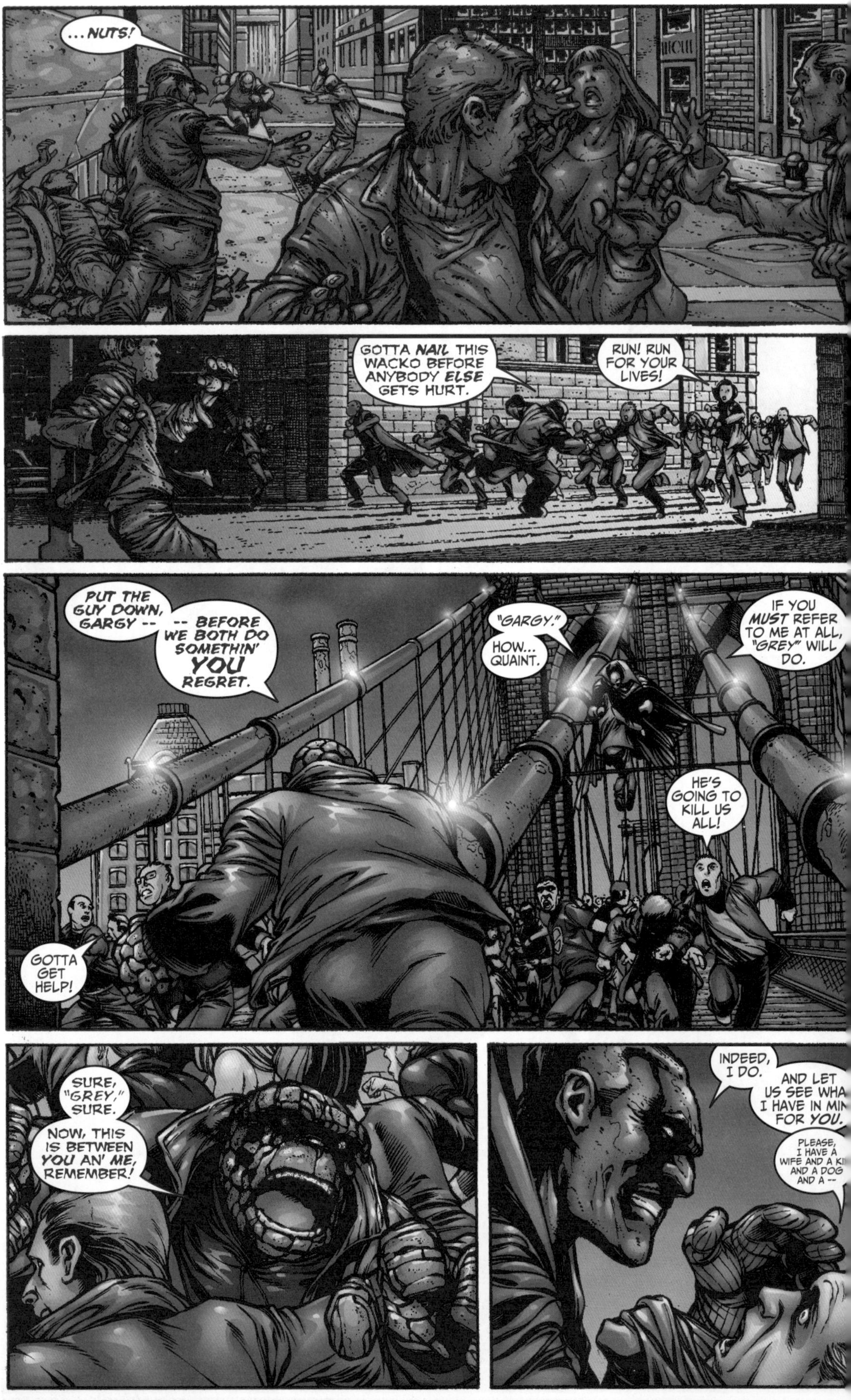
...NUTS!
GOTTA NAIL THIS WACKO BEFORE ANYBODY ELSE GETS HURT.
RUN! RUN FOR YOUR LIVES!
PUT THE GUY DOWN, GARGY --
-- BEFORE WE BOTH DO SOMETHIN' YOU REGRET.
"GARGY."
HOW... QUAINT.
IF YOU MUST REFER TO ME AT ALL, "GREY" WILL DO.
HE'S GOING TO KILL US ALL!
GOTTA GET HELP!
SURE, "GREY," SURE.
NOW, THIS IS BETWEEN YOU AN' ME, REMEMBER!
INDEED, I DO.
AND LET US SEE WHA I HAVE IN MIN FOR YOU.
PLEASE, I HAVE A WIFE AND A KI AND A DOG AND A --

-- CATKKK...

OH, I DO *SO* LOVE THE *SMELL* OF FLESH AND STONE.

THE BAXTER BUILDING. OUTER SPACE.

SURE WE GOT ENOUGH *ROOMS*, REED?

THE *ECHOES* HAVE *ECHOES*.

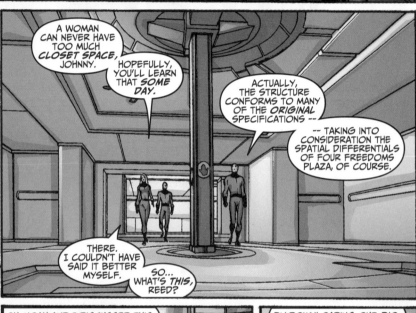

A WOMAN CAN NEVER HAVE TOO MUCH *CLOSET SPACE*, JOHNNY.

HOPEFULLY, YOU'LL LEARN THAT *SOME* DAY.

ACTUALLY, THE STRUCTURE CONFORMS TO MANY OF THE *ORIGINAL* SPECIFICATIONS --

-- TAKING INTO CONSIDERATION THE SPATIAL DIFFERENTIALS OF FOUR FREEDOMS PLAZA, OF COURSE.

THERE. I COULDN'T HAVE SAID IT BETTER MYSELF.

SO... WHAT'S *THIS*, REED?

OH, NOAH AND I DISCUSSED THIS AT LENGTH. I'M GLAD TO SEE HE INCORPORATED IT.

TRY AND THINK OF OUR NEW HOME AS A *"LIVING BUILDING"*.

BY DOWNLOADING OUR *BIO-SIGNATURES*, THE BAXTER BUILDING WILL GO *ONLINE* --

-- EFFECTIVELY BECOMING EXTENSIONS OF OURSELVES.

ONCE OPERATIONAL, ALL OF THE ONBOARD TECHNOLOGY WILL ACTIVATE *ONLY* WHEN IT RECOGNIZES ONE OF US.

HEY, THIS REMINDS ME OF WHEN WE *FIRST* STARTED.

REMEMBER HOW YOU HAD US PUT OUR HANDS TOGETHER, REED?

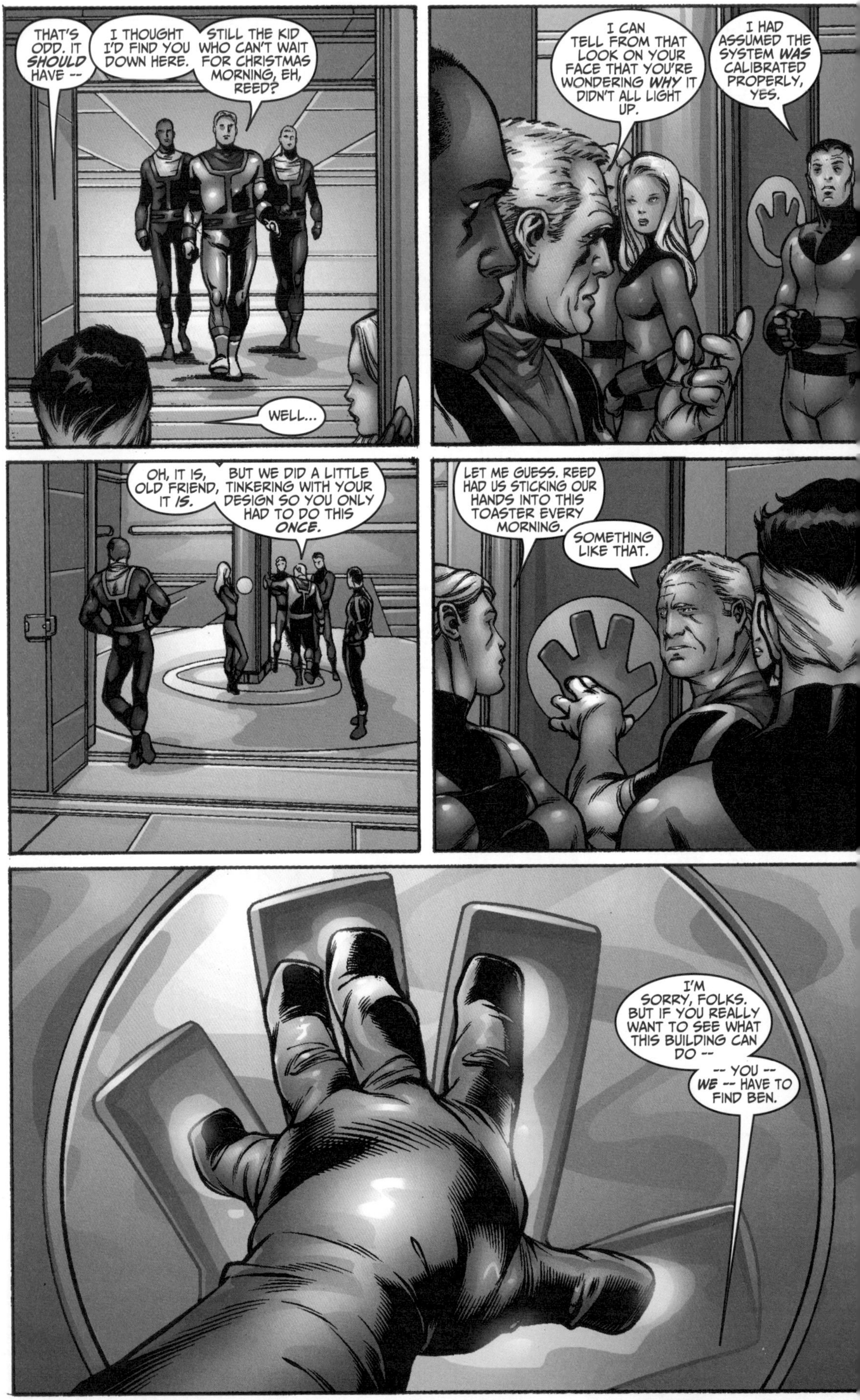
THAT'S ODD. IT SHOULD HAVE --
I THOUGHT I'D FIND YOU DOWN HERE.
STILL THE KID WHO CAN'T WAIT FOR CHRISTMAS MORNING, EH, REED?
WELL...
I CAN TELL FROM THAT LOOK ON YOUR FACE THAT YOU'RE WONDERING WHY IT DIDN'T ALL LIGHT UP.
I HAD ASSUMED THE SYSTEM WAS CALIBRATED PROPERLY, YES.
OH, IT IS, OLD FRIEND, IT IS.
BUT WE DID A LITTLE TINKERING WITH YOUR DESIGN SO YOU ONLY HAD TO DO THIS ONCE.
LET ME GUESS. REED HAD US STICKING OUR HANDS INTO THIS TOASTER EVERY MORNING.
SOMETHING LIKE THAT.
I'M SORRY, FOLKS. BUT IF YOU REALLY WANT TO SEE WHAT THIS BUILDING CAN DO --
-- YOU -- WE -- HAVE TO FIND BEN.

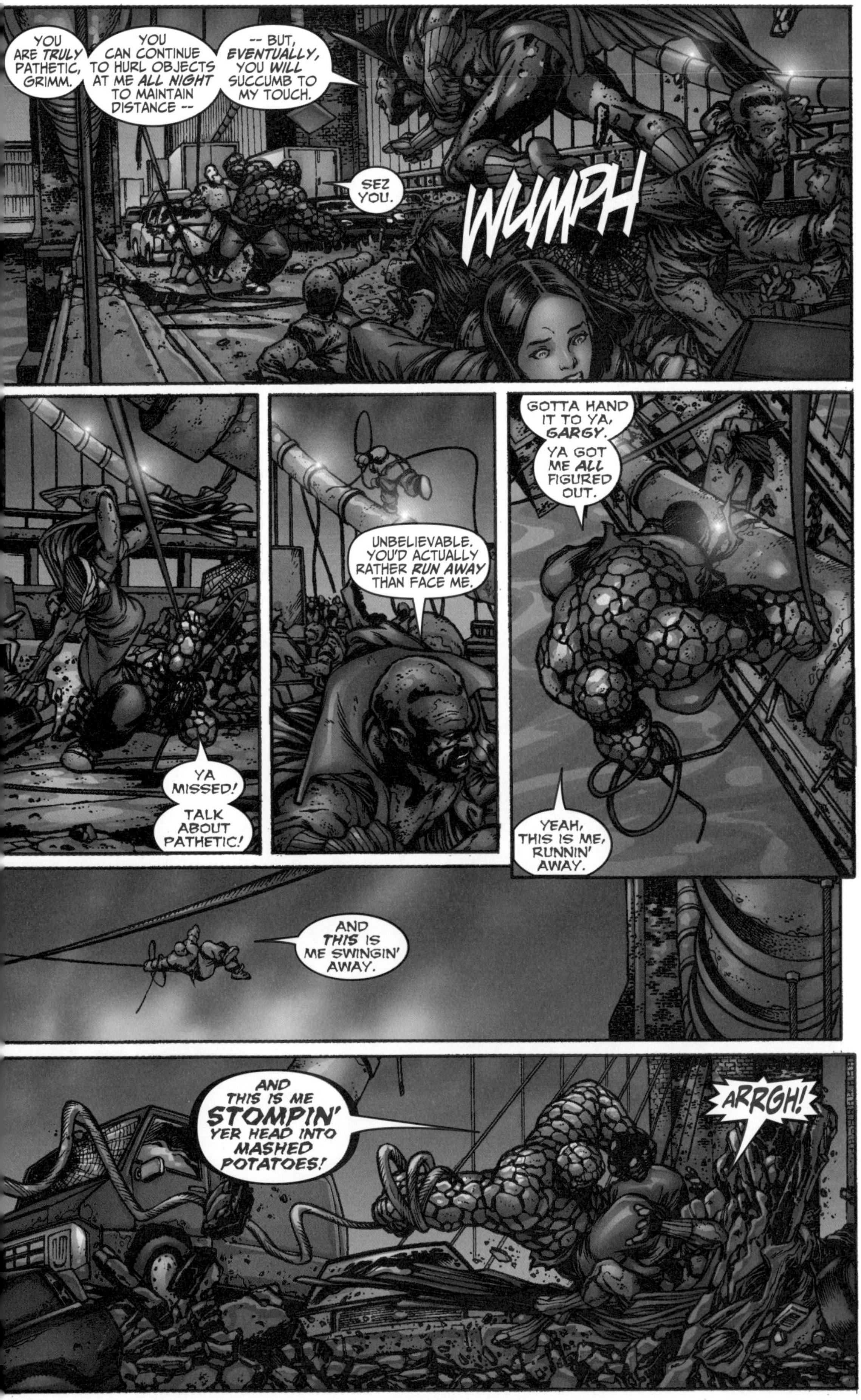

YOU ARE *TRULY* PATHETIC, GRIMM.
YOU CAN CONTINUE TO HURL OBJECTS AT ME *ALL NIGHT* TO MAINTAIN DISTANCE --
-- BUT, *EVENTUALLY*, YOU *WILL* SUCCUMB TO MY TOUCH.
SEZ YOU.
WUMPH
YA MISSED!
TALK ABOUT PATHETIC!
UNBELIEVABLE. YOU'D ACTUALLY RATHER *RUN AWAY* THAN FACE ME.
GOTTA HAND IT TO YA, *GARGY*.
YA GOT ME *ALL* FIGURED OUT.
YEAH, THIS IS ME, RUNNIN' AWAY.
AND *THIS* IS ME SWINGIN' AWAY.
AND THIS IS ME *STOMPIN'* YER HEAD INTO *MASHED POTATOES!*
ARRGH!

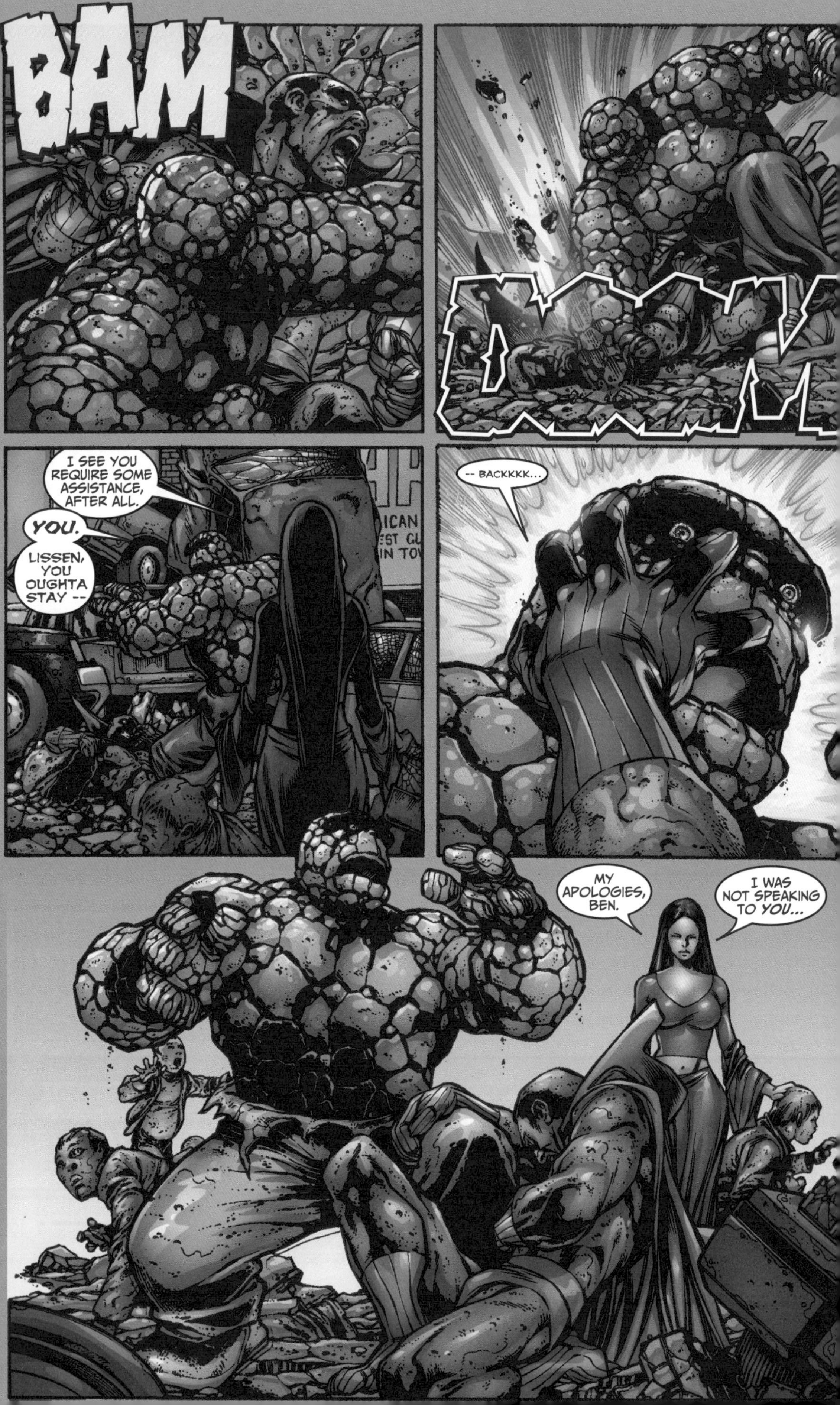
BAM
I SEE YOU REQUIRE SOME ASSISTANCE, AFTER ALL.
YOU.
LISSEN, YOU OUGHTA STAY --
-- BACKKKK...
MY APOLOGIES, BEN.
I WAS NOT SPEAKING TO YOU...

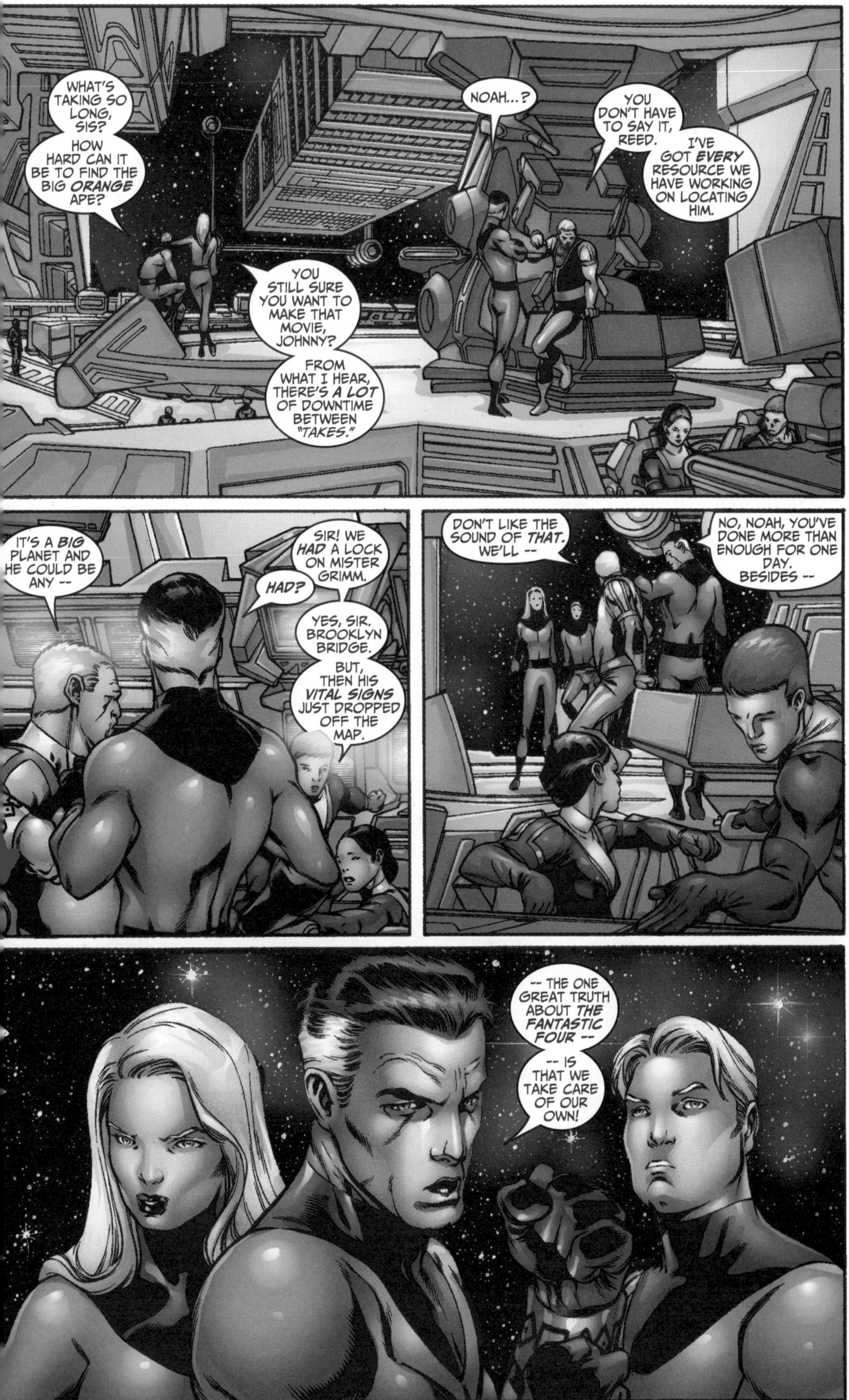
WHAT'S TAKING SO LONG, SIS?
HOW HARD CAN IT BE TO FIND THE BIG ORANGE APE?
YOU STILL SURE YOU WANT TO MAKE THAT MOVIE, JOHNNY?
FROM WHAT I HEAR, THERE'S A LOT OF DOWNTIME BETWEEN "TAKES."
NOAH...?
YOU DON'T HAVE TO SAY IT, REED.
I'VE GOT EVERY RESOURCE WE HAVE WORKING ON LOCATING HIM.
IT'S A BIG PLANET AND HE COULD BE ANY --
SIR! WE HAD A LOCK ON MISTER GRIMM.
HAD?
YES, SIR. BROOKLYN BRIDGE.
BUT, THEN HIS VITAL SIGNS JUST DROPPED OFF THE MAP.
DON'T LIKE THE SOUND OF THAT. WE'LL --
NO, NOAH, YOU'VE DONE MORE THAN ENOUGH FOR ONE DAY.
BESIDES --
-- THE ONE GREAT TRUTH ABOUT THE FANTASTIC FOUR --
-- IS THAT WE TAKE CARE OF OUR OWN!

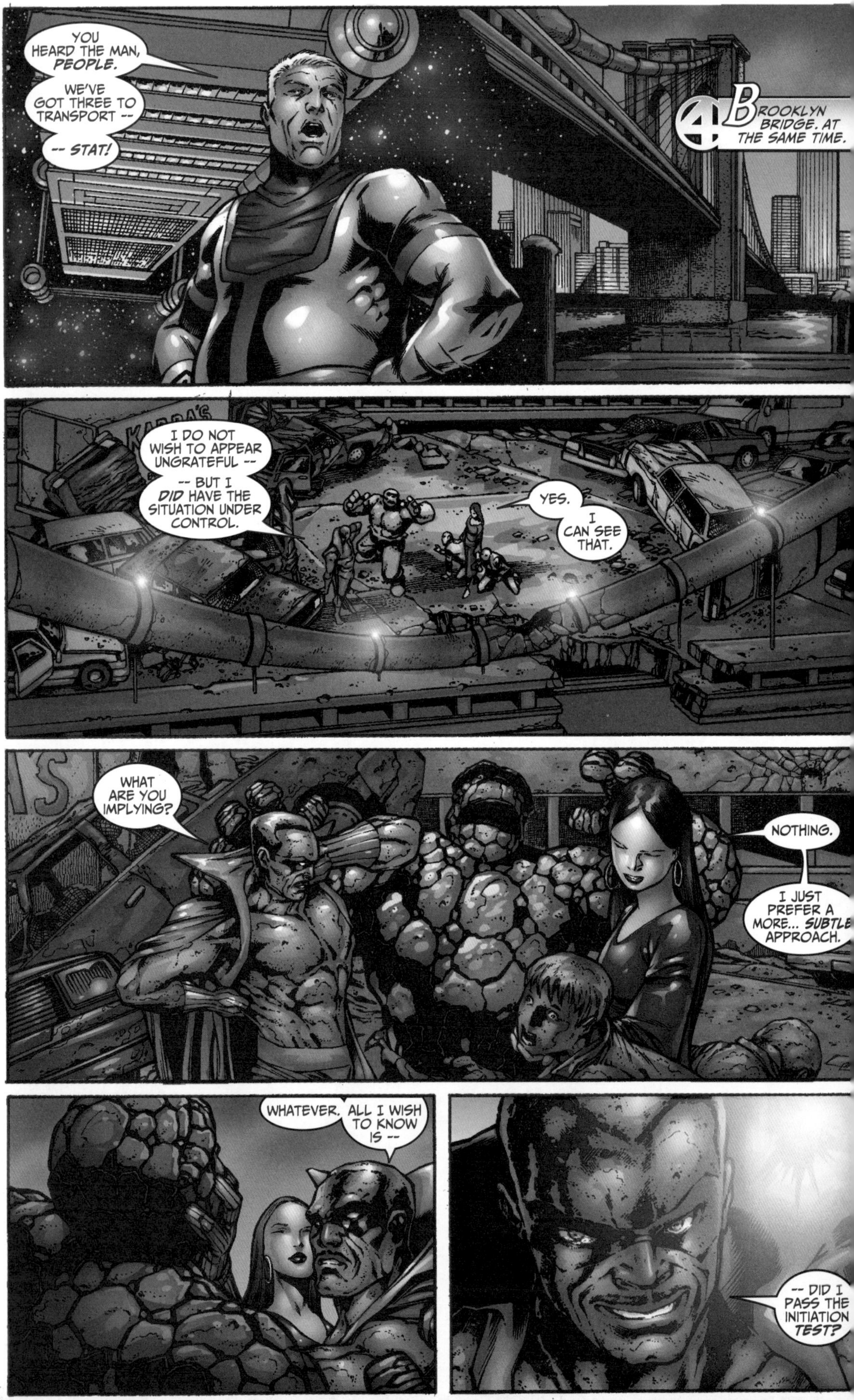

YOU HEARD THE MAN, PEOPLE.
WE'VE GOT THREE TO TRANSPORT --
-- STAT!
BROOKLYN BRIDGE. AT THE SAME TIME.
I DO NOT WISH TO APPEAR UNGRATEFUL --
-- BUT I DID HAVE THE SITUATION UNDER CONTROL.
YES.
I CAN SEE THAT.
WHAT ARE YOU IMPLYING?
NOTHING.
I JUST PREFER A MORE... SUBTLE APPROACH.
WHATEVER.
ALL I WISH TO KNOW IS --
-- DID I PASS THE INITIATION TEST?

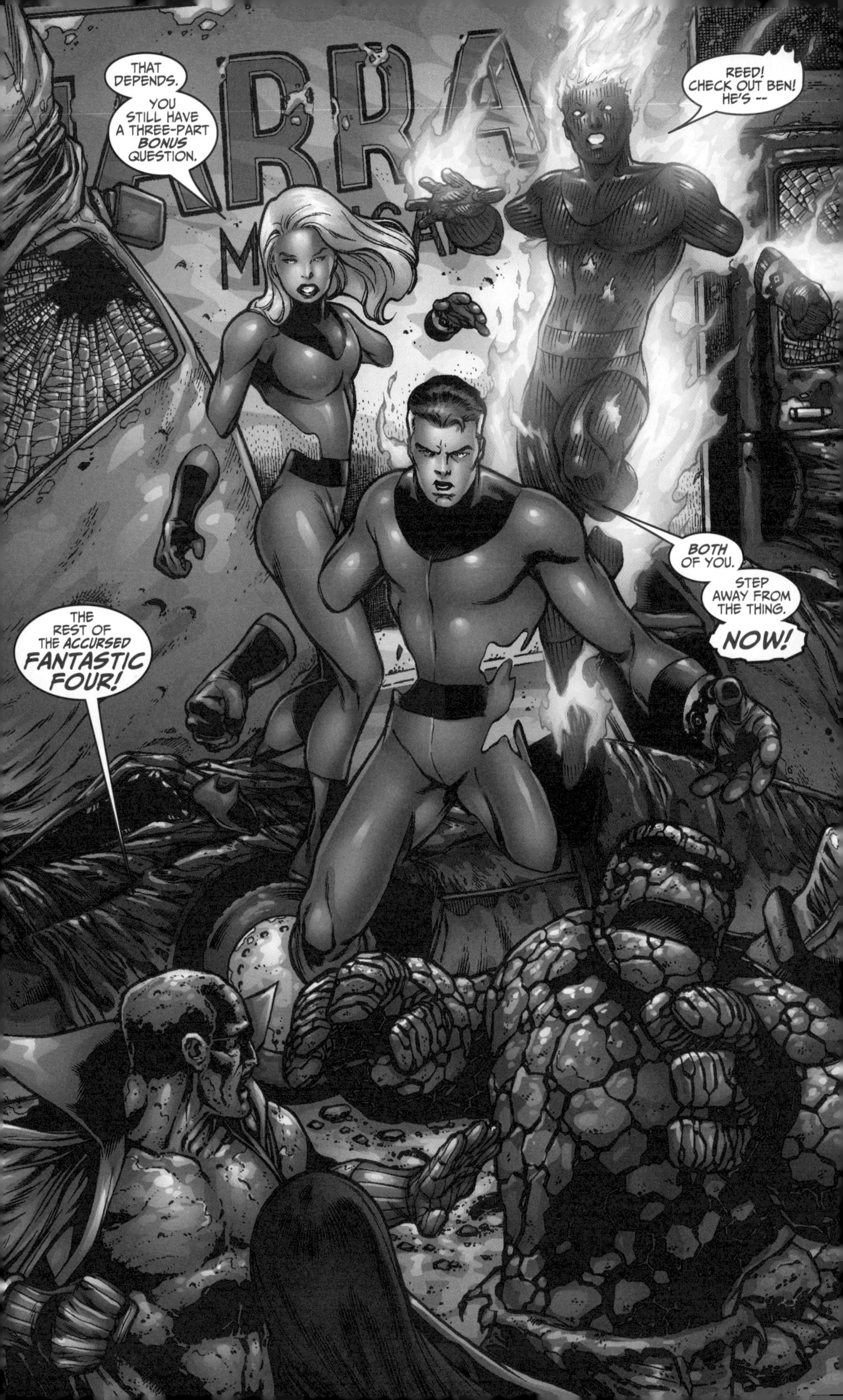
THAT DEPENDS.
YOU STILL HAVE A THREE-PART BONUS QUESTION.
REED! CHECK OUT BEN! HE'S --
BOTH OF YOU.
STEP AWAY FROM THE THING.
NOW!
THE REST OF THE ACCURSED FANTASTIC FOUR!

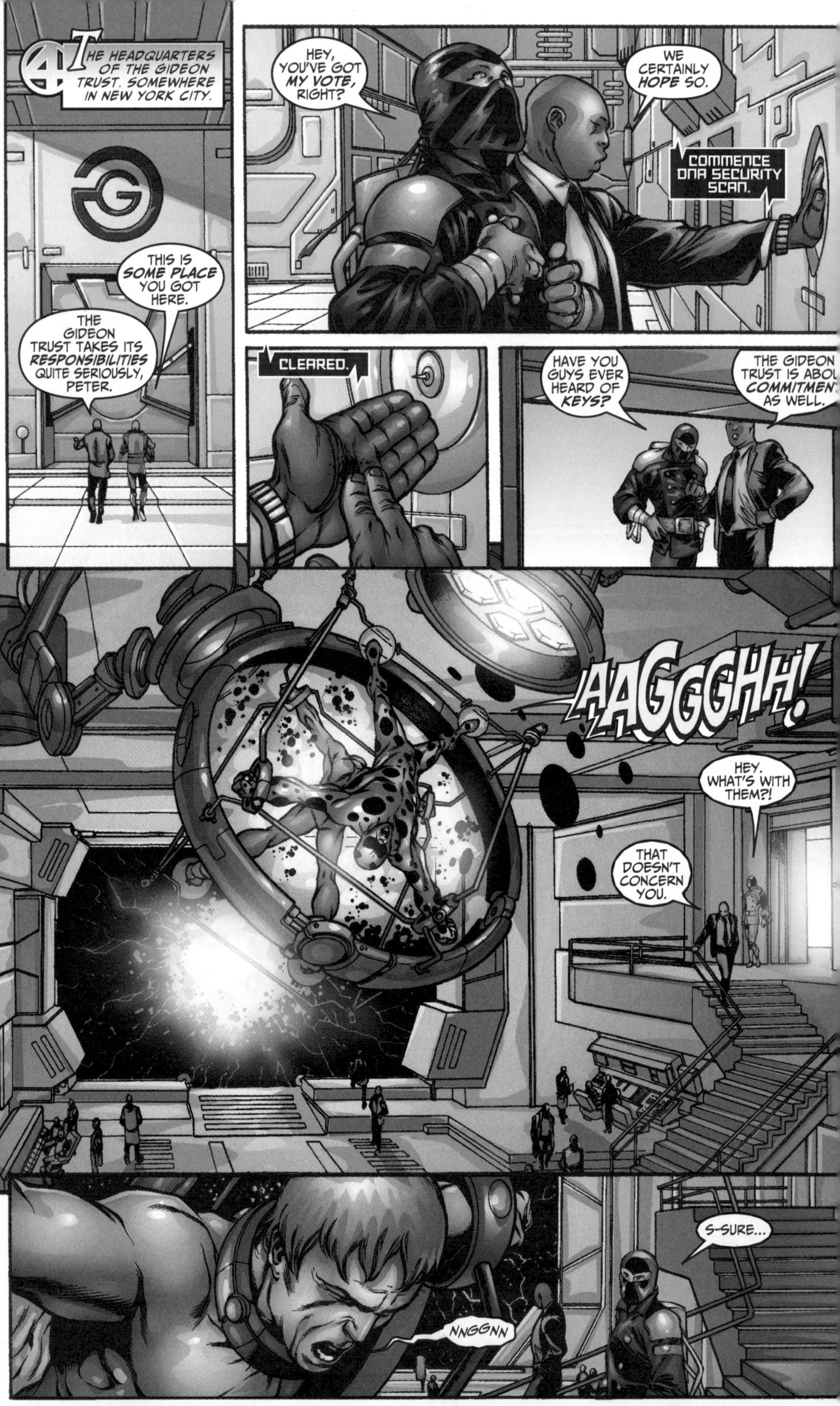
THE HEADQUARTERS OF THE GIDEON TRUST. SOMEWHERE IN NEW YORK CITY.
THIS IS SOME PLACE YOU GOT HERE.
THE GIDEON TRUST TAKES ITS RESPONSIBILITIES QUITE SERIOUSLY, PETER.
HEY, YOU'VE GOT MY VOTE, RIGHT?
WE CERTAINLY HOPE SO.
COMMENCE DNA SECURITY SCAN.
CLEARED.
HAVE YOU GUYS EVER HEARD OF KEYS?
THE GIDEON TRUST IS ABOU COMMITMEN AS WELL.
AAGGGHH!
HEY. WHAT'S WITH THEM?!
THAT DOESN'T CONCERN YOU.
S-SURE...
NNGGNN

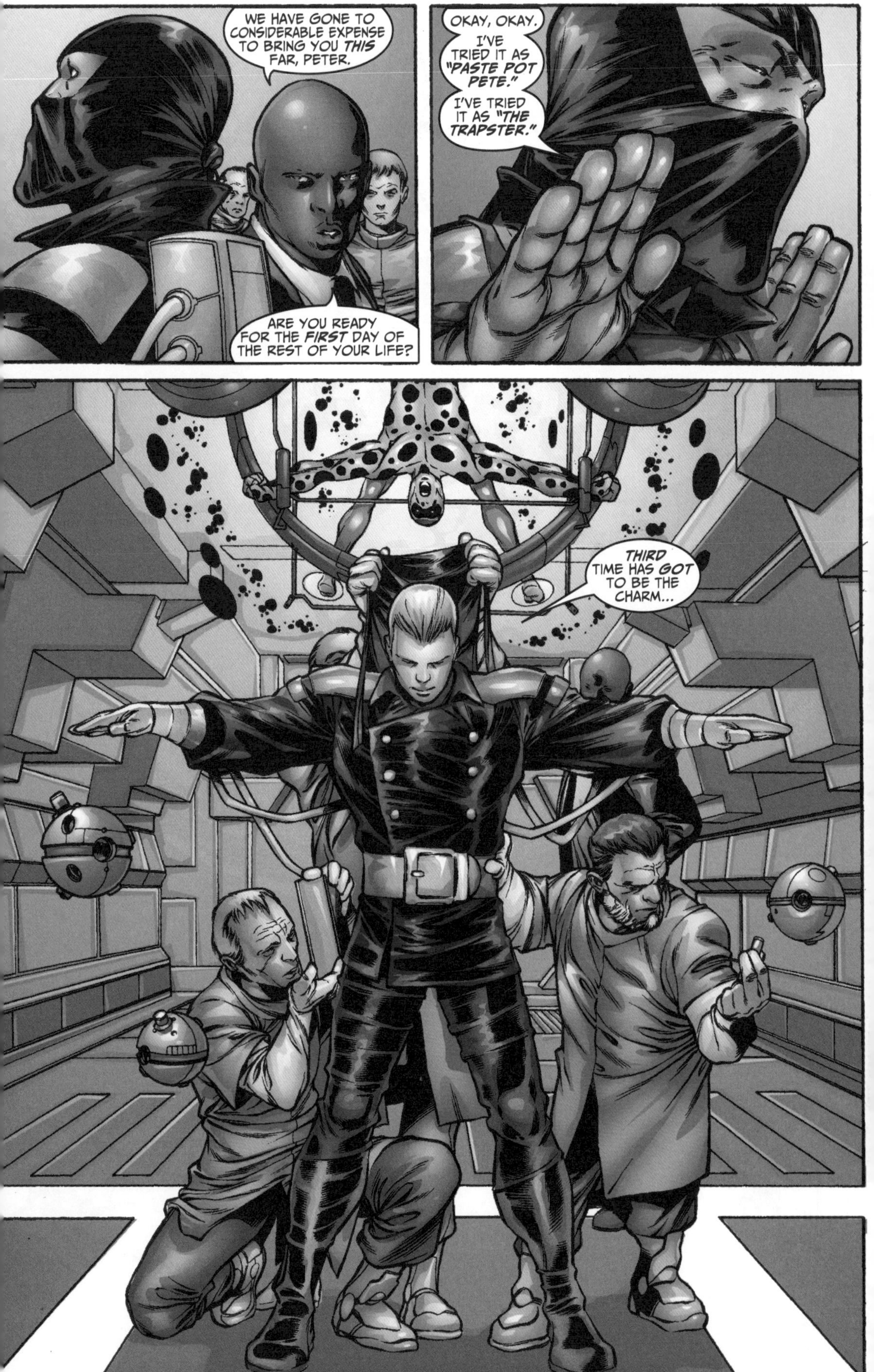
WE HAVE GONE TO CONSIDERABLE EXPENSE TO BRING YOU *THIS* FAR, PETER.
ARE YOU READY FOR THE *FIRST* DAY OF THE REST OF YOUR LIFE?
OKAY, OKAY.
I'VE TRIED IT AS *"PASTE POT PETE."*
I'VE TRIED IT AS *"THE TRAPSTER."*
THIRD TIME HAS *GOT* TO BE THE CHARM...

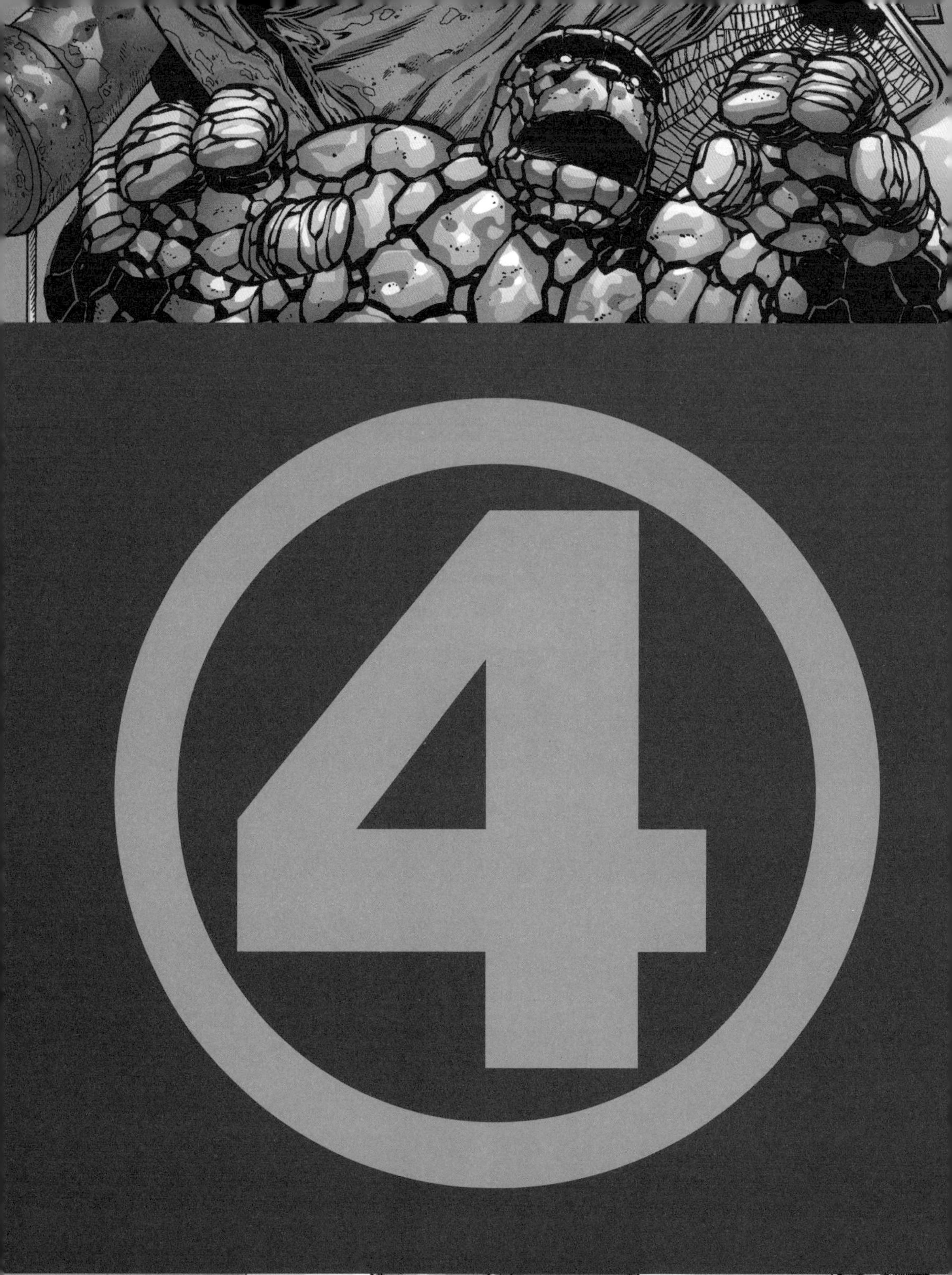

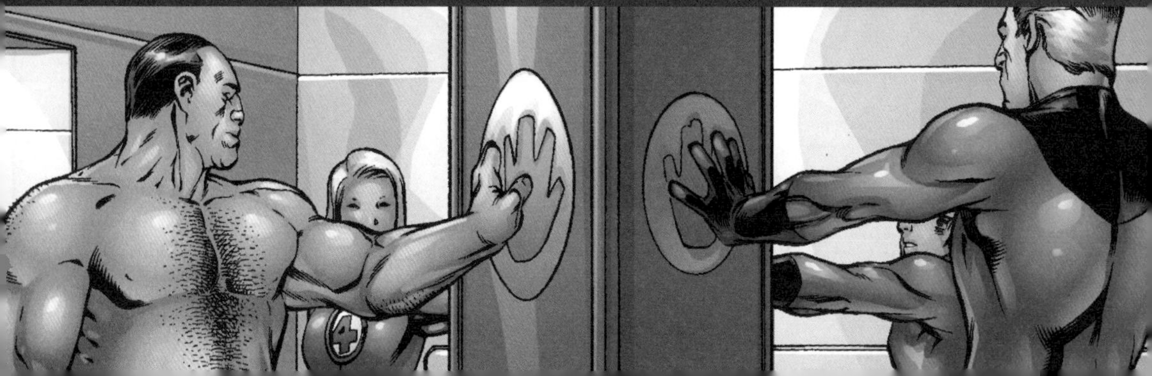

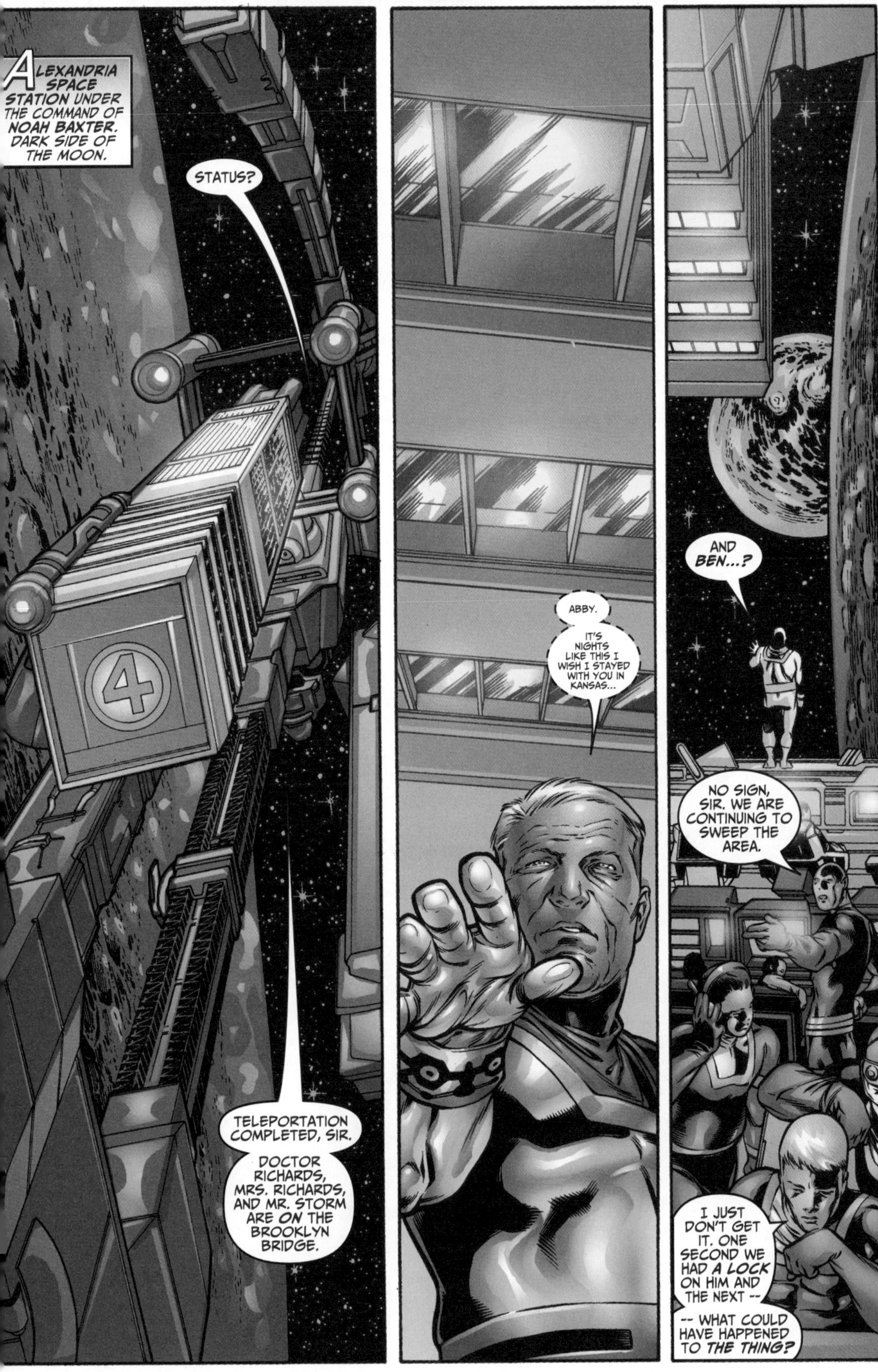
ALEXANDRIA SPACE STATION UNDER THE COMMAND OF NOAH BAXTER. DARK SIDE OF THE MOON.
STATUS?
TELEPORTATION COMPLETED, SIR.
DOCTOR RICHARDS, MRS. RICHARDS, AND MR. STORM ARE ON THE BROOKLYN BRIDGE.
ABBY.
IT'S NIGHTS LIKE THIS I WISH I STAYED WITH YOU IN KANSAS...
AND BEN...?
NO SIGN, SIR. WE ARE CONTINUING TO SWEEP THE AREA.
I JUST DON'T GET IT. ONE SECOND WE HAD A LOCK ON HIM AND THE NEXT --
-- WHAT COULD HAVE HAPPENED TO THE THING?

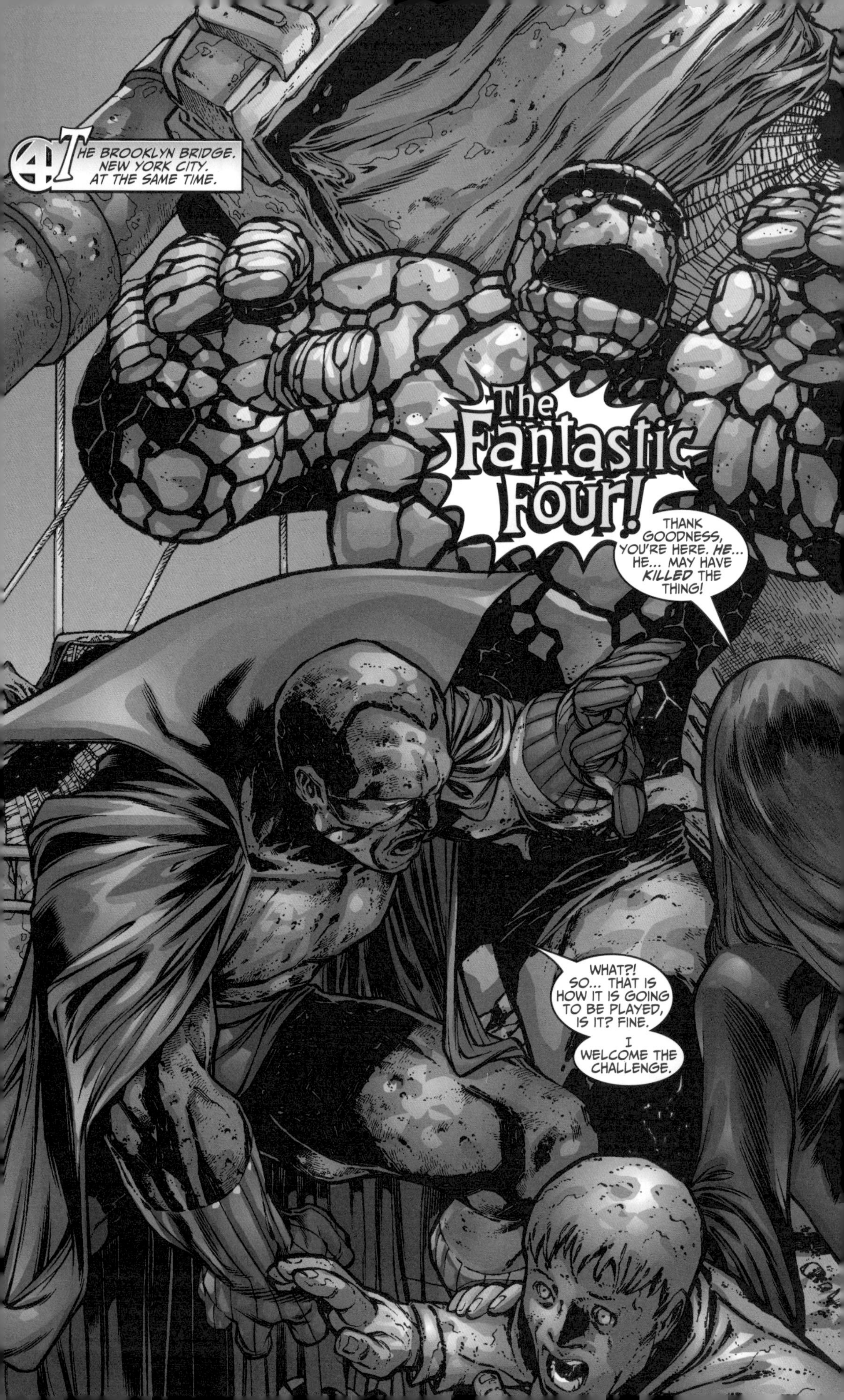
THE BROOKLYN BRIDGE. NEW YORK CITY. AT THE SAME TIME.
The Fantastic Four!
THANK GOODNESS, YOU'RE HERE. HE... HE... MAY HAVE KILLED THE THING!
WHAT?! SO... THAT IS HOW IT IS GOING TO BE PLAYED, IS IT? FINE.
I WELCOME THE CHALLENGE.

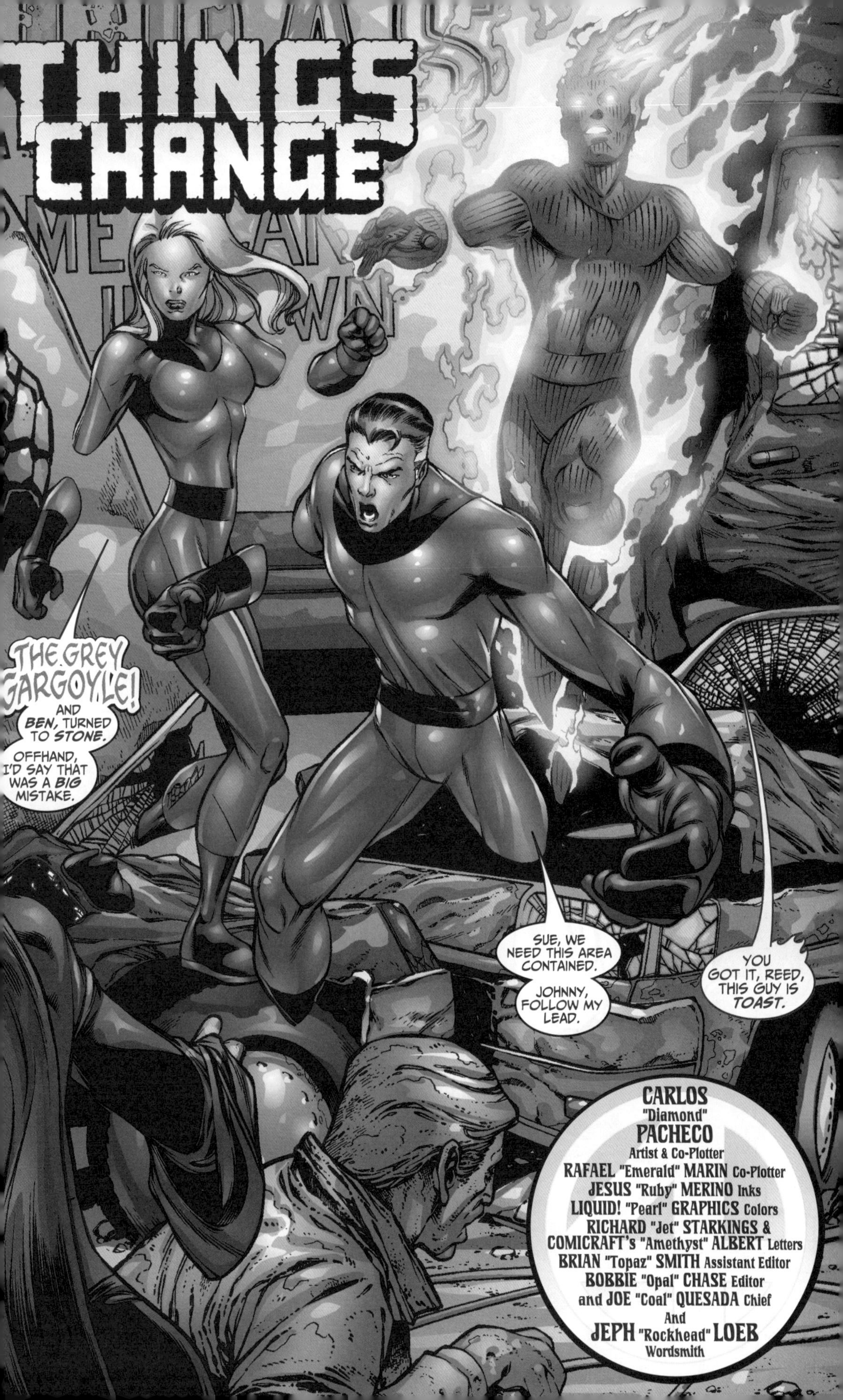
THINGS CHANGE
THE GREY GARGOYLE!
AND BEN, TURNED TO STONE.
OFFHAND, I'D SAY THAT WAS A BIG MISTAKE.
SUE, WE NEED THIS AREA CONTAINED.
JOHNNY, FOLLOW MY LEAD.
YOU GOT IT, REED, THIS GUY IS TOAST.
CARLOS "Diamond" PACHECO Artist & Co-Plotter
RAFAEL "Emerald" MARIN Co-Plotter
JESUS "Ruby" MERINO Inks
LIQUID! "Pearl" GRAPHICS Colors
RICHARD "Jet" STARKINGS & COMICRAFT's "Amethyst" ALBERT Letters
BRIAN "Topaz" SMITH Assistant Editor
BOBBIE "Opal" CHASE Editor
and JOE "Coal" QUESADA Chief
And
JEPH "Rockhead" LOEB Wordsmith

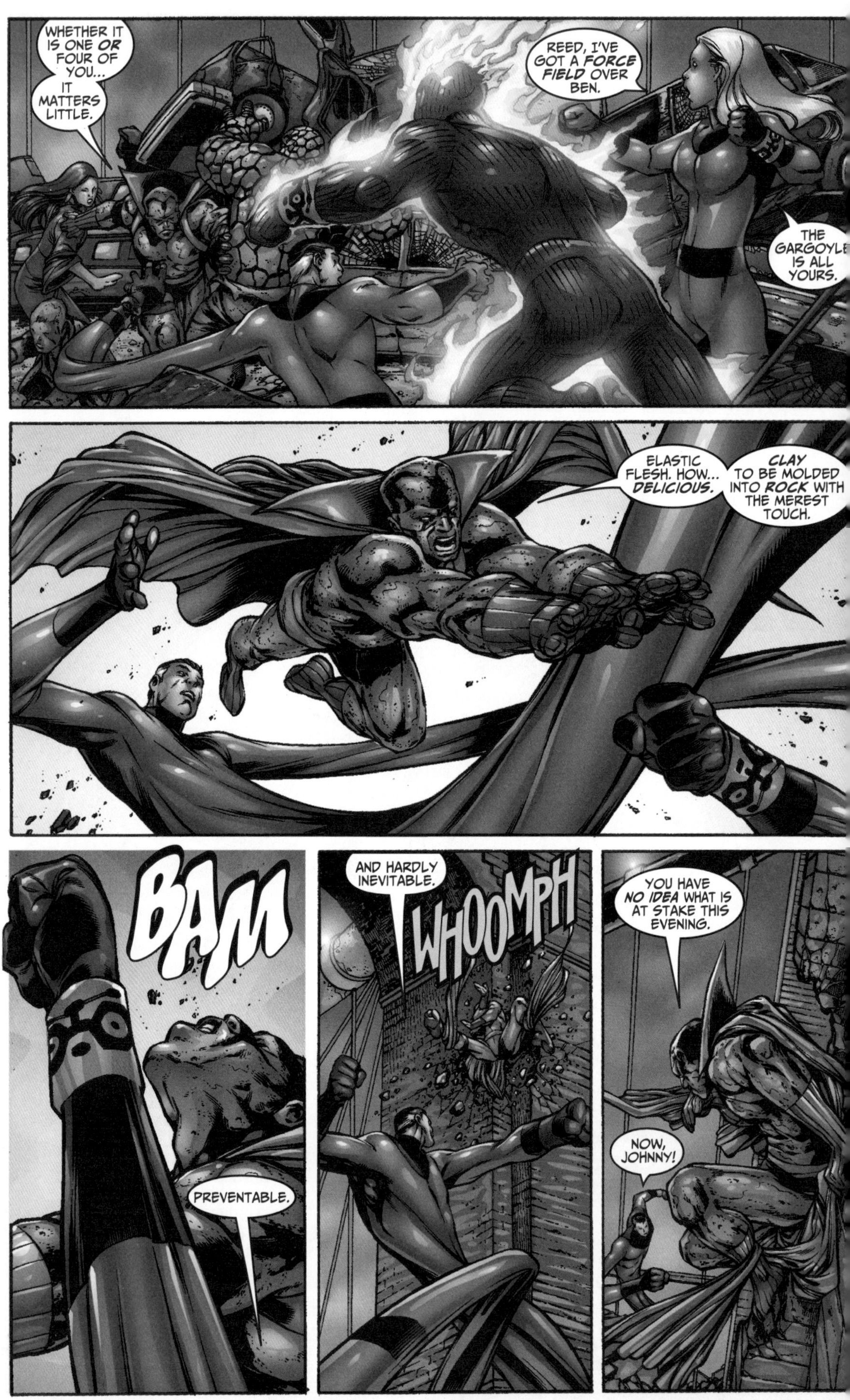
WHETHER IT IS ONE OR FOUR OF YOU...
IT MATTERS LITTLE.
REED, I'VE GOT A FORCE FIELD OVER BEN.
THE GARGOYLE IS ALL YOURS.
ELASTIC FLESH. HOW... DELICIOUS.
CLAY TO BE MOLDED INTO ROCK WITH THE MEREST TOUCH.
BAM
PREVENTABLE.
AND HARDLY INEVITABLE.
WHOOMPH
YOU HAVE NO IDEA WHAT IS AT STAKE THIS EVENING.
NOW, JOHNNY!

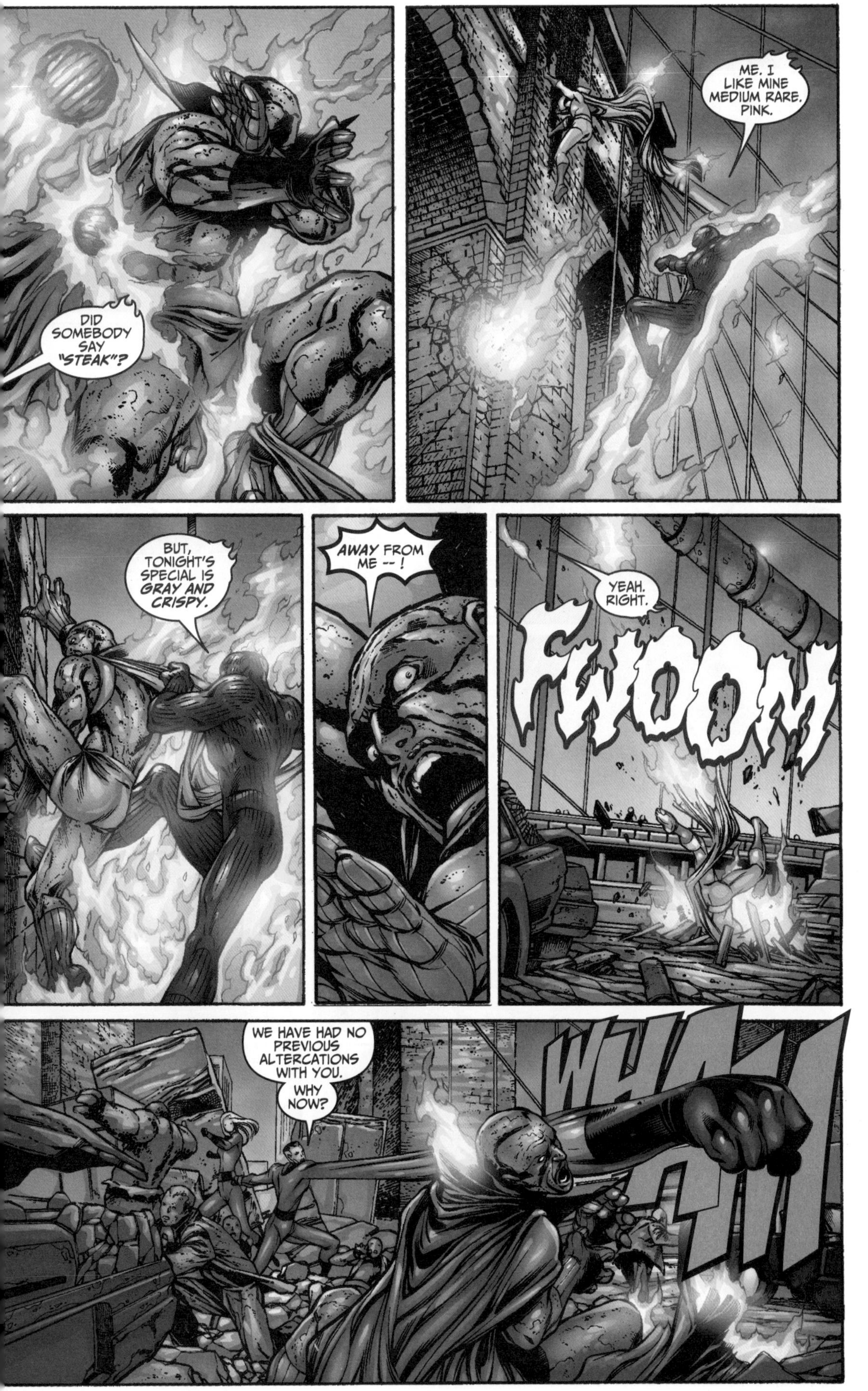

DID SOMEBODY SAY "STEAK"?
ME. I LIKE MINE MEDIUM RARE. PINK.
BUT, TONIGHT'S SPECIAL IS GRAY AND CRISPY.
AWAY FROM ME -- !
YEAH. RIGHT.
FWOOM
WE HAVE HAD NO PREVIOUS ALTERCATIONS WITH YOU.
WHY NOW?

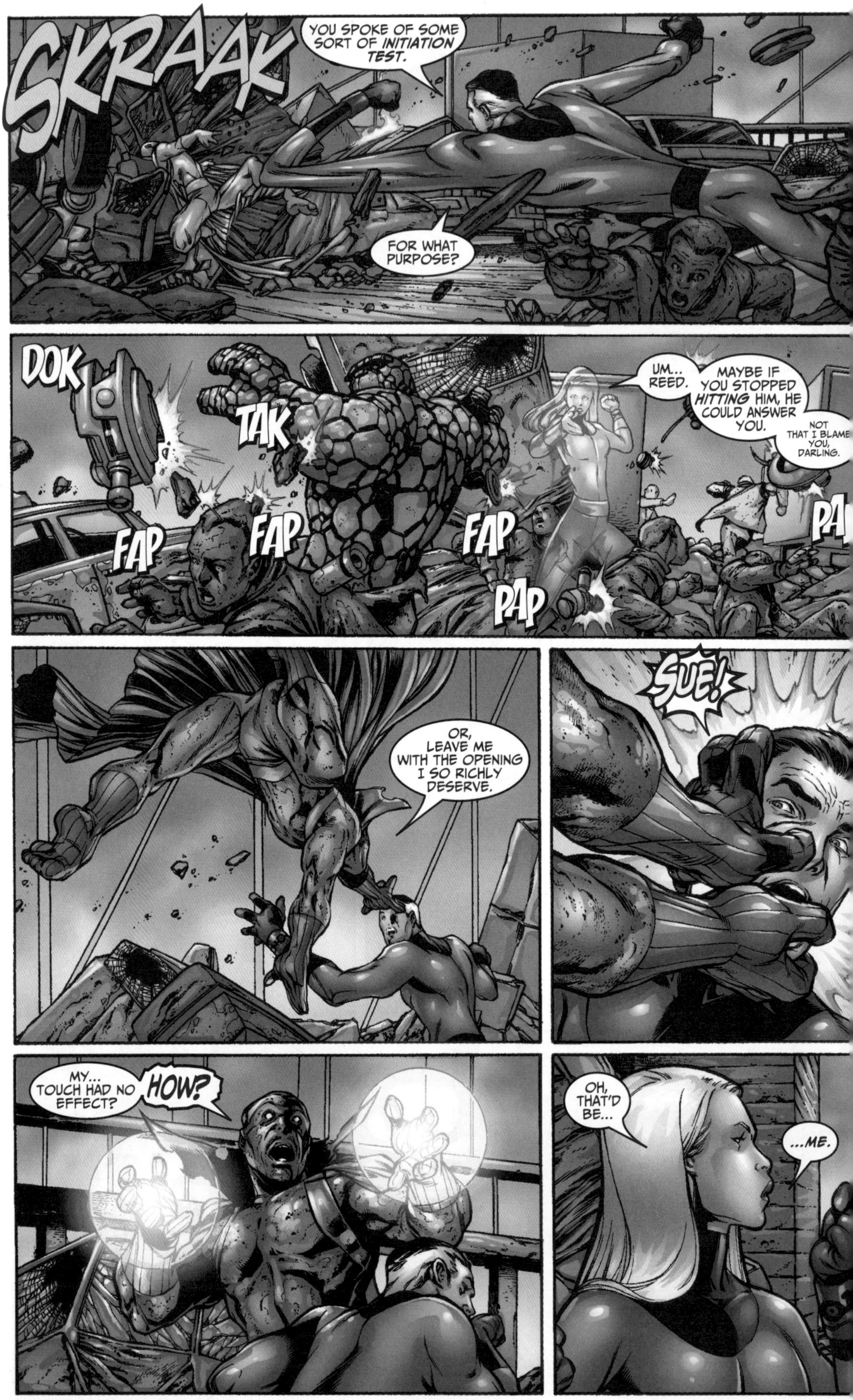
SKRAAK
YOU SPOKE OF SOME SORT OF INITIATION TEST.
FOR WHAT PURPOSE?
DOK
TAK
FAP
FAP
FAP
PAP
UM... REED.
MAYBE IF YOU STOPPED HITTING HIM, HE COULD ANSWER YOU.
NOT THAT I BLAME YOU, DARLING.
PA
OR, LEAVE ME WITH THE OPENING I SO RICHLY DESERVE.
SUE!
MY... TOUCH HAD NO EFFECT?
HOW?
OH, THAT'D BE...
...ME.

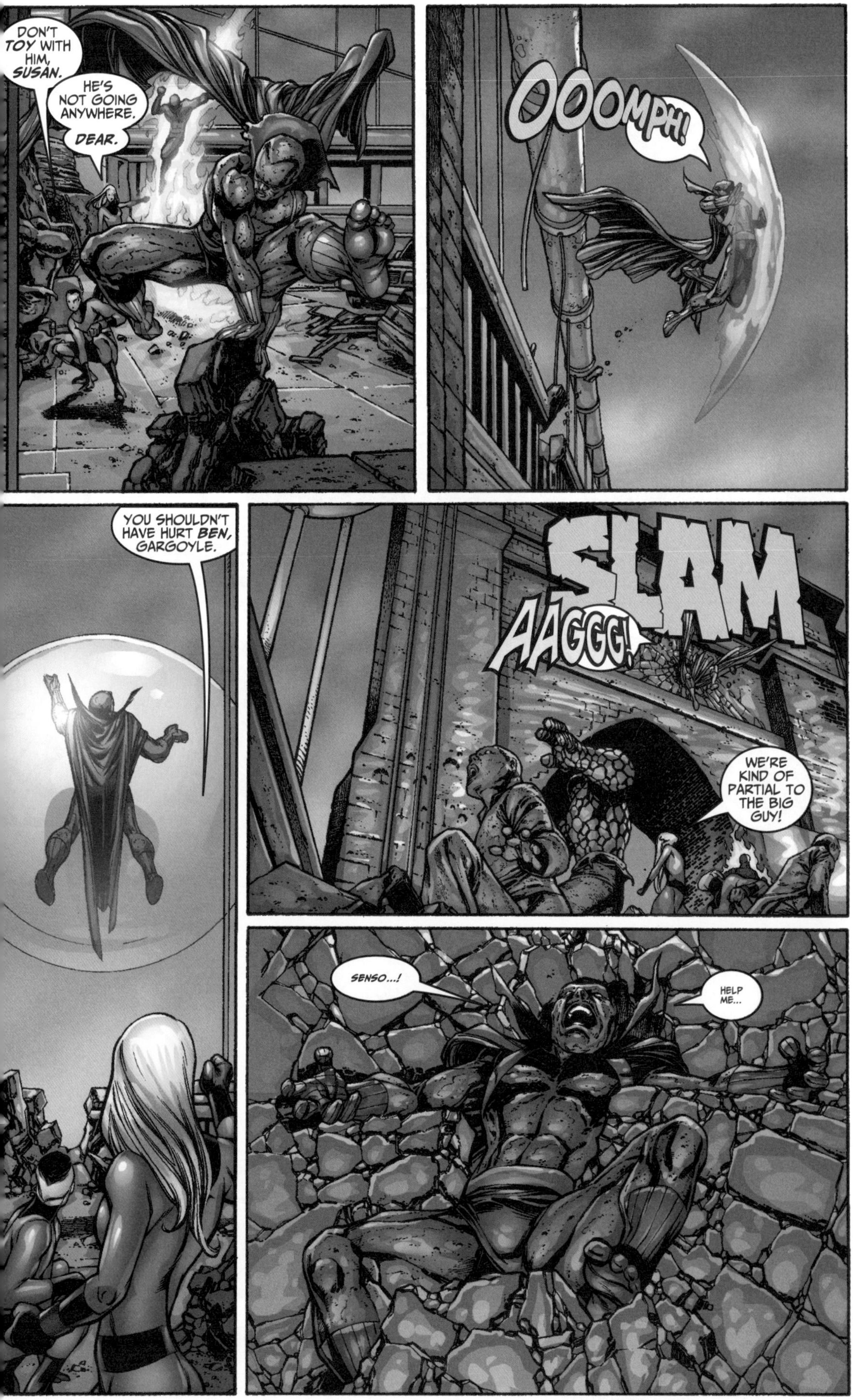
DON'T TOY WITH HIM, SUSAN.
HE'S NOT GOING ANYWHERE.
DEAR.
OOOOMPH!
YOU SHOULDN'T HAVE HURT BEN, GARGOYLE.
SLAM
AAGGG!
WE'RE KIND OF PARTIAL TO THE BIG GUY!
SENSO...!
HELP ME...

"SENSO"? WHO OR WHAT DO YOU SUPPOSE *THAT* MEANS?

WASN'T THERE A *WOMAN* STANDING WITH THE GARGOYLE?

I'LL DO A FLYBY AND SEE IF I CAN SCOPE HER OUT.

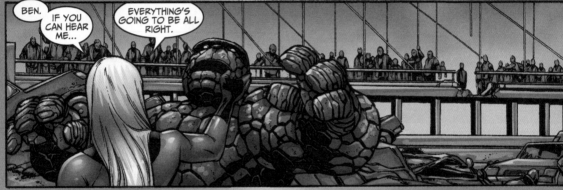

BEN. IF YOU CAN HEAR ME...

EVERYTHING'S GOING TO BE ALL RIGHT.

THEY SAVED US.

THEY'RE THE GREATEST!

WAIT'LL I TELL MY KIDS I SAW THEM IN ACTION!

LIFE IS FILLED WITH LITTLE DISAPPOINTMENTS, GREY.

IT'S WHAT MAKES IT SO... INTERESTING.

THE HEADQUARTERS OF THE GIDEON TRUST. SOMEWHERE IN NEW YORK CITY.

UGGNN...

...*THAT* WAS... UNPLEASANT...

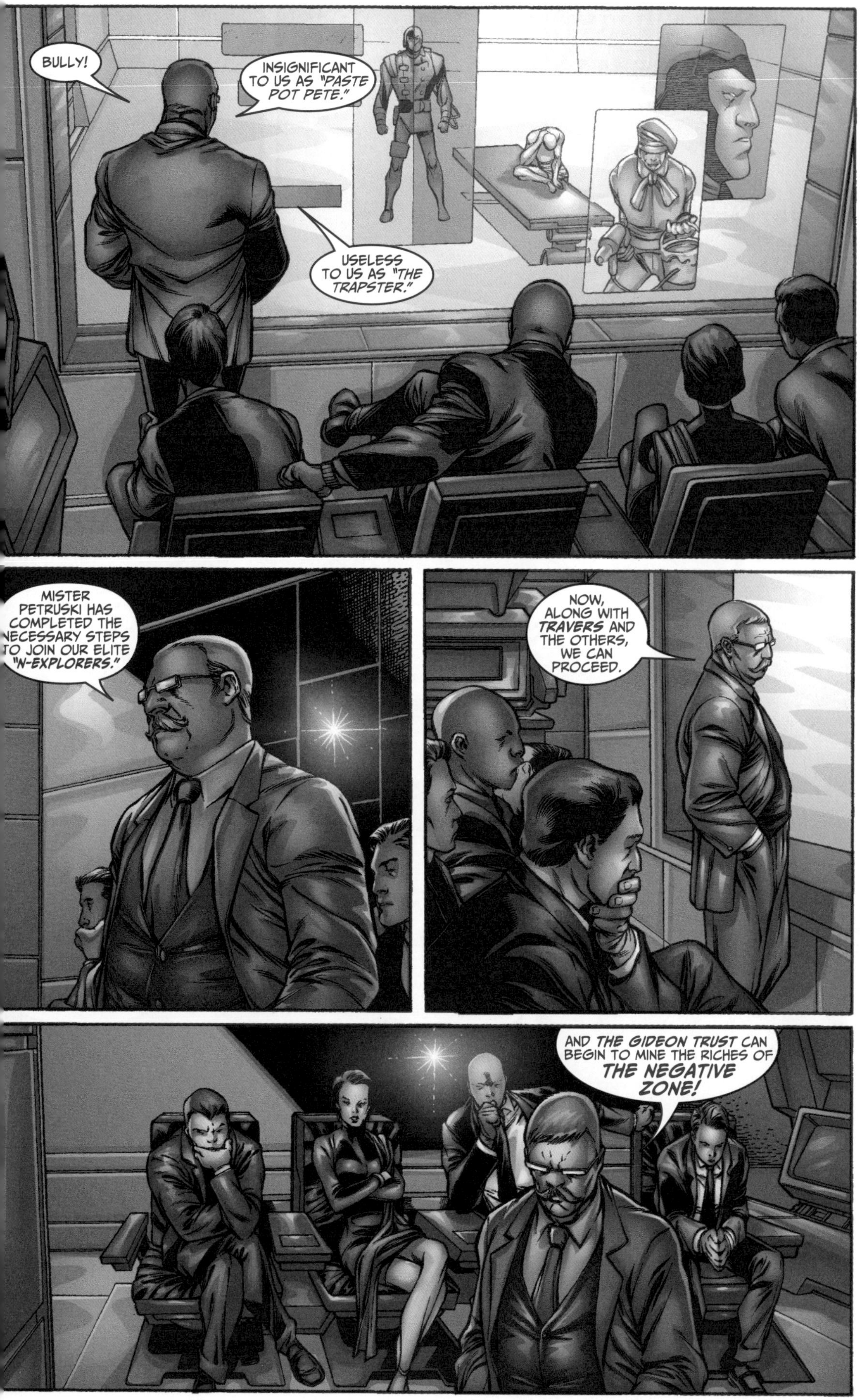
BULLY!
INSIGNIFICANT TO US AS "PASTE POT PETE."
USELESS TO US AS "THE TRAPSTER."
MISTER PETRUSKI HAS COMPLETED THE NECESSARY STEPS TO JOIN OUR ELITE "N-EXPLORERS."
NOW, ALONG WITH TRAVERS AND THE OTHERS, WE CAN PROCEED.
AND THE GIDEON TRUST CAN BEGIN TO MINE THE RICHES OF THE NEGATIVE ZONE!

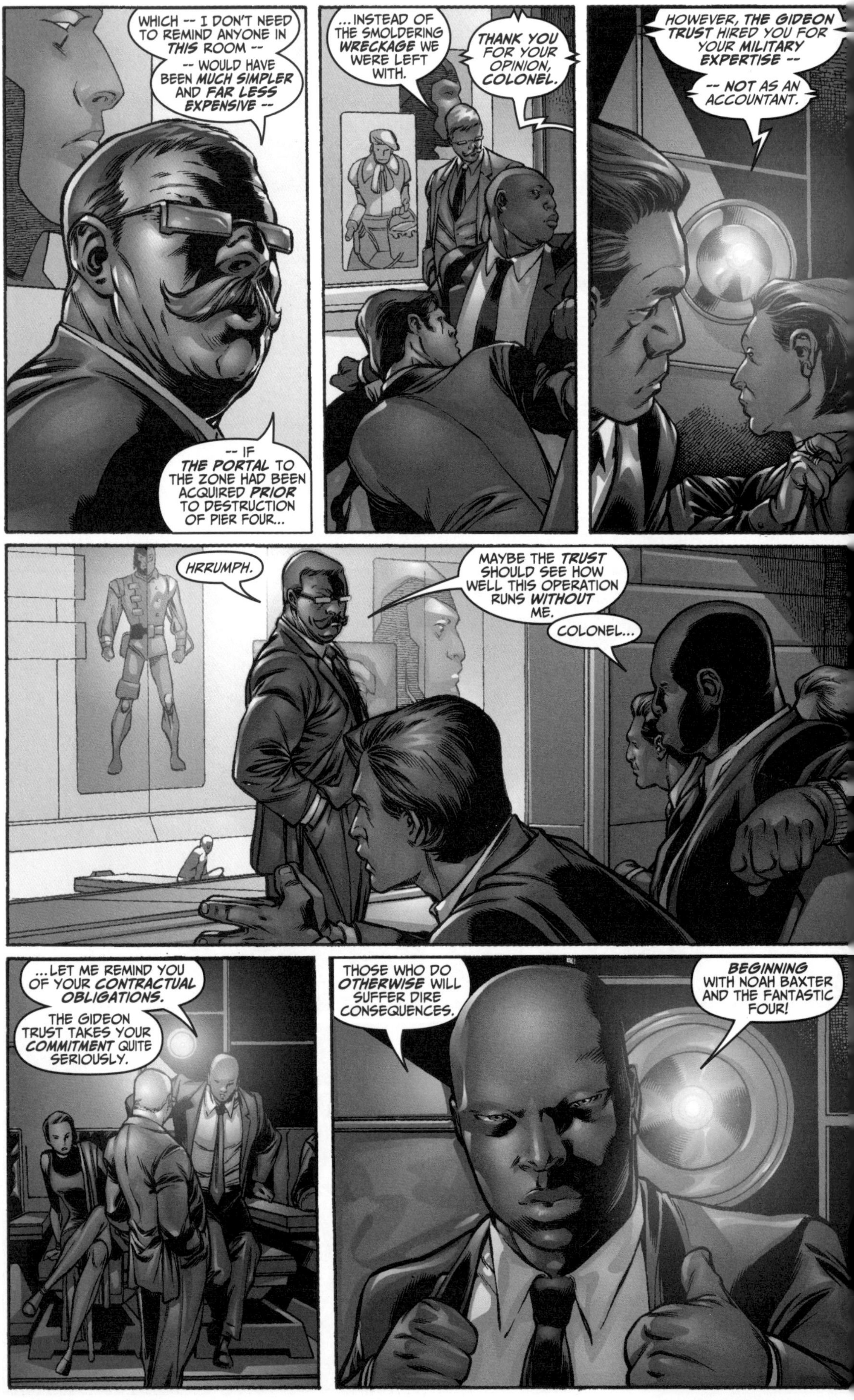
WHICH -- I DON'T NEED TO REMIND ANYONE IN THIS ROOM --
-- WOULD HAVE BEEN MUCH SIMPLER AND FAR LESS EXPENSIVE --
-- IF THE PORTAL TO THE ZONE HAD BEEN ACQUIRED PRIOR TO DESTRUCTION OF PIER FOUR...
...INSTEAD OF THE SMOLDERING WRECKAGE WE WERE LEFT WITH.
THANK YOU FOR YOUR OPINION, COLONEL.
HOWEVER, THE GIDEON TRUST HIRED YOU FOR YOUR MILITARY EXPERTISE --
-- NOT AS AN ACCOUNTANT.
HRRUMPH.
MAYBE THE TRUST SHOULD SEE HOW WELL THIS OPERATION RUNS WITHOUT ME.
COLONEL...
...LET ME REMIND YOU OF YOUR CONTRACTUAL OBLIGATIONS.
THE GIDEON TRUST TAKES YOUR COMMITMENT QUITE SERIOUSLY.
THOSE WHO DO OTHERWISE WILL SUFFER DIRE CONSEQUENCES.
BEGINNING WITH NOAH BAXTER AND THE FANTASTIC FOUR!

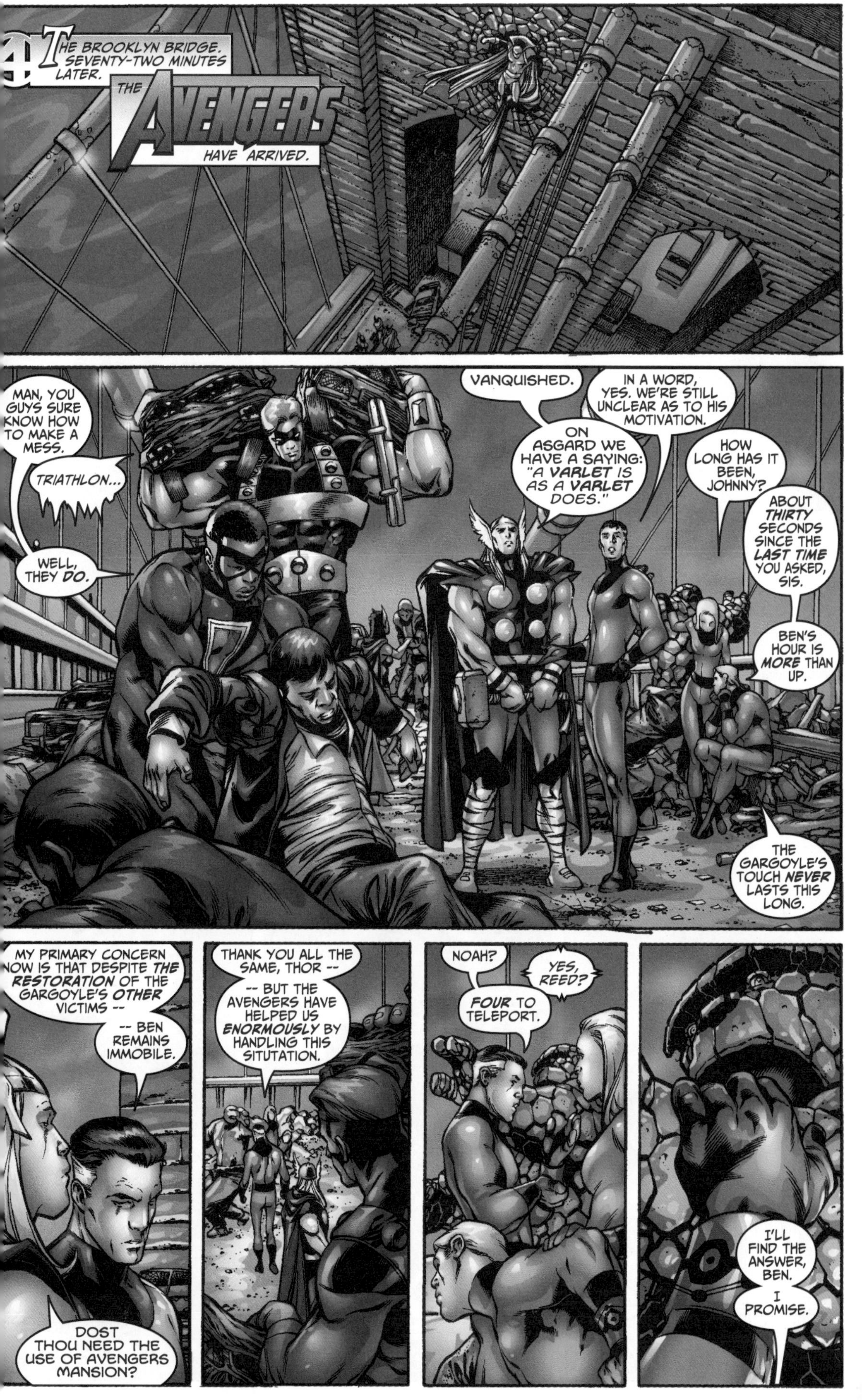
THE BROOKLYN BRIDGE. SEVENTY-TWO MINUTES LATER.
THE AVENGERS HAVE ARRIVED.
MAN, YOU GUYS SURE KNOW HOW TO MAKE A MESS.
TRIATHLON...
WELL, THEY DO.
VANQUISHED.
ON ASGARD WE HAVE A SAYING: "A VARLET IS AS A VARLET DOES."
IN A WORD, YES. WE'RE STILL UNCLEAR AS TO HIS MOTIVATION.
HOW LONG HAS IT BEEN, JOHNNY?
ABOUT THIRTY SECONDS SINCE THE LAST TIME YOU ASKED, SIS.
BEN'S HOUR IS MORE THAN UP.
THE GARGOYLE'S TOUCH NEVER LASTS THIS LONG.
MY PRIMARY CONCERN NOW IS THAT DESPITE THE RESTORATION OF THE GARGOYLE'S OTHER VICTIMS --
-- BEN REMAINS IMMOBILE.
DOST THOU NEED THE USE OF AVENGERS MANSION?
THANK YOU ALL THE SAME, THOR --
-- BUT THE AVENGERS HAVE HELPED US ENORMOUSLY BY HANDLING THIS SITUTATION.
NOAH?
YES, REED?
FOUR TO TELEPORT.
I'LL FIND THE ANSWER, BEN.
I PROMISE.

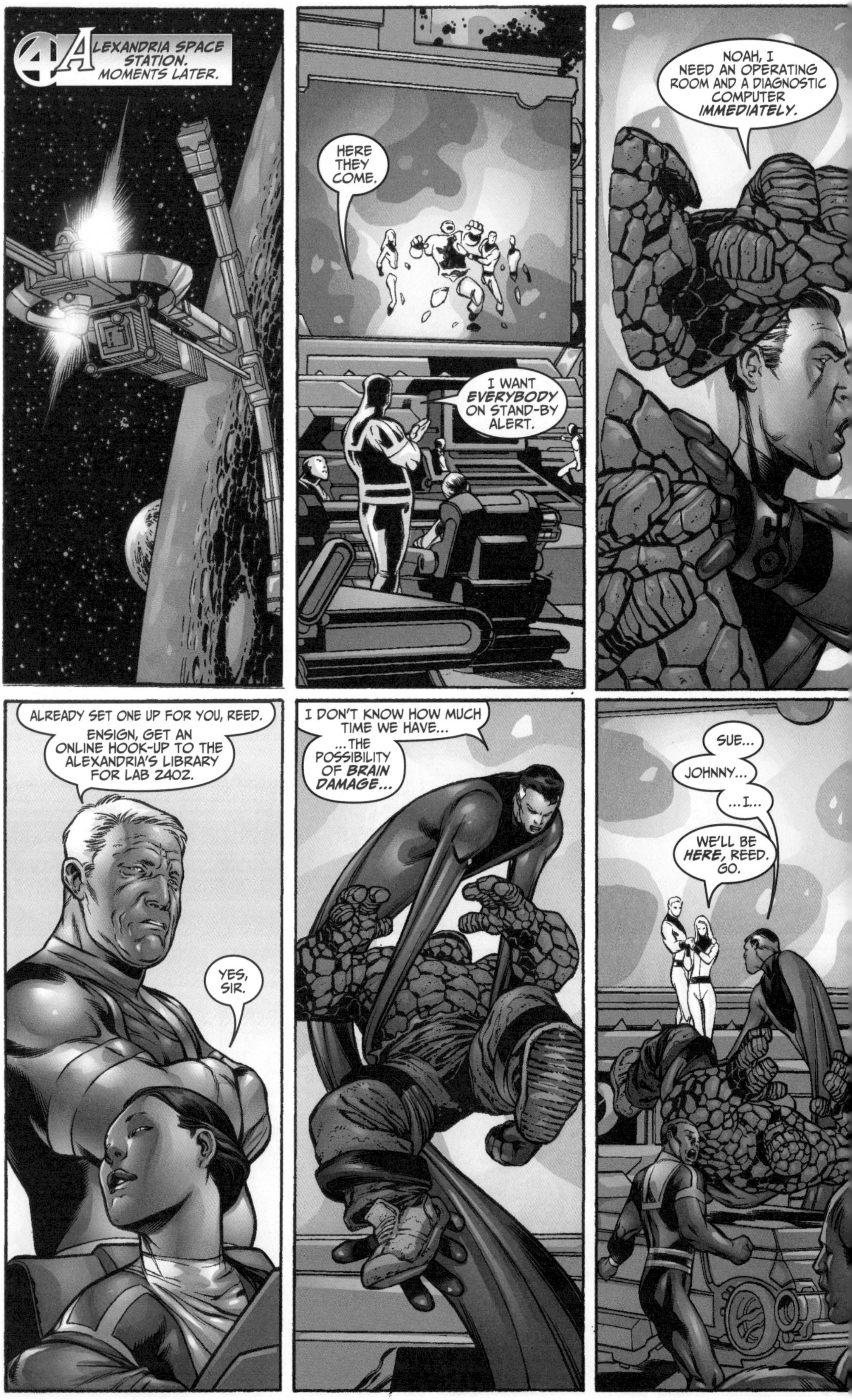
ALEXANDRIA SPACE STATION. MOMENTS LATER.
HERE THEY COME.
I WANT EVERYBODY ON STAND-BY ALERT.
NOAH, I NEED AN OPERATING ROOM AND A DIAGNOSTIC COMPUTER IMMEDIATELY.
ALREADY SET ONE UP FOR YOU, REED. ENSIGN, GET AN ONLINE HOOK-UP TO THE ALEXANDRIA'S LIBRARY FOR LAB 2402.
YES, SIR.
I DON'T KNOW HOW MUCH TIME WE HAVE...
...THE POSSIBILITY OF BRAIN DAMAGE...
SUE...
JOHNNY...
...I...
WE'LL BE HERE, REED. GO.

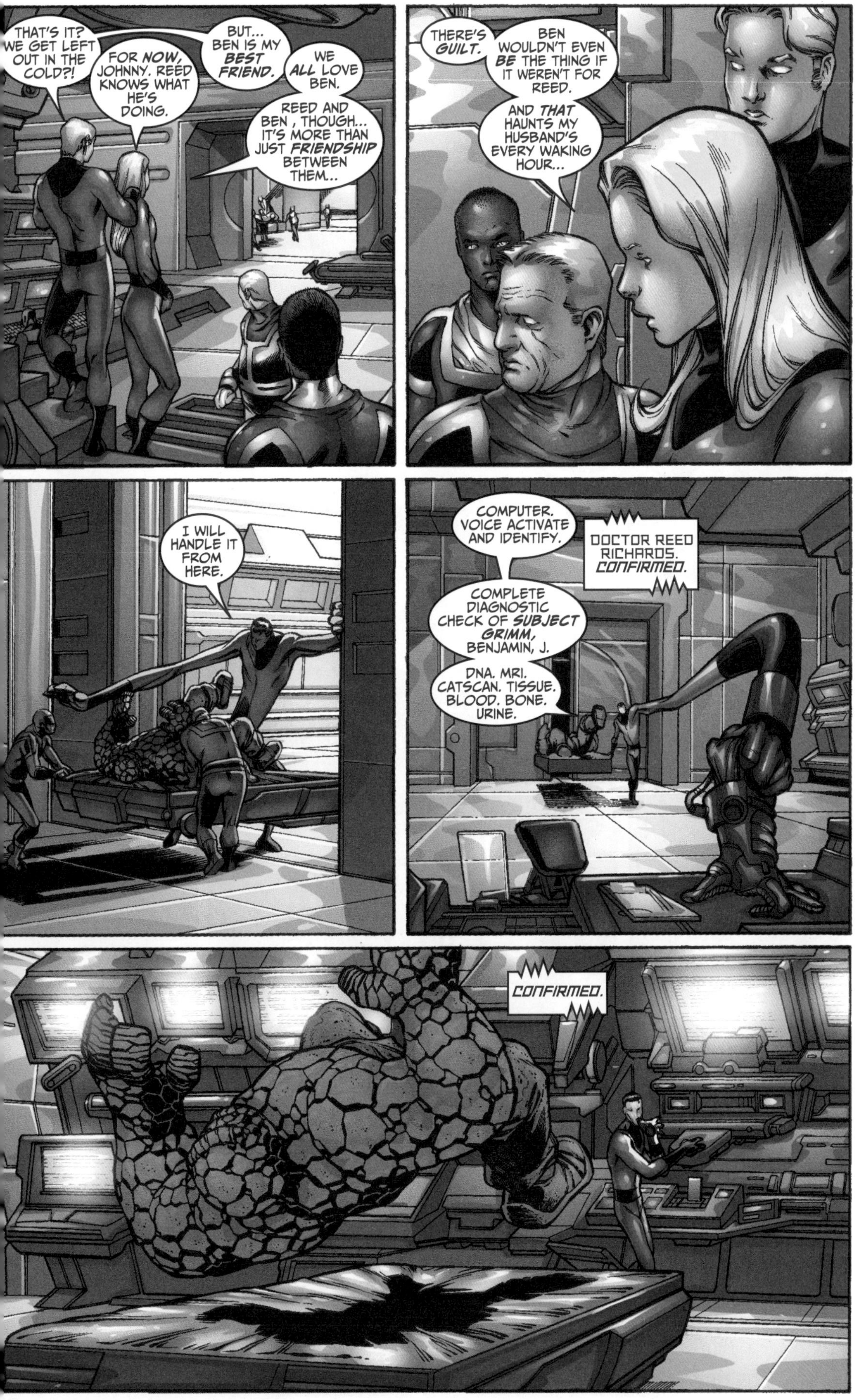
THAT'S IT? WE GET LEFT OUT IN THE COLD?!
FOR *NOW*, JOHNNY. REED KNOWS WHAT HE'S DOING.
BUT... BEN IS MY *BEST FRIEND.*
WE *ALL* LOVE BEN.
REED AND BEN, THOUGH... IT'S MORE THAN JUST *FRIENDSHIP* BETWEEN THEM...
THERE'S *GUILT.*
BEN WOULDN'T EVEN *BE* THE THING IF IT WEREN'T FOR REED.
AND *THAT* HAUNTS MY HUSBAND'S EVERY WAKING HOUR...
I WILL HANDLE IT FROM HERE.
COMPUTER. VOICE ACTIVATE AND IDENTIFY.
DOCTOR REED RICHARDS. *CONFIRMED.*
COMPLETE DIAGNOSTIC CHECK OF *SUBJECT GRIMM,* BENJAMIN, J.
DNA. MRI. CATSCAN. TISSUE. BLOOD. BONE. URINE.
CONFIRMED.

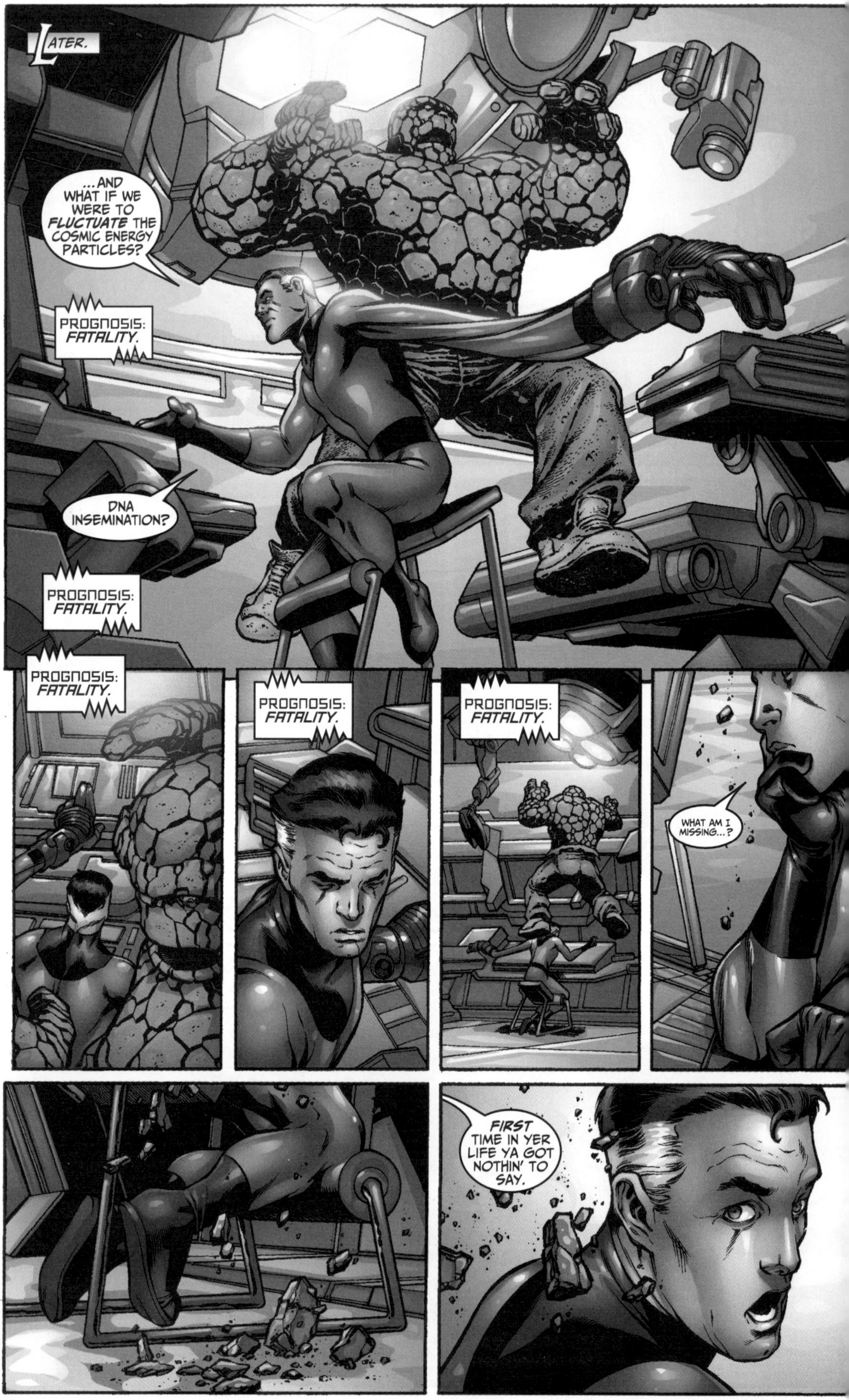
LATER.
...AND WHAT IF WE WERE TO FLUCTUATE THE COSMIC ENERGY PARTICLES?
PROGNOSIS: FATALITY.
DNA INSEMINATION?
PROGNOSIS: FATALITY.
PROGNOSIS: FATALITY.
PROGNOSIS: FATALITY.
PROGNOSIS: FATALITY.
WHAT AM I MISSING...?
FIRST TIME IN YER LIFE YA GOT NOTHIN' TO SAY.

SUE. JOHNNY. COME IN HERE. I NEED YOU!

THAT'S OUR CUE, SIS.

LOCKED!

NOAH! IF YOU CAN HEAR ME, OPEN THIS G.D. DOOR!

FOOM

REED!

WHAT'S ALL THE HUBBUB?

BEN...?

BEN! IT'S YOU! YOU -- YOU!

IN THE FLESH, SUZIE GAL.

YOU UGLY MUG, LOOK AT YOUR UGLY MUG!

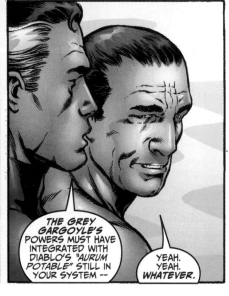

THE GREY GARGOYLE'S POWERS MUST HAVE INTEGRATED WITH DIABLO'S "AURUM POTABLE" STILL IN YOUR SYSTEM --

YEAH. YEAH. WHATEVER.

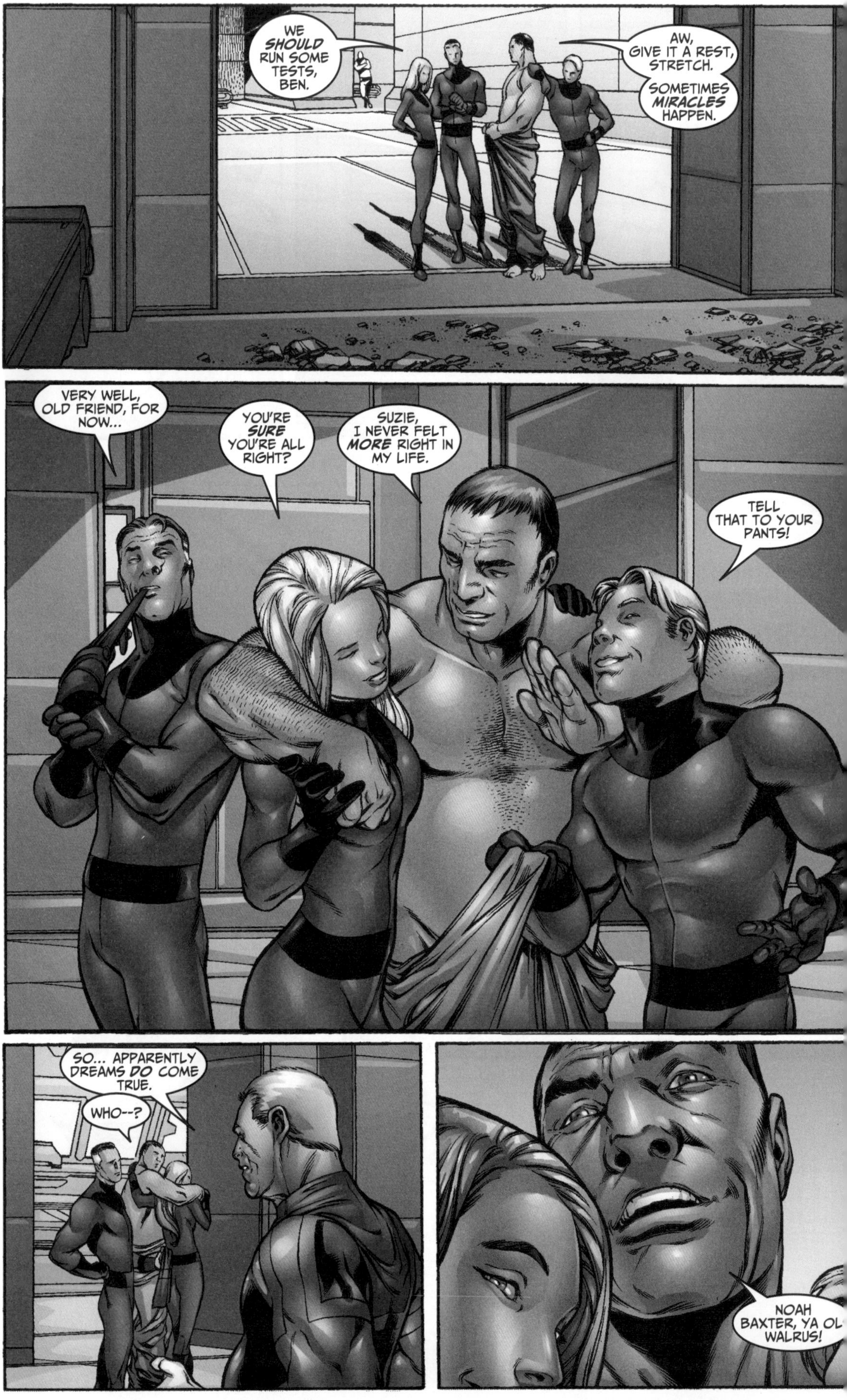
WE SHOULD RUN SOME TESTS, BEN.
AW, GIVE IT A REST, STRETCH.
SOMETIMES MIRACLES HAPPEN.
VERY WELL, OLD FRIEND, FOR NOW...
YOU'RE SURE YOU'RE ALL RIGHT?
SUZIE, I NEVER FELT MORE RIGHT IN MY LIFE.
TELL THAT TO YOUR PANTS!
SO... APPARENTLY DREAMS DO COME TRUE.
WHO--?
NOAH BAXTER, YA OL WALRUS!

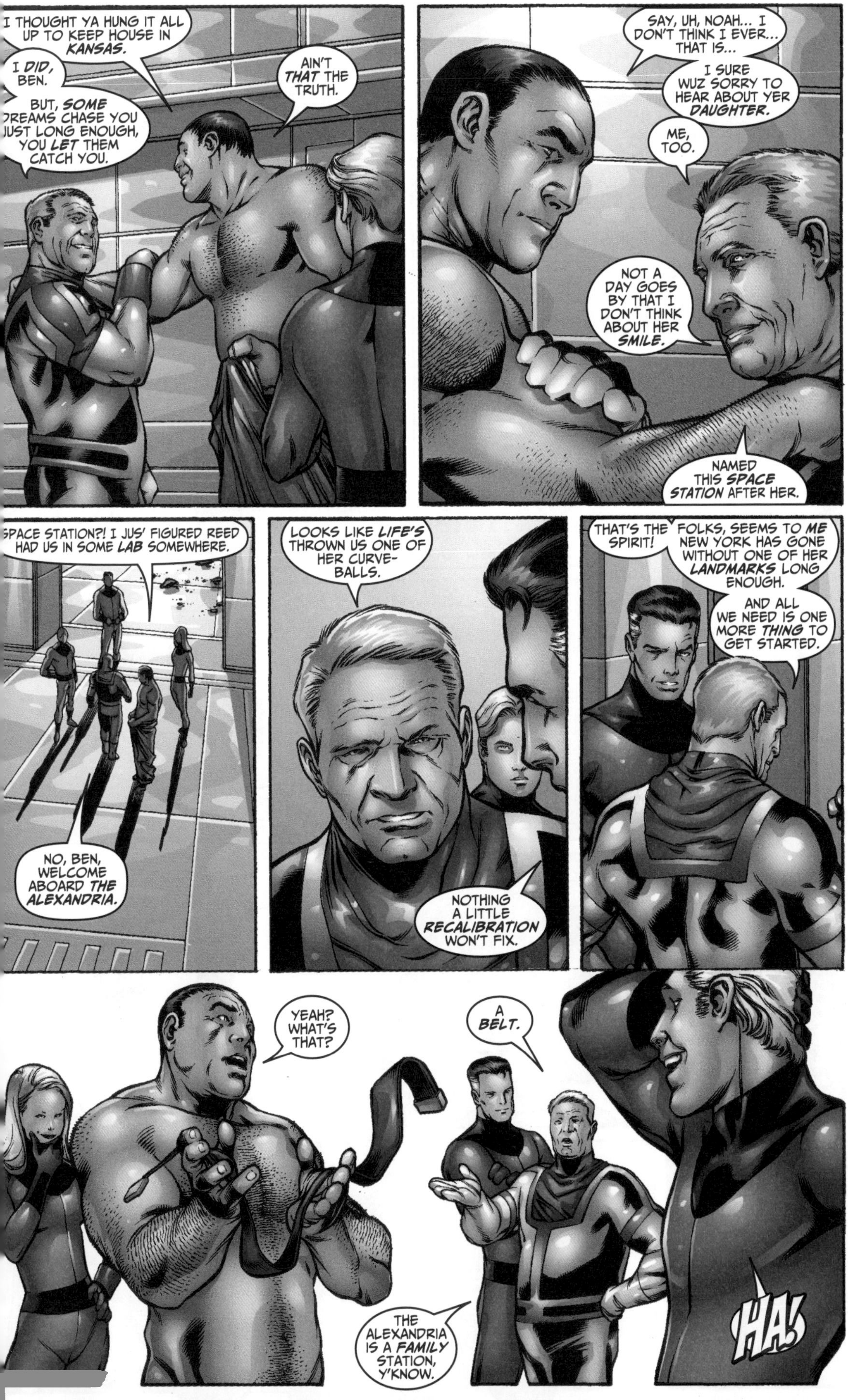
I THOUGHT YA HUNG IT ALL UP TO KEEP HOUSE IN KANSAS.
I DID, BEN.
BUT, SOME DREAMS CHASE YOU JUST LONG ENOUGH, YOU LET THEM CATCH YOU.
AIN'T THAT THE TRUTH.
SAY, UH, NOAH... I DON'T THINK I EVER... THAT IS...
I SURE WUZ SORRY TO HEAR ABOUT YER DAUGHTER.
ME, TOO.
NOT A DAY GOES BY THAT I DON'T THINK ABOUT HER SMILE.
NAMED THIS SPACE STATION AFTER HER.
SPACE STATION?! I JUS' FIGURED REED HAD US IN SOME LAB SOMEWHERE.
NO, BEN, WELCOME ABOARD THE ALEXANDRIA.
LOOKS LIKE LIFE'S THROWN US ONE OF HER CURVE-BALLS.
NOTHING A LITTLE RECALIBRATION WON'T FIX.
THAT'S THE SPIRIT!
FOLKS, SEEMS TO ME NEW YORK HAS GONE WITHOUT ONE OF HER LANDMARKS LONG ENOUGH.
AND ALL WE NEED IS ONE MORE THING TO GET STARTED.
YEAH? WHAT'S THAT?
A BELT.
THE ALEXANDRIA IS A FAMILY STATION, Y'KNOW.
HA!

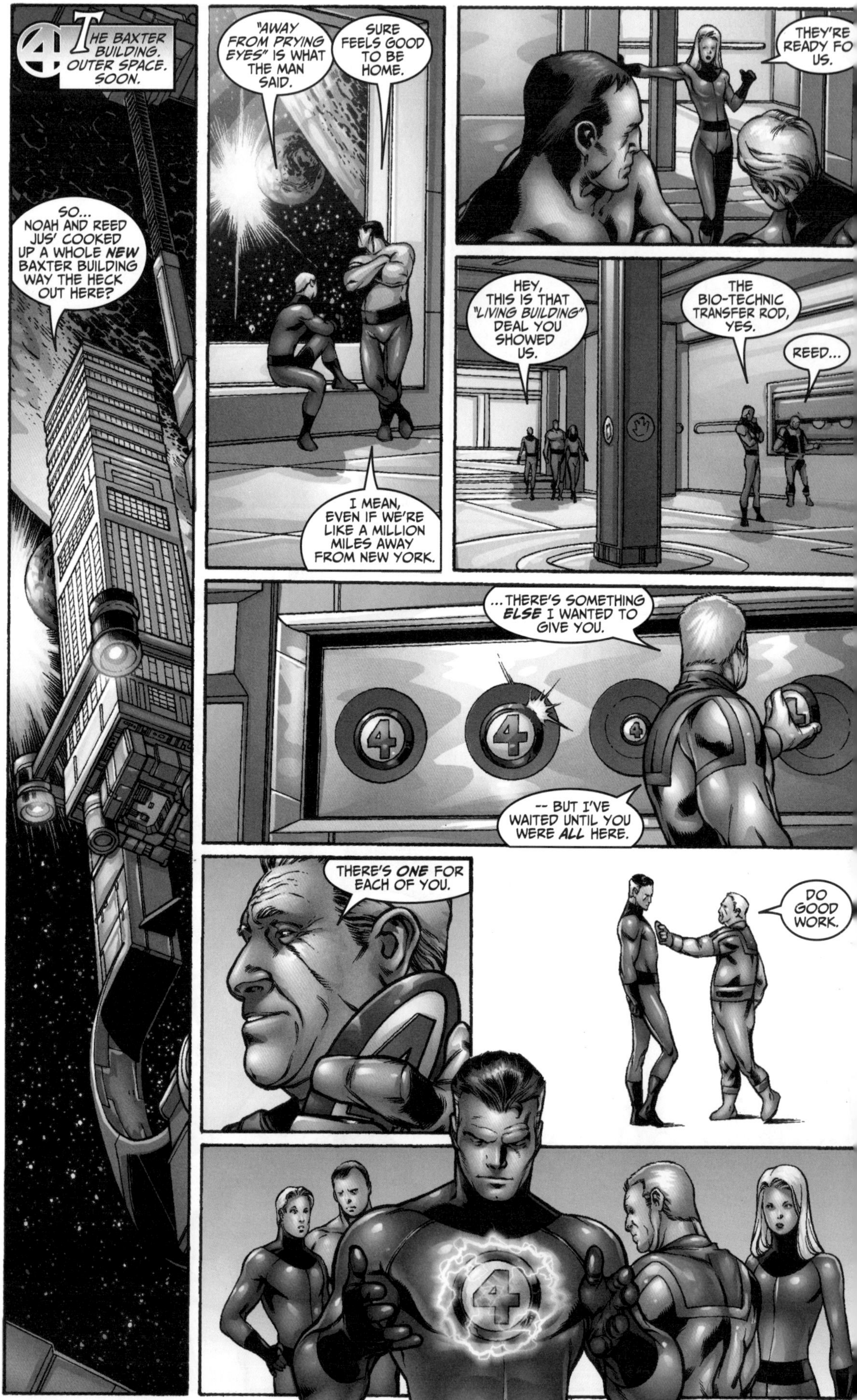
THE BAXTER BUILDING. OUTER SPACE. SOON.
SO... NOAH AND REED JUS' COOKED UP A WHOLE NEW BAXTER BUILDING WAY THE HECK OUT HERE?
"AWAY FROM PRYING EYES" IS WHAT THE MAN SAID.
SURE FEELS GOOD TO BE HOME.
I MEAN, EVEN IF WE'RE LIKE A MILLION MILES AWAY FROM NEW YORK.
THEY'RE READY FO US.
HEY, THIS IS THAT "LIVING BUILDING" DEAL YOU SHOWED US.
THE BIO-TECHNIC TRANSFER ROD, YES.
REED...
...THERE'S SOMETHING ELSE I WANTED TO GIVE YOU.
-- BUT I'VE WAITED UNTIL YOU WERE ALL HERE.
THERE'S ONE FOR EACH OF YOU.
DO GOOD WORK.

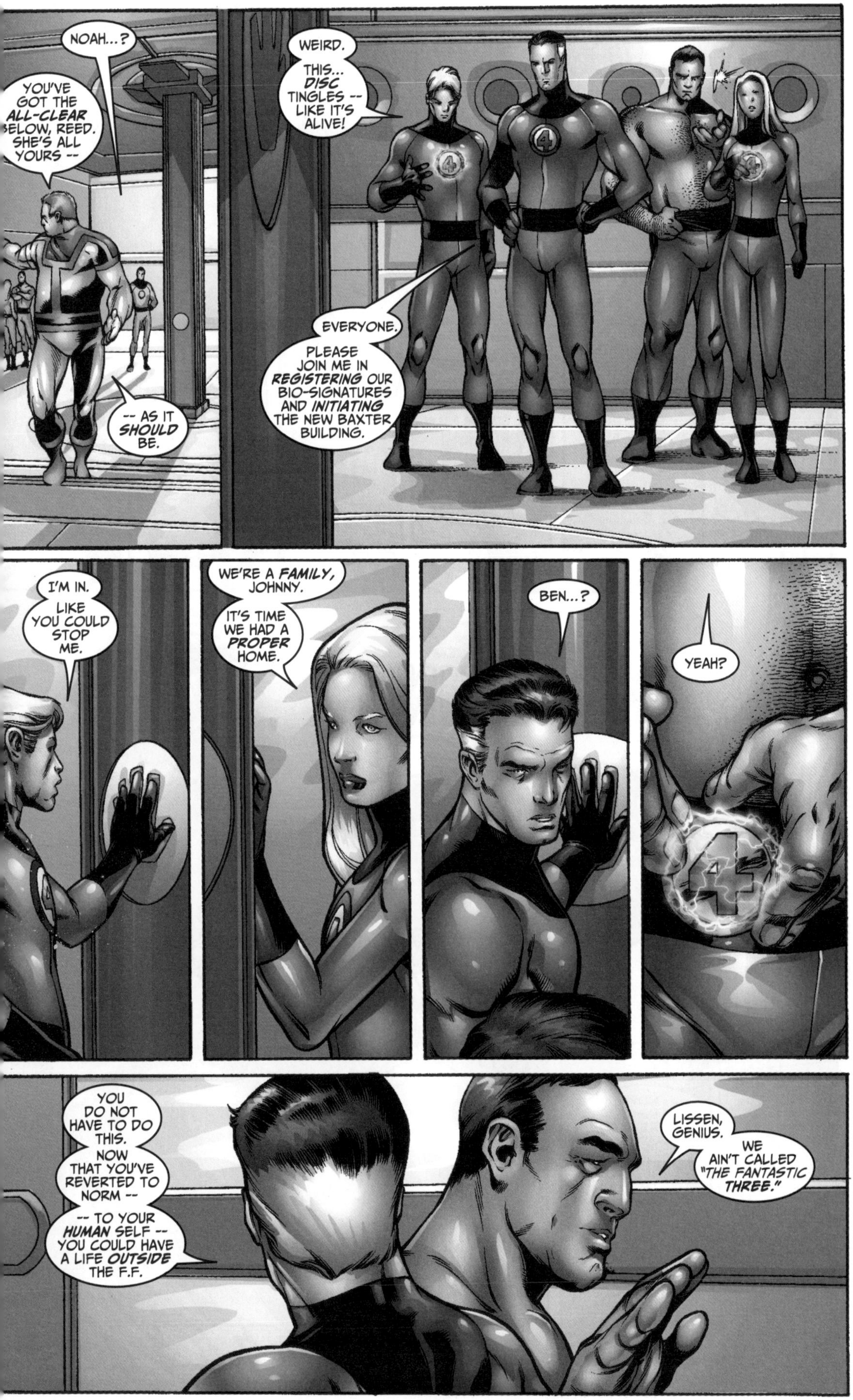
NOAH...?
YOU'VE GOT THE ALL-CLEAR BELOW, REED. SHE'S ALL YOURS --
-- AS IT SHOULD BE.
WEIRD.
THIS... DISC TINGLES -- LIKE IT'S ALIVE!
EVERYONE.
PLEASE JOIN ME IN REGISTERING OUR BIO-SIGNATURES AND INITIATING THE NEW BAXTER BUILDING.
I'M IN.
LIKE YOU COULD STOP ME.
WE'RE A FAMILY, JOHNNY.
IT'S TIME WE HAD A PROPER HOME.
BEN...?
YEAH?
YOU DO NOT HAVE TO DO THIS.
NOW THAT YOU'VE REVERTED TO NORM --
-- TO YOUR HUMAN SELF -- YOU COULD HAVE A LIFE OUTSIDE THE F.F.
LISSEN, GENIUS.
WE AIN'T CALLED "THE FANTASTIC THREE."

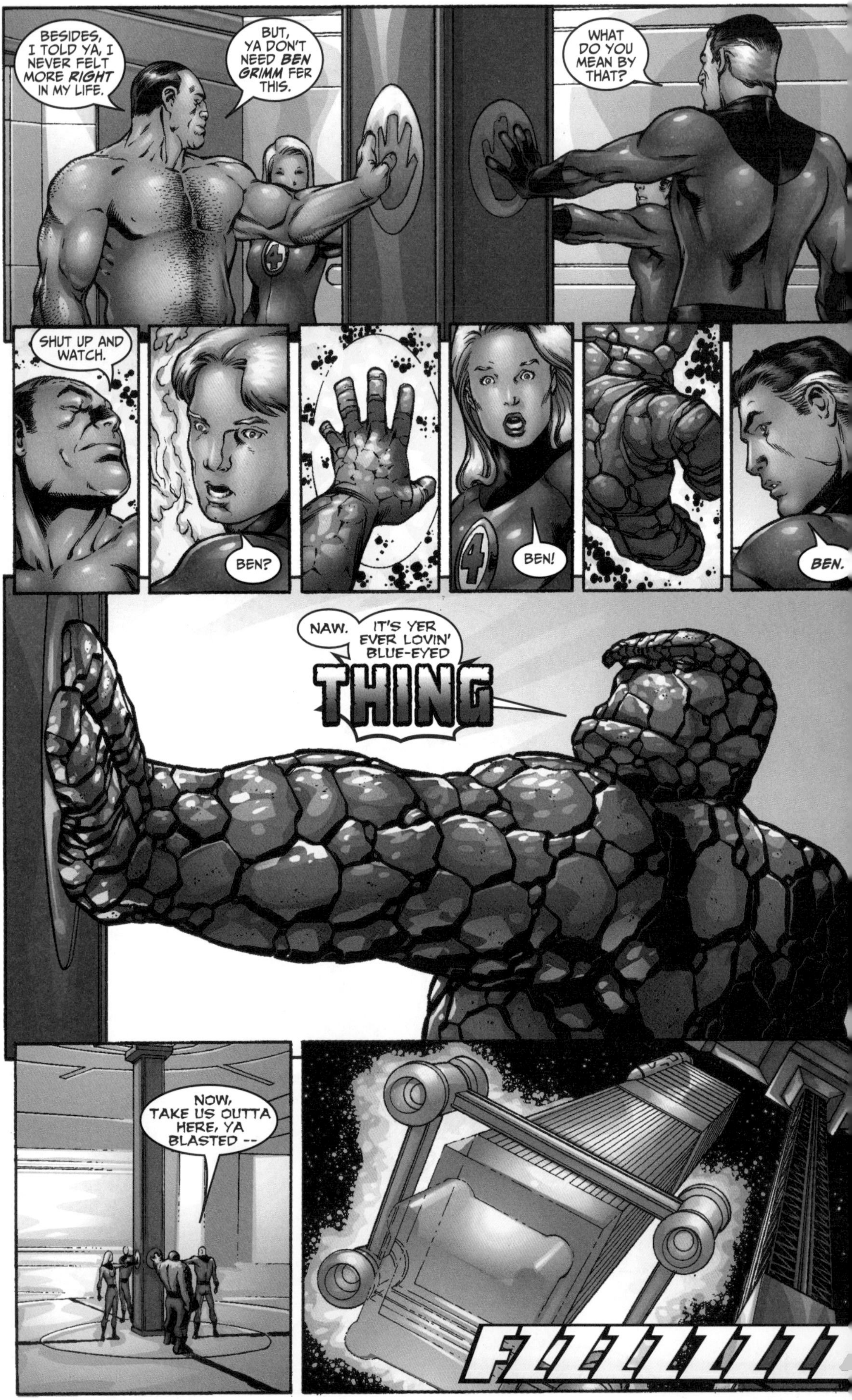

BESIDES, I TOLD YA, I NEVER FELT MORE RIGHT IN MY LIFE.
BUT, YA DON'T NEED BEN GRIMM FER THIS.
WHAT DO YOU MEAN BY THAT?
SHUT UP AND WATCH.
BEN?
BEN!
BEN.
NAW.
IT'S YER EVER LOVIN' BLUE-EYED
THING
NOW, TAKE US OUTTA HERE, YA BLASTED --
FZZZZZZZ

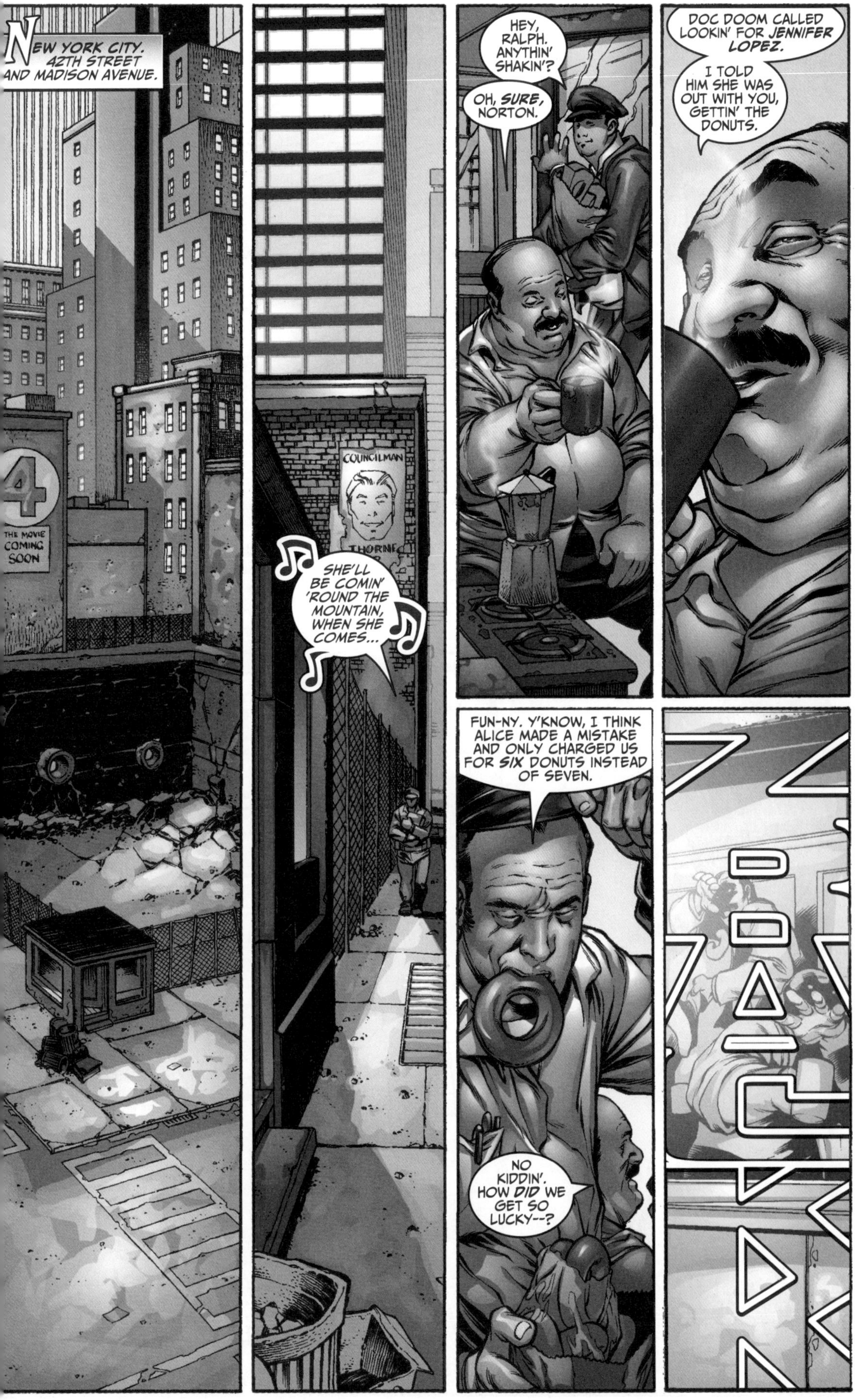

NEW YORK CITY. 42TH STREET AND MADISON AVENUE.
4
THE MOVIE COMING SOON
COUNCILMAN
THORNE
SHE'LL BE COMIN' 'ROUND THE MOUNTAIN, WHEN SHE COMES...
HEY, RALPH. ANYTHIN' SHAKIN'?
OH, SURE, NORTON.
DOC DOOM CALLED LOOKIN' FOR JENNIFER LOPEZ.
I TOLD HIM SHE WAS OUT WITH YOU, GETTIN' THE DONUTS.
FUN-NY. Y'KNOW, I THINK ALICE MADE A MISTAKE AND ONLY CHARGED US FOR SIX DONUTS INSTEAD OF SEVEN.
NO KIDDIN'. HOW DID WE GET SO LUCKY--?

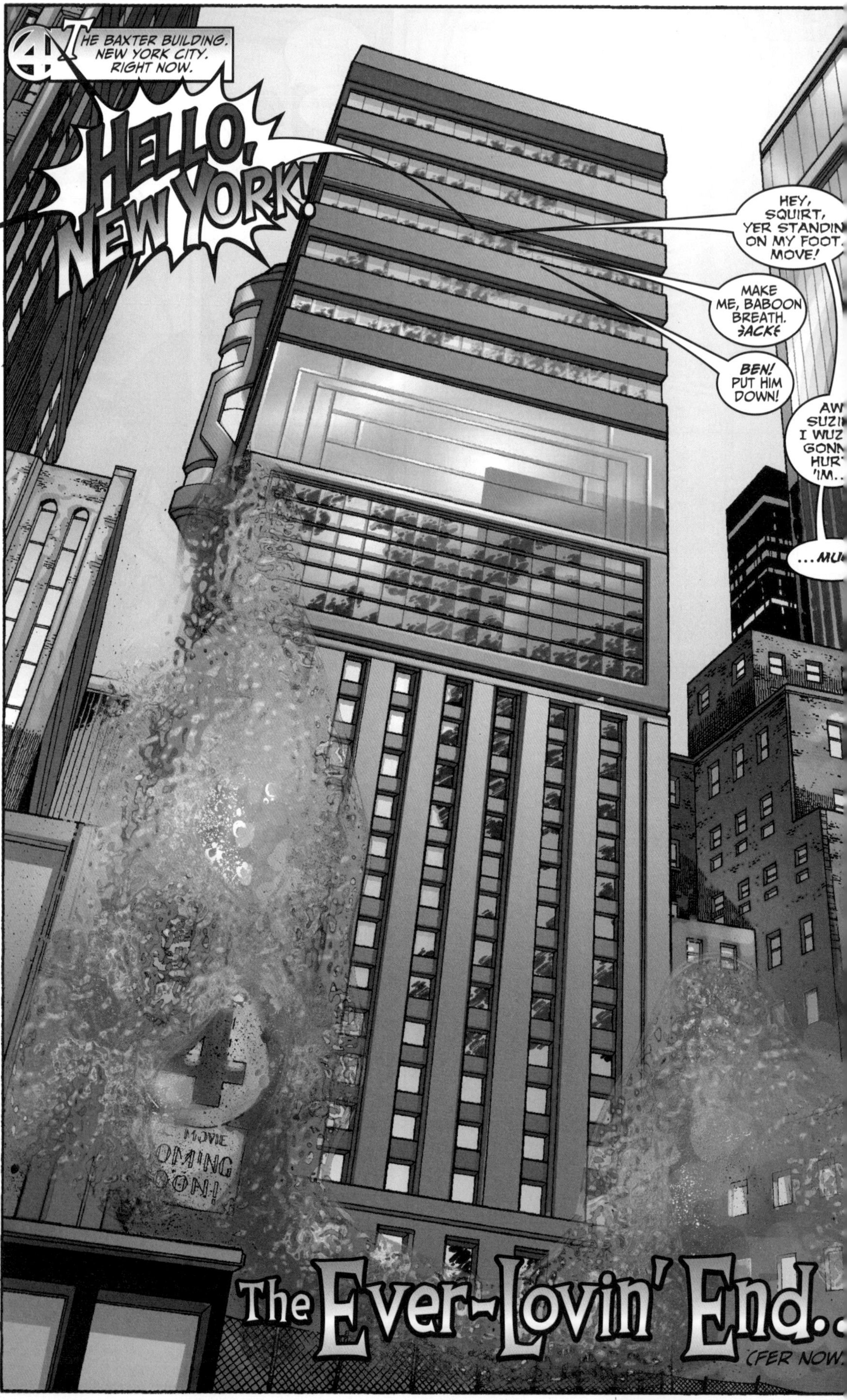
THE BAXTER BUILDING. NEW YORK CITY. RIGHT NOW.
HELLO, NEW YORK!
HEY, SQUIRT, YER STANDIN ON MY FOOT. MOVE!
MAKE ME, BABOON BREATH. ACK
BEN! PUT HIM DOWN!
AW SUZI I WUZ GONN HUR 'IM...
...MU
MOVIE OMING ON!
The Ever-Lovin' End...
(FER NOW